UKCAT

FOR

DUMMIES®

UKCAT FOR DUMMIES®

by Dr Chris Chopdar and Dr Neel Burton

A John Wiley and Sons, Ltd, Publication

UKCAT For Dummies®

Published by
John Wiley & Sons, Ltd
The Atrium
Southern Gate
Chichester
West Sussex
PO19 8SQ
England

Email (for orders and customer service enquires): cs-books@wiley.co.uk

Visit our home page on www.wiley.com

For general information on our other products and services, please contact our Customer Care Department within the U.S. at 877-762-2974, outside the U.S. at 317-572-3993, or fax 317-572-4002.

For technical support, please visit www.wiley.com/techsupport.

Wiley also publishes its books in a variety of electronic formats and by print-on-demand. Some content that appears in standard print versions of this book may not be available in other formats. For more information about Wiley products, visit us at www.wiley.com.

British Library Cataloguing in Publication Data: A catalogue record for this book is available from the British Library

ISBN: 978-1-119-96584-8 (paperback), ISBN: 978-1-119-96655-5 (ebook), ISBN: 978-1-119-96657-9 (ebook), ISBN: 978-1-119-96656-2 (ebook)

Printed and bound in Great Britain by TJ International, Padstow, Cornwall

10 9 8 7 6 5 4 3 2

About the Authors

Dr Chris Chopdar MA (Oxon), BMBCh (Oxon), MRCPsych is co-founder of Get into Medical School Ltd, which has a strong track record of getting prospective medical students into the university of their choice. He enjoys teaching courses both in Oxford and at schools and colleges across the UK. Chris got his medical degree from Oxford University, and also has a Master's degree in Physiological Sciences from his time there.

He returned to Oxford as a psychiatrist after brief stints working in other parts of the country. Chris continues in clinical practice, combining this work with interests in interview technique and the psychological motifs inherent in clothing.

Dr Neel Burton BSc, MBBS, MRCPsych, MA(Phil), AKC is co-founder of Get into Medical School Ltd, designed its UKCAT course, and coaches individual candidates. Having qualified in Medicine from the University of London, he is now a psychiatrist, philosopher, and writer.

Neel lives and teaches in Oxford, where he also runs the Oxford Wine Academy and the Meaning of Madness course. He is the recipient of the Society of Authors' Richard Asher Prize, the British Medical Association's Young Authors' Award, and the Medical Journalists' Association Open Book Award. He is happy to talk at charities, schools, universities, and other public gatherings.

More information on **Get into Medical School**, and the courses it offers, can be found at www.getintomedicalschool.org.

Dedication

We would like to dedicate this book to the many students we've taught over the years. Their intellectual curiosity makes teaching a pleasure, and through the teaching, we ourselves continue to learn.

Authors' Acknowledgements

The Roman philosopher and statesman Seneca once said, "A gift consists not in what is done or given, but in the intention of the giver or doer". Your authors have been fortunate indeed in the intentions of those around them.

Chris would particularly like to thank his father for his ongoing encouragement and support, and his late mother for instilling in him a sense of curiosity about the world.

Chris and Neel extend their joint gratitude to the entire *For Dummies* team at Wiley, who have proven themselves both pleasant and efficient to work with throughout the process of bringing this book to publication. Special thanks go to commissioning editor Mike Baker and development editor Jo Jones for their shared ability to balance attention to detail with overall vision. We're grateful to the whole editing team for their relentless focus, which improved the book immeasurably. Thanks also to the illustrators, who must have sometimes felt like pulling their hair out with frustration when faced with the task of neatly reproducing the complicated diagrams used in the practice tests. We certainly appreciate their efforts, and are confident that so will all those students who successfully use this book to prepare for the UKCAT.

Publisher's Acknowledgements

We're proud of this book; please send us your comments through our Dummies online registration form located at www.dummies.com/register/.

Some of the people who helped bring this book to market include the following:

Commissioning, Editorial, and Media Development

Project Editor: Jo Jones

Commissioning Editor: Mike Baker

Assistant Editor: Ben Kemble

Development Editor: Colette Holden

Copy Editor: Martin Key

Technical Editors: Sam Harrison, Amy Nicklin

Proofreader: Kim Vernon

Production Manager: Daniel Mersey

Publisher: David Palmer

Cover Photo: © iStock / mustafa deliormanli

Cartoons: Ed McLachlan

Composition Services

Project Coordinator: Kristie Rees

Layout and Graphics: Carl Byers, Carrie Cesavice, Sennett Vaughan Johnson, Corrie Niehaus, Christin Swinford, Laura Westhuis, Erin Zeltner

Proofreader: Melissa Cossell

Indexer: Ty Koontz

Special Help

Brand Reviewer: Carrie Burchfield

Publishing and Editorial for Consumer Dummies

    Kathleen Nebenhaus, Vice President and Executive Publisher

    Kristin Ferguson-Wagstaffe, Product Development Director

    Ensley Eikenburg, Associate Publisher, Travel

    Kelly Regan, Editorial Director, Travel

Publishing for Technology Dummies

    Andy Cummings, Vice President and Publisher

Composition Services

    Debbie Stailey, Director of Composition Services

Contents at a Glance

Table of Contents

Introduction

∙ ∙

You want to be a doctor or a dentist. You clearly love a challenge!

Medicine and dentistry are varied careers with some interesting science underpinning daily practice, and with the opportunity to meet a wide cross-section of society and help people through difficult times. The jobs can be tough but also highly rewarding if you approach them positively.

Before you head off to medical or dental school, you need to prove to universities that you deserve the chance of training with them. The selection process is long and, to be honest, sometimes unnecessarily frustrating. But if you take things one step at a time, you can get through it successfully.

A key part of this is scoring well in the United Kingdom Clinical Aptitude Test (UKCAT). The UKCAT is a fairly new exam, taken as part of the selection process for many medical and dental courses that measures your innate talent to cope with the kind of material you learn during your medical or dental training.

Universities want to know that you can interpret written material, perform basic math operations, spot patterns quickly, and use complex information to make challenging decisions. These are all skills that doctors and dentists put into practice every day of their working lives.

For instance, as a doctor or dentist you may have to rapidly extract relevant information from a colleague's clinical letter, calculate the right dose of a drug to administer based on a patient's weight, or interpret a range of lab test results to make a diagnosis and deduce a patient's likely prognosis.

The UKCAT doesn't expect you to be able to do all those things already but it tries to ensure that you have the ability to learn how to do them when the time comes. Fortunately, as with every test that is theoretically meant to check natural aptitude, the truth is that your test score improves as you become familiar with the style of questioning.

Practice pays dividends.

We regularly teach prospective applicants to medical and dental school on how to prepare for the UKCAT. Most students are pretty anxious about sitting such a different kind of exam. The UKCAT isn't the sort of test for which you can simply learn a set of facts and expect to do well. Understanding what the UKCAT involves means practising a lot of questions, figuring out *why* certain answers are correct, and then applying that knowledge in the real exam to reach your potential and get your best possible score. We've written this book to give you the framework you need to succeed on the UKCAT.

About This Book

UKCAT For Dummies is for intelligent, motivated individuals who want to rapidly familiarise themselves with the nature of the UKCAT and get plenty of focused practice answering the kinds of questions they're likely to face on the day of the exam.

The book breaks down the different parts of the test into smaller chapters. You can read each chapter in isolation to quickly get up to speed on a section you find tricky, or you can work through the book from cover to cover to get an overview of the entire test.

We teach prospective medical students how to get into medical school (see Chapter 12 for more information), but we're also psychiatrists, and we want to leverage that background to show you some techniques to cope with exam stress. These techniques will help you in the UKCAT and also the other exams you face over the coming years as you study to be a doctor or dentist.

In book we include the following:

- Background information on the UKCAT.
- The skills each component of the UKCAT tests.
- A large number of sample questions for each subtest, with worked-through answers to help you understand the solutions.
- Complete timed practice tests so that you gain the necessary experience to be comfortable with the time limit when the crunch comes.
- Strategies for taking tests and managing your anxiety.
- Broader tips and strategies to help you navigate the sometimes confusing world of medical and dental school applications.

Conventions Used in This Book

You won't find too many strange conventions in this book. We keep things as straightforward as possible so you can focus on the content instead of trying to figure out what we mean by using a particular font. Having said that, we do use the following basic conventions:

We use *italics* to highlight important words.

We use **bold text** to indicate key concepts in lists and to indicate correct answers in the answer section.

Keep in mind that some web addresses are long, extending over two lines of text – just ignore the line break when you type out these addresses.

We use the terms *applicant*, *candidate*, and *student* interchangeably. We do the same with *aptitude*, *talent* and *innate ability*. We also sometimes refer to 'UKCAT' rather than 'the UKCAT', in our attempts to improve readability.

What You're Not to Read

Feel free to skim anything in the sidebars – grey boxes with text in them – if you're in a rush. The information in these boxes either gives you some extra background information or relates a light-hearted anecdote. Taking occasional short breaks as you study is a good thing, however, and reading these sidebars helps you do just that.

Foolish Assumptions

Anyone who writes a book has to make some assumptions about their readers.

In this book we assume that you intend to sit the UKCAT, with a goal to becoming either a doctor or a dentist. If that's not the case, you can breathe a sigh of relief and put this book down!

We also assume that you're prepared to put in some work. Little in life is handed to you on a plate, and a place in medical or dental school is no exception. If you want that place, you need to have to invest time and effort, not only on this book and the UKCAT but also on the broader application process too.

We should mention that the sample questions in this book are designed for applicants to help them acquire the skills needed to answer a range of potential questions. The questions are not designed to be used by test administrators.

How This Book is Organised

This book is divided into four parts to make the information more manageable. Most of the divisions are self-explanatory, but the information in this section should help you quickly identify the part you're looking for.

Part 1: Understanding UKCAT

If you love the idea of medicine or dentistry but feel a bit lost regarding the practicalities of applying, start here.

In Chapter 1 we sketch out the process of applying to medical and dental school and show where UKCAT fits into that process. We also give you pointers about the other things successful applicants need to think about.

In Chapter 2 we give a more detailed breakdown of the UKCAT itself, including what's in the test, how much time you have, and whether the test has a pass mark.

In Chapter 3 we show you how to optimise your ability to do well in any test. Regardless of the subject matter, you can use certain strategies to improve your performance in any time-limited examination. In fact, you probably know some of these techniques already.

Part II: Examining the Subtests

The chapters in Part II cover each of the subtests of the UKCAT in turn. Each chapter consists of some basic theory, followed by a large number of sample questions with fully worked-through answers and explanations to highlight how to apply those theoretical principles to score highly on the test.

Reading between the lines: The verbal reasoning subtest

Chapter 4 is all about the verbal reasoning subtest. We explain the aptitudes this subtest explores, and how to refine those talents through plenty of practice questions. We identify the concepts behind the passages, showing you how to think logically and to infer meaning.

Making it all add up: The quantitative reasoning subtest

In Chapter 5 we explain the quantitative reasoning subtest. This test is about solving numerical problems. We explain the kinds of information you may be presented with, and how to extract the data you need. Plenty of practice questions let you make sure that your skills are improving.

Looking at pretty patterns: The abstract reasoning subtest

In the abstract reasoning subtest, UKCAT challenges you to quickly infer relationships between abstract shapes arranged into patterns. Abstract reasoning is probably the scariest part of the test to many people. The key to doing well is training your mind to approach this subtest in a specific way. In Chapter 6 we help you learn this strategy, with lots of practice questions to prove to yourself that you can do it.

Deciphering the code: The decision analysis subtest

The trickiest part of the decision analysis subtest is that the questions are designed to get progressively harder as you work through them. The questions get more complex, and more ambiguous, forcing you to go through increasingly difficult decision-making processes before arriving at an answer. In Chapter 7 we explore the nature of decision-making and demonstrate how practice questions improve your confidence in your answers.

Part III: Practice Tests

Chapters 8–11 contain two full-length practice tests that you can do under timed conditions, with worked-through solutions to refer to afterwards.

Part IV: The Part of Tens

Every *For Dummies* book comes with a Part of Tens. These chapters contain sets of concise tips designed to boost your productivity. In the Part of Tens in this book we focus on strategies to reduce your anxiety and strategies to maximise your studying efficiency.

Icons Used in This Book

Throughout this book we use various icons in the margins to flag up important information. Here's what the icons mean:

We use this icon to highlight the most important information and insights in the book. We recommend that you read this material carefully.

Knowledge is important, but strategy can help you answer questions more efficiently by improving your familiarity with the test. We indicate these strategic shortcuts with this icon.

UKCAT can be tricky at times. We use this icon to flag up potential pitfalls that many candidates fall into. Avoiding these mistakes improves your score relative to your competition, increasing your chances of impressing the universities receiving your scores.

UKCAT is underpinned by a lot of research and testing. You don't really need to know much about it to do well in the test, but sometimes knowing why an examiner asks you questions that seem superficially random is helpful. This icon marks out those aspects of the test.

Where to Go from Here

You can read this book from cover to cover for a full overview of the UKCAT. Or you can cherry-pick the parts and chapters that address the bits of the text you're most worried about.

Closer to exam time, you may want to do the practice tests under timed conditions to replicate the feel of the actual exam and check that you're on track – head to Chapters 8, 9, 10, and 11.

The book's structure is flexible enough to be used whichever way meets your needs best.

We also recommend that you do the practice exam on the UKCAT website (www.ukcat.ac.uk/pages/details.aspx?page=practiceQuestions) and the practice tests in this book. Trying the practice exam gives you valuable experience with the software that you use on test day itself.

For more advice about applying to medical school in general, have a look at the resources on www.medschoolsonline.co.uk, www.medschools online.co.uk and for dental schools try www.dentalschoolscouncil. ac.uk/uk_dental_schools.htm.

We wish you the best of luck in the UKCAT and in your future career. And remember: One day we may be under your medical or dental care, so we have every interest in you doing very well indeed.

Part I
Understanding UKCAT

— THE FOUR HORSEMEN OF THE UKCAT—

In this part . . .

Part I is all about the basics. Before you get to test day, before you even start answering practice questions, you need to understand what the UKCAT is designed to test, how it's structured, how to apply and most importantly, whether a career in medicine or dentistry is right for you.

By the time you've got to this book, you've already sat and succeeded at a great many exams. With the right knowledge and plenty of practice you'll do well on the UKCAT.

Chapter 1 explores the challenge ahead, and helps you decide whether it's the right fight for you.

Chapter 1

The UKCAT and University

*Y*ou can easily drift into a career path without really thinking about whether the career is right for you. This chapter explains what Medicine and Dentistry are like as careers, and what role UKCAT plays in the application process to these courses.

Looking at the Lifestyle

Getting into university to study medicine or dentistry is tough. Doctors and dentists are some of the most respected members of society. Medical and dental jobs retain an air of glamour and mystique in the eyes of the general public. And although the reality is often more challenging and more pedestrian than the fantasy of medical drama, these careers do have some unique benefits.

As a doctor or dentist, you earn extraordinary privileges. As well as receiving an excellent grounding in the sciences, you develop your communication skills, sharpen your deductive skills, and discover all sorts of intimate details about complete strangers along the way.

Medicine and dentistry are two of the few professions where you can incorporate both science and art into your daily working life. A career in medicine or dentistry comes with more job security than most jobs provide, along with an historically comfortable salary.

These jobs have downsides too. Doctors and dentists often cope with the less enjoyable disciplines of bureaucracy and organisational restructuring. They also face perennial threats to training time, remuneration, and education budgets. More fundamentally, the jobs are often exhausting, physically, mentally, and emotionally. Dealing with some of the most troubled and unwell people in the country every day can take its toll. Ask yourself whether that's something you want to do, and why – a bit of honest soul-searching now may save you from agony later on.

If you still want to apply to medical or dental school, you need to overcome one of the toughest university degree application systems. Things weren't always so complicated. When we started out, all we needed was a bit of relevant work experience, solid A-level predictions, and the ability to sound intelligent and vaguely enthusiastic in an interview. If you applied to Oxford you needed to navigate the little matter of the Oxford Entrance Exam but if you performed well, you got an offer based on two Es in your A-levels.

Barriers to admission are far higher today. Tomorrow's doctors and dentists have to show intelligence and initiative, communication skills and commitment, and resilience and reliability. You need to demonstrate both breadth and depth of work experience, take part in significant extracurricular activities, have excellent AS results and A-level predictions, be prepared to take on large tuition fees with their associated loans, and be naturally talented and have practised enough to perform well in the extra exams universities make you sit such as the BioMedical Admissions Test (BMAT) and the United Kingdom Clinical Aptitude Test (UKCAT).

This increasing complexity isn't due only to more people applying for courses. The situation is also because universities increasingly struggle to distinguish between good and great candidates on the basis of A-level predictions and results alone. We wait to see whether the recent introduction of the A* grade shifts the balance back to A-level results, but currently many universities consider good UKCAT scores vital. Because university admissions policies tend to change particularly slowly, there may be an organisational inertia against streamlining entrance requirements for fear that doing so would lead to a reduction in the quality of applicants to the best universities. Therefore, UKCAT is likely to remain a key part of the selection procedures for the foreseeable future.

Getting a good UKCAT score is crucial to your chances of success.

We often hear first-hand how worrying the UKCAT is to candidates. The good news is that with preparation, you can improve your eventual performance markedly. In this book we aim to help you do just that.

Applying to Read Medicine or Dentistry

If you've weighed the pros and cons of a career in medicine or dentistry and decided that's what you really want to do, you need to know exactly how to go about it. The application process is long, and it starts early.

Use this section as a jumping-off point to research the medical fields further.

Considering the timeline

In Figure 1-1 we show a rough timeline of when to do what if you want to apply to medical or dental school. Use it to keep the big picture of the application process in mind.

Picking your A-levels

Unless you're reading this book at a remarkably early stage, you've probably already chosen your A-levels. If you still have time to optimise your choices for medicine or dentistry, remember that chemistry is mandatory, and having biology really helps too. Many medical and dental applicants study physics or mathematics at A-level, but these subjects aren't essential for getting into medical or dental school.

An increasing number of candidates sit more than three A-levels. Languages, psychology, and business studies are popular options for potential medical and dental students to demonstrate breadth of ability.

The choice is yours, but you need to expect to score highly in your chosen subject areas if you want even a hope of getting into medical or dental school.

Having the highest grades is much more important than having many grades. Assuming that you will do well in chemistry and biology, choose your other A-level(s) based on the subjects you're likely to get As and A*s in, instead of just trying to cram in more sciences. General Studies doesn't count towards your A-level total for Medicine or Dentistry so you must sit at least three other subjects.

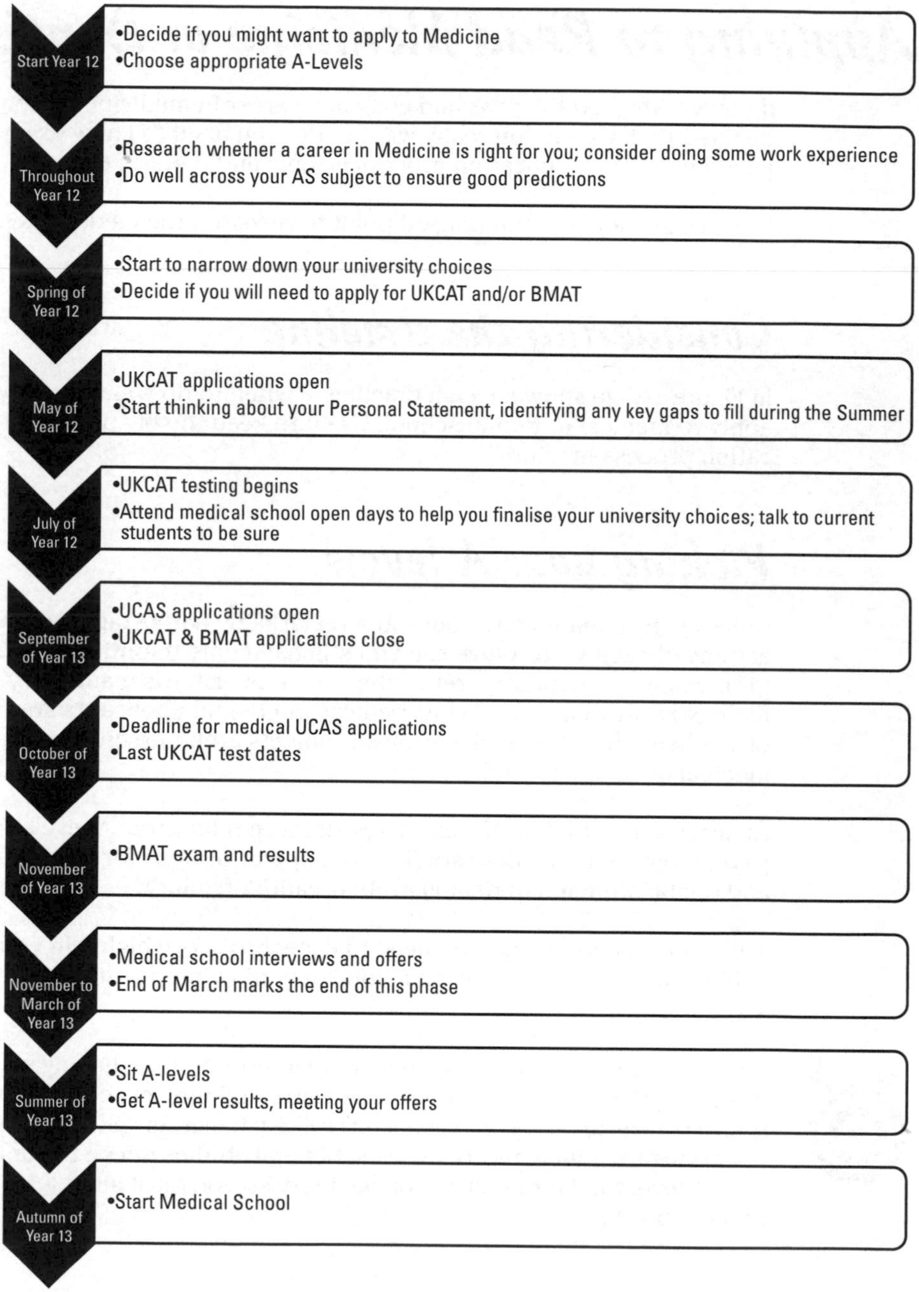

Start Year 12	•Decide if you might want to apply to Medicine •Choose appropriate A-Levels
Throughout Year 12	•Research whether a career in Medicine is right for you; consider doing some work experience •Do well across your AS subject to ensure good predictions
Spring of Year 12	•Start to narrow down your university choices •Decide if you will need to apply for UKCAT and/or BMAT
May of Year 12	•UKCAT applications open •Start thinking about your Personal Statement, identifying any key gaps to fill during the Summer
July of Year 12	•UKCAT testing begins •Attend medical school open days to help you finalise your university choices; talk to current students to be sure
September of Year 13	•UCAS applications open •UKCAT & BMAT applications close
October of Year 13	•Deadline for medical UCAS applications •Last UKCAT test dates
November of Year 13	•BMAT exam and results
November to March of Year 13	•Medical school interviews and offers •End of March marks the end of this phase
Summer of Year 13	•Sit A-levels •Get A-level results, meeting your offers
Autumn of Year 13	•Start Medical School

Figure 1-1:
Timeline for applying to medical or dental school.

Choosing a university

The UK has 32 medical schools and 18 dental schools. All these schools provide a good standard of education. The exact name of the degree (and therefore the letters you get after your name on qualification) varies a little between institutions, but after completion of one of their courses you're a fully-qualified doctor or dentist entitled to register provisionally with the General Medical Council or General Dental Council and able to begin working in the UK.

Choosing between schools on the basis of a given year's statistics on applicant-to-place ratios is dangerous. Prospective students often spend hours searching through data tables stating how many applicants each medical or dental school gets in an attempt to calculate their chances of success. This strategy is deeply flawed: the raw statistics tell you little about the real nature of the competitive selection process at each university.

For instance, the applicant-to-place ratios at Oxford and Cambridge tend to be about half that of, say, Brighton. That doesn't mean Brighton is harder to get into. Other factors interfere, such as only the best candidates daring to apply to Oxbridge and maybe people using Brighton as a 'reserve' option because the university's based in a vibrant part of the country.

We recommend that you choose a medical or dental school based largely on its course structure, its teaching style and whether you think that you can meet its typical entrance requirements. The location of the school may also be relevant.

Be realistic but positive when choosing a medical or dental school. You have four slots on your Universities and Colleges Admission Service (UCAS) form to use on medical or dental schools, so you may feel that you can dare to aim high with one of your choices, on the basis that you feel more secure about your chances on your other choices.

Read each university's prospectus, attend open days so you get a feel for the environment, and talk to current students for an unvarnished report on what life's like for people living and studying there.

If you like the idea of research, consider applying to a school that offers an intercalated BSc degree. These courses often include a strong research element. Courses with intercalated degrees mean that you graduate at the end of your time at the university with a BSc degree as well as your medical or dental degree, at the cost of only one extra year at university.

The Oxford MA

Oxford University is unusual in that although your intercalated degree is called a BSc (Bachelor of Sciences) as you actually do the course, the degree conferred is a BA (Bachelor of Arts). This odd result is because Oxford traditionally doesn't award BSc degrees.

Another quirk of Oxford's system is that you can upgrade your BA to an MA (Master of Arts) if you pay a small fee seven years after you first started your course. Oxford has some valid historical reasons for this anomaly, but one of the more amusing whimsical explanations is that Oxford considered its undergraduate teaching to be of such high quality that you needed a further four years after graduation to fully internalise all its lessons, by which time you were surely worthy of a Master's degree.

Writing a good personal statement

The only information a medical or dental school has on you is your UCAS application form and your UKCAT and/or BMAT results. Therefore, you can probably see the importance of doing well in the UKCAT and how crucial your UCAS form is. Most of the UCAS form is fairly straightforward, but the personal statement can distinguish you from everyone else.

Your personal statement must be engaging to read. It should highlight your reasons for choosing medicine or dentistry, how you've demonstrated your commitment to the career, and the soft skills (which we explain in the later section 'Working on your soft skills') you've acquired so far. Do not expect to write your personal statement in an afternoon.

Start writing your personal statement months before the application deadline. Starting early gives you time to identify any gaps early and undertake the necessary work to plug the holes, helping you to create a more compelling and coherent personal statement.

We recommend you give the statement a linear narrative structure, with a beginning, middle, and end. Each paragraph should flow smoothly from the previous one, yet also make sense in isolation.

By the conclusion, the reader must be convinced that you've a realistic and enthusiastic view of medicine or dentistry and have proven to your and their satisfaction that you've worked hard to get the real-life experience to formulate that viewpoint. The reader must also feel confident that you have not only the academic skills but also the communication and leadership skills that go along with being a doctor or dentist. Describing the personal insights you've gained by reflecting on your work experience and extracurricular activities can go a long way toward demonstrating this level of maturity.

Although many universities use a standardised marking scheme to grade your personal statement, good writing skills are still vital, because the reader can easily identify and score the areas they're looking for in a well-written personal statement.

Bad spelling, poor grammar, and inferior use of language have torpedoed many a personal statement. Bad writing comes across as immature and lacking in confidence. We also suggest that you avoid bizarre or highly controversial opinions, as they may expose a poorly thought-through position on a sensitive topic.

Getting work experience

Work experience needs to demonstrate your commitment to medicine or dentistry as a career. In many respects, where you go and how long you work are less important than being able to explain what you learned.

If possible, try to get experience both in the high-powered side of medicine and dentistry (operating theatres, consultant clinics, cosmetic dentistry, maybe even management meetings) and at the 'coal face' of hospice work and Emergency Departments (the modern name for Accident & Emergency or Casualty). This not only broadens your understanding of your future career, but also and lets you compare and contrast the two settings. If you express these insights clearly and concisely in your personal statement, you'll come across as a much more rounded and mature applicant than someone who simply lists what they did on their work experience.

Arranging work placements can be tricky. If your school or social circle lacks good contacts, a sensible starting point is to make an appointment with your local GP or dentist to talk through your interest in a career in medicine or dentistry.

Work experience rarely organises itself: you have to make the effort to reach out to people and organisations in your local community who can help. Many opportunities exist for motivated individuals. Remember that charities and the non-profit sector are often keen for free and enthusiastic help.

Working on your soft skills

A high level of academic ability and productive work experience make for a strong package. To become a doctor or dentist, however, you also need to prove that you have *soft skills*: leadership potential, communication skills, and charisma.

These soft skills improve with practice. For most people, the easiest way to get that practice is to get involved in extracurricular activities that encourage the development of these traits. Think about any sports you do, clubs you belong to and groups such as Scouts and Cadets and you can probably channel all these settings to give you some soft skills experience. This experience can be a great store of anecdotes for you to talk about on your personal statement and in your interview.

Sitting entrance exams such as UKCAT

Almost all applicants to medical and dental school need to sit extra exams in addition to their A-levels. Oxford, Cambridge, Imperial, and UCL request that medical applicants sit BMAT. The vast majority of the other medical schools and nine of the dental schools require you to sit UKCAT.

As you have four potential slots on your UCAS form, your choices may span the range of these schools. For medical applicants, that can mean the need to sit both exams. That makes for a hectic and exhausting year.

UKCAT and BMAT test different domains. BMAT focuses more on raw current academic ability, whereas UKCAT assesses aptitude and potential. Both UKCAT and BMAT performance improve with practice and familiarity, so if you need to sit UKCAT, keep reading this book.

Preparing for interviews

If you've got an interview with a medical or dental school, you're doing well. Most of the cull in applicant numbers takes place before this stage, so you're ahead of most of your competition by the time the school invites you for an interview.

Performing at your best in interviews can be difficult, even if you're experienced. You have to be consistent with the information on your personal statement but still come across as fresh, enthusiastic, and personable.

Ask your friends and family to practise interviews with you. If you have a teacher at school willing to conduct mock interviews, that can be a great way to get constructive feedback on your strengths and weaknesses. Dedicated interview skills workshops (such as those offered by us at www.getinto medicalschool.org) can provide this feedback and help you focus on the key messages you need to get across to the interviewer.

Chapter 2

Dissecting UKCAT

· ·

· ·

*B*efore sitting the UKCAT, you need to know what's in it and how to apply. This chapter provides that information.

Exploring the Origins of UKCAT

The United Kingdom Clinical Aptitude Test (UKCAT) is, as its name suggests, a test of aptitude, which means that the test is theoretically designed to reward candidates with a natural talent for the tested skills.

The UKCAT universities knew that they had lots of information about their applicants' current academic achievements, in the form of GCSE and A-level (or Scottish Higher) results and predictions. But in addition they wanted to assess a wider range of mental abilities identified as useful in medicine and dentistry, including critical thinking, logical reasoning and inference.

The universities hoped that an aptitude test, the results of which would be considered alongside the pre-existing academic record during the selection process, would help them choose the most suitable candidates to join their medical and dental courses.

UKCAT is described as a *psychometric test*, which means that the test tries to measure your thought processes or, more accurately, how those thought processes affect your performance on a set of standardised tasks. By grouping those tasks into different subtests, the results show the examiner something about how your ability varies across different dimensions of mental activity.

The UKCAT Consortium

The UKCAT is run by the UKCAT Consortium, a company registered at the University of Nottingham, whose members and directors are drawn from the 26 universities that use UKCAT as part of their selection procedures for medical and dental applicants. This corporate structure ensures that a strong link is maintained between the eventual users of the test results and the compilers of the test itself. The UKCAT is a relatively new test that started in 2006.

The test is entirely computerised and physically administered by Pearson VUE, a for-profit subsidiary of the wider media group of Pearson PLC. Pearson VUE administers computerised testing not only for UKCAT but also for a whole array of other organisations and businesses. For example, if you've sat your UK driving theory test, you've already used Pearson VUE computerised testing services.

A further hope was that the UKCAT would be a fairer way of narrowing down the applicant field, as an aptitude test is a good predictor of underlying talent. This type of test minimises the effect of background and schooling on a candidate's academic achievement.

Sitting the UKCAT

The UKCAT is designed for applicants to medical and dental university courses. The test is a required part of the selection process for the courses and universities listed in Table 2-1. In Table 2-2, we explain what the UCAS (Universities and Colleges Admissions Service) course codes in Table 2-1 actually mean.

Table 2-1	Universities and Courses Requiring UKCAT
University	**UCAS Course Code**
University of Aberdeen	A100, A201
Brighton and Sussex Medical School	A100
Barts and The London School of Medicine and Dentistry	A100, A101, A200, A201
Cardiff University	A100, A104, A200, A204
University of Dundee	A100, A104, A200, A204
University of Durham	A100

University	UCAS Course Code
University of East Anglia	A100, A104
University of Edinburgh	A100
University of Glasgow	A100, A200
Hull York Medical School	A100
Keele University	A100, A104
King's College London	A100, A101, A102, A202, A205
Imperial College London Graduate Entry	A101
University of Leeds	A100
University of Leicester	A100, A101
University of Manchester	A104, A106, A204, A206
University of Newcastle	A100, A101, A206
University of Nottingham	A100, A108
University of Oxford Graduate Entry	A101
Peninsula College of Medicine and Dentistry	A100
Queen's University Belfast	A100, A200
University of Sheffield	A100, A104, A200
University of Southampton	A100, A101, A102
University of St Andrews	A100, A990, B900
St George's, University of London	A100
Warwick University Graduate Entry	A101

Table 2-2	UCAS Course Codes

UCAS Code	Course
A100	Medicine
A101	Medicine (graduate entry 4-year programmes everywhere, except King's Extended Medical Degree)
A102	Medicine (widening access 6-year programme at Southampton; graduate professional entry 4-year programme at King's)
A104	Medicine (including initial pre-medical/foundation year)
A108	Medicine (including foundation year, Nottingham only)
A200	Dentistry
A201	Dentistry (graduate entry 4-year programmes)

(continued)

Table 2-2 *(continued)*

UCAS Code	Course
A204	Dentistry (including pre-dental/foundation year, except King's, where it is for medical graduates)
A205	Dentistry (King's only)
A206	Dentistry (Newcastle and Manchester)
A990	North American Medical Programme (St Andrews only)
B900	International Foundation for Medicine (St Andrews only, 1-year programme)

In short, UKCAT is required for undergraduate medical entry everywhere in the UK except Birmingham, Bristol, Cambridge, Imperial, Liverpool, Oxford, Swansea, and UCL. However, Imperial, Oxford, and Warwick require UKCAT for their graduate medical courses.

For Cambridge, Imperial, Oxford, and UCL medical undergraduate courses, you need to sit the BioMedical Admissions Test (BMAT) instead of the UKCAT. (Check out the BMAT website for more information at www.bmat.org.uk.) If you wish to avoid any sort of extra exam altogether, your only options are Birmingham, Bristol, Liverpool and Swansea.

Finding out whether you're exempt from taking the UKCAT

If your course and institution are listed in Tables 2-1 and 2-2, you have to sit the UKCAT, provided that you live and are educated in one of the following countries:

Australia, Austria, Bahrain, Bangladesh, Belgium, Botswana, Brunei, Bulgaria, Cameroon, Canada, China, Cyprus, Czech Republic, Denmark, Egypt, Estonia, Finland, France, Germany, Ghana, Gibraltar, Greece, Hong Kong, Hungary, India, Indonesia, Ireland, Israel, Italy, Japan, Jordan, Kenya, Kuwait, Latvia, Lithuania, Luxembourg, Malaysia, Malta, Mauritius, Netherlands, New Zealand, Nigeria, Norway, Pakistan, Poland, Portugal, Qatar, Republic of Korea, Romania, Saudi Arabia, Singapore, Slovakia, Slovenia, South Africa, Spain, Sri Lanka, Sweden, Switzerland, Taiwan, Thailand, Uganda, United Arab Emirates, United Kingdom of Great Britain and Northern Ireland, United Republic of Tanzania, and the United States of America.

Does UKCAT work?

To a critical eye, it can be debated as to whether UKCAT actually succeeds in its aim of testing underlying aptitude and so is whether its inclusion in the selection process adds to the fairness of the eventual outcome of determining who is accepted into medical and dental training.

In its favour, the test certainly doesn't contain any curriculum or science content. It focuses on exploring the cognitive areas it aims to test. The UKCAT Consortium takes great care to ensure that the test questions are written by appropriate experts and then tests the questions extensively for validity and reliability. The UKCAT Consortium also tries to minimise the possibility of cultural bias. We can therefore say the test has good intentions.

However, the very existence of the UKCAT adds an extra hurdle to applying to medical or dental school. People from backgrounds not historically likely to apply to these medical or dental schools may be put off applying by the knowledge that they've to sit yet another exam, whereas people from schools or families with experience and knowledge of the system may be more motivated and understand the process better. In addition, the UKCAT has an entrance fee of £65 or £80 (or £100 for non-EU candidates), depending on when you sit the exam, which may prevent some people from registering to do the UKCAT. Bursaries to cover the cost are available in some circumstances. (See 'Registering for the UKCAT' later in this chapter for more details.)More fundamentally, some people question how pure an aptitude test the UKCAT is. A perfect aptitude test should not reward revision or practice. A test designed to reveal underlying mental capability should always give similar results for the same person, no matter how prepared that person is. The UKCAT Consortium takes great pains to emphasise that revision is not required for the test. However, the Consortium's website states: 'You should take the time to familiarise yourself with the test. We strongly advise you to practise answering the types of questions that will be presented in the UKCAT, to familiarise yourself with the question styles, multiple-choice format and varying requirements of each subtest.' Plus, re-applicant candidates tend on average to improve their scores in the second year.

By buying this book, you're already one step ahead in realising that practising any test, even an aptitude test, results in better test scores.

If your home isn't in the roll call above, you're exempt from the requirement to sit the UKCAT. If you're exempt, you still need to contact UKCAT using a form available on the UKCAT website (www.ukcat.ac.uk). UKCAT then issue you with a reference number and contact the universities you apply to on your behalf to inform them of your exemption.

Getting the dates right

You have to take the UKCAT in the same year as that of your application cycle.

For example, candidates applying in 2012 for entry in 2013 (or for deferred entry in 2014) sit the UKCAT in 2012. Your test score is valid only for one application cycle. If you reapply the following year, you need to sit the UKCAT again that year.

The logic behind the need to resit an aptitude test from one year to the next somewhat escapes us. As aptitude is an innate talent, it shouldn't vary significantly between years. Nonetheless, the UKCAT rules are clear about resitting, so be sure to stick to them.

The exact dates for UKCAT registration, testing and publication of results cycle vary from year to year, though usually only by a few days. UKCAT is good at maintaining its own website with the relevant dates for the current year. UKCAT's website is www.ukcat.ac.uk and has a lot of useful information, not just test dates.

As an example of the approximate times of year to be aware of, in Table 2-3 we show the dates from the 2012 cycle.

Table 2-3	Key UKCAT dates, 2012
Event	*Date*
Registration opens	1 May 2012
Bursary applications open	1 May 2012
Testing begins	3 July 2012
Registration deadline	21 September 2012
Bursary application deadline	21 September 2012
Exemption application deadline	21 September 2012
Last testing date	5 October 2012
UCAS application deadline	15 October 2012

We recommend that you aim to sit the UKCAT fairly early in the cycle. Then, if you fall ill or for some other reason can't make your initial test date, you still have time to rebook to a later date. An early test date means that you have to start your preparation sooner, but the insurance you gain by having room to manoeuvre is probably worth the trade-off.

If you need to cancel or reschedule your test, log into Pearson VUE's website (www.pearsonvue.co.uk). Rescheduling is free of charge, provided you give at least a full working day's notice between the time of rescheduling and the original day of your test. If you cancel or try to reschedule with less than a day's notice, you're counted as a no-show and are liable for the full fee (and then have to pay a further fee for the rescheduled test).

Registering for the UKCAT

UKCAT registration is entirely computerised. Navigate to UKCAT's website at www.ukcat.ac.uk and click the Sign In link on the Registration page. Registration is only possible within the period indicated in Table 2-3. You will be seamlessly transferred to Pearson VUE's website and guided through a series of online forms to create an account to access the system, register, and pay for the test. Registering is no more intimidating than opening an account with any online shopping site, so don't panic!

The UKCAT application fee is £65 if you sit the test in the summer part of the application cycle, and £80 if you sit the test in the autumn. If you're not from an EU country, the fee rises to £100, regardless of when you sit the test. You can pay securely online with any major credit or debit card. You don't have an offline option, so if you don't have access to one of these cards, you need to look into getting a temporary or prepaid card from your bank or from other organisations like the Post Office.

Many potentially eligible applicants don't realise that UKCAT operates an extensive bursary system covering many EU candidates for the full cost of the test fee. In fact, poor level of awareness around the bursary system was one of the areas highlighted in a candidate survey carried out by UKCAT. You can apply for a bursary by completing the form at www.ukcat.ac.uk/pages/bursaryApplicationForm.aspx. You can only apply during the registration window indicated in Table 2-3.

Historically, bursaries were available for those in receipt of the Educational Maintenance Allowance (EMA) or Adult Learning Grant (ALG). Recipients of Income Support and some other benefits were also eligible for bursaries. Both EMA and ALG have now been closed and, at time of writing, UKCAT have not confirmed what kind of new requirements are going to govern bursary eligibility from 2012 onwards. Candidates should check the bursary website link when the application period opens for the latest information.

The process of applying has historically required documentary evidence (generally a letter from the relevant government agency) to verify your eligibility for the bursary. After you demonstrated eligibility, UKCAT sent you a voucher code to enter into the normal booking system during your application process instead of paying. The processes for 2012 bursaries and beyond are likely to be similar, with only the detail of the eligible benefits to change.

If you've already paid, you may still be able to get a refund. Contact Pearson VUE Customer Services directly on (+44) 0161 855 7409.

If you can demonstrate that you've special educational needs, you can sit the UKCATSEN instead. The UKCATSEN has the same content as the UKCAT but gives you 25 per cent more time to complete the exam. Mobility and other needs can also be accommodated by UKCAT if you contact the organisation in advance.

Don't register for the UKCATSEN if you do not have special educational needs. Not only is this unethical behaviour, but you will be found out. UKCAT does not expect you to provide clinical evidence to verify your eligibility for UKCATSEN, but the universities do require such evidence. Your test results will be declared null and void if you can't provide evidence of special educational needs at this stage. The evidence needed is typically in the form of a certificate from a qualified medical practitioner or other relevant health professional.

Doing the UKCAT

You can find UKCAT test centres across the UK and in the countries where UKCAT is not exempted. You should be able to find one relatively close to you via the UKCAT website.

Make sure that you know where you're going on test day! We can't think of anything worse than turning up to an exam late, or rushing to get there and feeling frazzled, sweaty and confused as a result.

For the UKCAT, we recommend being 15–30 minutes early, as you need to go through some formalities before you start the exam.

Bring photographic proof of identity with you, such as a valid adult passport with your own signature (children's passports aren't accepted) or a photo-card driving licence. If you've neither of these, ask your school to provide an appropriately certified form letter.

You don't need to take anything else with you. In fact, you're not permitted to take anything else into the test room itself. This prohibition includes coats, bags, phones, wallets, watches, keys and sweets.

Although this situation seems excessive to casual observers, and certainly doesn't take place at many other examinations, at least you're now fore-warned and won't be surprised when the invigilator insists you leave your priceless family heirloom Rolex in a locker.

For the exam, your workstation consists of a computer, a laminated non-erasable notepad and pen, and a chair. You can ask for a set of headphones or earplugs if the ambient noise is too loud for you to concentrate.

UKCAT recently revised its procedures to avoid the need to issue handheld calculators to candidates. Instead, you now have access to a software-based calculator on your workstation computer.

Become comfortable with punching numbers on a screen-based calculator rather than your familiar handheld device so you don't slow down too much during the numerical portions of the exam.

You can leave the room for invigilator-escorted comfort breaks, but the test is not paused during this time, so try to avoid doing so. The time pressure is already one of the toughest things about the exam: you don't want to make it worse.

After the test, you get your results immediately as the UKCAT is computer-marked.

UKCAT automatically forward the results to the universities on your UCAS application that require a UKCAT score. If you want an extra transcript of your results, you can order one for a fee.

You cannot retake the test in the same application cycle.

Deconstructing UKCAT

The UKCAT is a computer-administered exam lasting just over an hour and a half. The test consists of four parts: Verbal Reasoning, Quantitative Reasoning, Abstract Reasoning and Decision Analysis, which are all covered in Part II of this book.

Each of the four parts of the UKCAT is in a multiple-choice format and is timed separately. This section covers the timings and scoring of the UKCAT.

Timing

Students consistently report that one of the hardest things about the UKCAT is the time pressure rather than the content. We show the timings for the UKCAT and the number of question items in each section in Table 2-4.

The demise of the non-cognitive analysis subtest

In previous years, the UKCAT also included a non-cognitive analysis section lasting about half-an-hour. This part aimed to test personal attributes; essentially, it was a form of personality testing to see whether you were suited to a career in medicine or dentistry.

This component of UKCAT was always controversial, and many people considered it to be open to manipulation and unlikely to yield useful information to universities. From 2011, the non-cognitive analysis section has been removed completely from the exam, though whether it has gone for good remains to be seen.

We don't doubt that understanding your own personality is hugely important. Good self-knowledge gives you insight on your interactions with the outside world and how those interactions affect your internal psyche. Such insight can help you choose the right career path and lifestyle to maximise your happiness.

But trying to assess your personality using a psychometric test before medical school had real problems. First, misrepresentation was possible, leading to inaccurate results. More fundamentally, however, many different types of people can have successful medical careers, provided they choose their specialties carefully and have the willpower and techniques to cope with those aspects of medical training and practice that don't naturally mesh with their personality.

Table 2-4	UKCAT Subtests		
Subtest	*Time Allowed*	*Number of Items*	*Time Per Item*
Verbal reasoning	22 minutes	44 items	30 seconds
Quantitative reasoning	23 minutes	36 items	38 seconds
Abstract reasoning	16 minutes	65 items	15 seconds
Decision analysis	32 minutes	26 items	74 seconds

The times per item should give you a general idea of how to pace yourself through each subtest. Naturally, some questions are harder than others, so you may find yourself spending a little longer on the harder ones. But if you take longer on these items, you have to be brisker with the simpler ones. The UKCAT is designed to allow the very best candidates to complete the entire test, although the pace required to do so is challenging.

If you sit the UKCATSEN, you've an extra 25 per cent of time for each section, but the test content remains unchanged.

Familiarising yourself with the pace required is an essential component of your revision. Try the practice test at the end of this book under timed exam conditions to see what we mean.

For further practice tests simulating UKCAT's own computer software, see
www.ukcat.ac.uk/pages/details.aspx?page=practiceQuestions.
Doing these tests helps familiarise you with the software environment of the
real exam.

Marking

The UKCAT is marked based on the number of correct responses you give
on the test. The test doesn't use *negative marking*. That means your score
doesn't go down if you give a wrong answer, but instead you just fail to gain
on that particular question.

If you don't know the answer, guess! You can't actively lose marks.

The number of correct responses is scaled into a mark for each subtest, rang-
ing from 300 to 900. The total score for the entire test therefore ranges from
1200 to 3600.

The UKCAT doesn't have a specific pass mark, and different universities have
different opinions on what they consider to be a good UKCAT score. (See the
section 'Weighing up' below for more on scoring.)

Weighing up

Each university within the UKCAT Consortium is free to decide for itself the
importance of your UKCAT score. Significant variation exists in how the various universities weight your score during their selection processes.

Some universities give the UKCAT score fairly short shrift, while other universities consider the score an absolutely vital part of the selection process and
demand high marks. For instance, the University of Sheffield is traditionally
in the latter camp: in its 2011 cycle, the University of Sheffield's cut-off point
for shortlisting was a total score of 2870.

Candidates often worry about this variation between universities, both before
they sit the test and after they receive their results. This worry is wasted
nervous energy, as you can do little in terms of how you approach the exam,
even if you've complete knowledge of the weighting formula of your preferred
university.

Instead of worrying, focus on practising as much as you can before the test,
staying calm and pacing yourself during the exam. Then put the results out
of your mind. After the test, concentrate on the things you can do to improve

your odds through the rest of the selection process like preparing for the interviews, doing work experience and keeping up to date with any major advances in the medical world.

Think of the application process as the London Marathon and the UKCAT as the equivalent of crossing Tower Bridge. The UKCAT is an important milestone, and you want to be doing well at that stage, but UKCAT isn't the end of the race. You can still recover, or fall back, after you sit the UKCAT. After you cross the bridge, put it out of your mind and focus on the rest of the race.

Chapter 3

Taking Tests: UKCAT Strategies that Work

In This Chapter
▶ Getting ready for the UKCAT
▶ Structuring your revision time
▶ Coping with test day

*F*ew people enjoy taking tests. For most people, tests are an annoyance and some people even find tests terrifying. But if you're serious about being a doctor or a dentist, you need to accept that tests are going to be part of your life for a long time to come.

You've probably already spent a good few years sitting, and likely doing well in, exams at school. After you do the UKCAT, depending on the course and universities you're applying to, you may also have to sit the BMAT, and then you have your A-levels.

In your preclinical years in medical or dental school, you'll have annual or more frequent exams. During your clinical years, the frequency of testing increases, culminating in your finals. If you reckon that's it, think again: you then need to sit postgraduate specialisation exams to get your Royal College Membership, which come in multiple parts taken over a period of years. Dentists also face an increasing number of opportunities to sub-specialise, with their own examinations.

Then you have annual appraisals for both medicine and dentistry, with doctors also now having to revalidate every five years to prove continued fitness to practise. Most of this work is about continuing professional education rather than formal test-taking, but the idea that you escape tests entirely after you leave medical or dental school is seriously flawed.

If you're reading this book, the UKCAT is probably important to you right now. After all, the test may be a significant part of whether you get into medical or dental school. Try to remember that in the long run, if you're successful in your ambitions, the UKCAT is one small test in a long line of other tests. Put the UKCAT in its place and don't let it take over your thoughts.

In this chapter, we suggest some strategies for the UKCAT to help you organise your study time effectively, work out which bits of the test you need to focus on, keep some semblance of a social life, and deal with test day itself.

Organising Yourself

The UKCAT is pretty good practice for life as a junior doctor. When you're on call, you're first in line to be bleeped to do various jobs all over the hospital. You have to figure out quickly which jobs are urgent, which jobs can wait a few minutes, and which jobs can wait until your regular rounds. And while budding dentists reading this book will avoid that scenario, you'll still have to deploy the same time-management and task-scheduling skills in your clinical practice or face a deeply unhappy waiting room! Prioritising your time and organising yourself to work within a tight schedule are skills that improve with forethought and practice.

Fitting in your UKCAT preparation requires the same skill. Your life is busy and you've a lot of things to do. You probably have many things on your mind right now – not only the UKCAT, A-levels, and UCAS forms, but also the small matter of finding time to be with your family and friends and basically having a life.

You need to figure out a way to schedule your studying without letting other aspects of your life suffer too much.

Work out how long you've got until your test date. Now think about the other tasks you have to do and try to give each one the necessary time. Using a calendar, wall planner, or your favourite app on your iPad, map out exactly where you need to be and what you need to do at different times over the coming weeks, including when you plan to be at your desk studying for the UKCAT.

To give UKCAT the time it needs, without letting it take over your entire life, try to set aside some time periods to focus specifically on the test. When you're not scheduled to work on the UKCAT, put it out of your mind and don't spend time wondering whether you've done enough work.

'Little and often' is better than trying to cram all your studying into the last few days before your test.

Dealing with Distractions

Be ruthless in eliminating diversions from your study time. We don't suggest you hire a professional assassin to ward off your younger siblings, but you do need to be a bit selfish about your needs.

Keep these studying tips in mind:

✔ Find a calm space to study (home, library, school).

✔ Turn off your phone.

✔ Avoid social networking websites.

✔ Lock your door.

✔ Ask people not to disturb you.

Don't give your friends and family the total brush-off though. Explain why you're setting such strict boundaries, and try to schedule time to spend with them. Having some fun with your friends helps you relax and feel happier, and also reassures them that you won't forget about them in your new high-flying career.

Focusing on Your Weakest Skills

Most people love doing things that they're familiar with and that they do well. Practising skills that you're good at can provide a sense of mastery and help your self-esteem, but without a clear study plan you may find yourself spending too much time on these areas just to boost your confidence.

You need to score well on all *four* subtests of the UKCAT. A near-maximum score on, say, quantitative reasoning won't be enough to compensate for a dreadful mark in abstract reasoning. (Individual tests are covered in Part II of this book.)

Spending time on the areas you currently do worst on is the easiest way to increase your total score.

Think about your study time as a resource. You've a set amount of productive hours to spend on revision. If you spend those hours working on an area you're already good at, you may improve your performance from 800 to 850, a 6.25 per cent increase.

But if you spend the same number of hours working on an area you're not so good at, you may improve your score from 400 to 600, a 50 per cent increase.

In terms of your total score, you could gain an extra 150 points by spending those precious hours on your weaker areas rather than your strongest areas. Obviously, these numbers aren't guarantees of what score you may get. They're indicative figures used to illustrate the general impact of aggressively targeting the bottlenecks in your knowledge. But the principle is sound.

Practising Taking Tests

The time pressure in UKCAT is severe. One of the best ways to ensure that you complete the UKCAT within the time allocated to each subtest is to practise taking the test under exam conditions. We include two full sample tests in Parts 3 and 4 of this book to help you practise.

UKCAT is a computer-administered test, with a software calculator. We suggest that you familiarise yourself with the UKCAT software interface by trying the sample tests on the UKCAT website (www.ukcat.ac.uk).

Staying Healthy

Preparing for tests can be exhausting, especially when you've a lot of other things on your plate at the same time. But nothing causes your test performance to suffer more than you being unwell and unable to concentrate.

Here are some 'dos' to keep you healthy during your UKCAT preparation:

- ✔ Eat regularly and healthily.
- ✔ Stay hydrated by drinking plenty of water.
- ✔ Get enough sleep.
- ✔ Schedule time for fun and relaxing activities.
- ✔ Consider using relaxation techniques. Some people enjoy using meditation or yoga to help stay focused. Others may prefer a playlist of relaxing music.

And here are some 'don'ts' to watch out for:

- ✔ Drinking too much coffee. Caffeine makes you feel jittery and you lose sleep.
- ✔ Being tempted to take any sort of illicit drug or stimulant.

✔ Working beyond the time scheduled for preparation. You just exhaust yourself.

✔ Having too many late nights. Your sleep pattern can become disordered.

✔ Overhyping the importance of UKCAT. This test is not the only determinant of your application's success.

Arriving for the Test

Make sure that you have a reasonably early night the day before your test. On the day of your test, set your alarm to wake you up, even if you normally get up on time naturally.

Try to eat normally, even if you don't feel hungry or you've a few butterflies in your stomach. If you don't have enough to eat, you won't be able to concentrate during the test. Complex carbohydrates are good, as they release their energy slowly across the day. Complex carbohydrates can be found in many breakfast foods like wholemeal bread and cereals, porridge, and bananas. The night before the UKCAT, you may want to include brown rice or potatoes in your evening meal. Just before your exam, eat an energy bar or fruit for a more instant energy boost.

Take your ID and some cash to deal with any unexpected emergencies en route to the test centre. Leave home a bit earlier than you need to in case the traffic is heavy or your train is delayed. If you arrive at the test centre too early, pop into a local cafe, have something to eat, and take the opportunity to relax a little before your test.

In any exam, you always see a few people desperately trying to do some last-minute preparation. We suggest that you don't join them as it will probably just raise your anxiety level. Try to focus on maintaining an even psychological keel. Steady, deep, controlled breathing can help keep you in the zone, without tipping over into last-minute panic.

And don't forget to go to the toilet before you start the test, even if you don't think that you need to. Sod's law dictates that if you don't go, you're going to feel the urge 10 minutes into your test.

Part II
Examining the Subtests

'I find it helps me with the abstract reasoning.'

In this part . . .

Time to get serious about the UKCAT.

This Part covers all the subtests of the UKCAT in turn and in detail. Each chapter is dedicated to one of the subtests and starts by covering the basic theory behind it.

This will help you get to grips with what the examiners are looking for and the skills you need to develop to answer questions efficiently. I'll also help you avoid some of the common pitfalls students encounter.

Each chapter then goes on to cover a large number of sample questions. Don't worry; there are fully worked-through answers and explanations! The observant reader will note that across the next four chapters there are as many questions as you will encounter in the UKCAT exam itself. Together with the full practice test in the next Part of the book, that's a very substantial pool of test questions for you to "enjoy" working through.

For the Verbal Reasoning chapter, I have to assume you already have a reasonable grasp of basic English. Beyond that, you need to keep your wits about you, concentrate and avoid rushing into answers. In the Quantitative Reasoning chapter, I'll help you bend the good set of mathematical skills you already have from your GCSEs to addressing UKCAT's specific question format. Many people find Quantitative Reasoning the easiest of the four subtests, but that confidence can easily lead to complacency.

Abstract Reasoning is the section of UKCAT that students tend to find the most intimidating. Whereas the Verbal and Quantitative Reasoning sections deal with basically familiar concepts, Abstract Reasoning is, well, Abstract. Its chapter tries to demystify this subtest by familiarising you with a common method to approach these questions. Finally, the last chapter in this Part is devoted to breaking the code of the Decision Analysis subtest.

Chapter 4

Reading Between the Lines: The Verbal Reasoning Subtest

....

In This Chapter

▶ Understanding what the verbal reasoning subtest looks for

▶ Exploring strategies to answer verbal reasoning questions quickly

▶ Practising verbal reasoning questions

....

*Y*ou already have the skill of verbal reasoning – in fact, you've been working on it your entire life. Verbal reasoning is the skill with which you understand and work out the meanings of written words, and draw conclusions based on what you read.

In short, verbal reasoning is what helps you understand meaning.

The UKCAT tests your verbal reasoning ability because this skill is vital for any clinician. Think of the average day of a dentist. She may start off slowly with a coffee, catching up on her email. One message is from a nursing colleague requesting advice about a patient. Another message is from a manager giving feedback from a recent administrative meeting. And then she has a pharmacy bulletin about a newly discovered adverse drug reaction.

Verbal reasoning lets the dentist quickly read all three messages, determine what each person wants and needs, and work out whether she needs to do anything to keep everyone happy. For instance, she may ask a few pertinent questions to get more details before giving the nurse some advice. She may send the manager a quick confirmation that she has read the email and mention a couple of problems that the administrators need to consider. And the information about the adverse drug reaction may prompt her to check that none of her patients on that drug show any early signs of the reaction.

Even before the dentist has left her desk in the morning, she's actively used verbal reasoning in her clinical practice. The UKCAT verbal reasoning subtest tests how well you may perform when faced with similar situations in the future. Universities want to see that you can rapidly take on board written information and use it correctly.

In this chapter, we give you the facts, strategies, and practice that you need to score highly in the UKCAT verbal reasoning subtest. We include a detailed explanation of the types of question found in the verbal reasoning subtest, some useful preparation strategies, essential tips for test day and plenty of practice passages, questions, and answers with full worked-through explanations.

Fathoming the Format of the Verbal Reasoning Subtest

The verbal reasoning subtest consists of 11 passages of prose. After each passage come 4 statements referring to the passage – giving a total of 44 statements. You've 22 minutes to complete the subtest.

You have to read each passage, think carefully about the information presented, and use the information to answer each statement. You then have to determine whether each statement is true or false, or whether you can't tell.

'Can't tell' means that you cannot be absolutely sure whether the statement is true or false – not that you find the question too difficult to answer.

The verbal reasoning subtest looks at your powers of comprehension and your ability to logically infer answers based on the information provided – not whether you already know the answers based on outside data. The subtest is about *judgement*. This subtle difference is one potential reason why many intelligent and well-read candidates make mistakes in the verbal reasoning subtest.

Base your answer solely on the information in the passage. Even if you already know something about the topic discussed in the passage, try to forget that extraneous knowledge and answer each statement using only the information provided in the passage. For example, if the text states that London is the capital of France, you need to 'believe' this statement when you use the passage to determine the correct answer.

Preparing for Success in the Verbal Reasoning Subtest

A good way to prepare for the verbal reasoning subtest is to practise reading dense, complicated material. Any well-written source of information is fine. The material doesn't have to be about medical or dental matters. In fact, at this stage of your studying, we recommend that you try to read as widely as possible in order to better understand the world around you.

A great starting point is the broadsheet newspapers – in other words, papers that don't have large supplements on TV talent contests or celebrities. Especially useful are the opinion columns of the broadsheets. Broadsheet columnists are paid considerable sums of money to write about topical events and draw parallels and conclusions about them. Most opinion columns are rather biased, because strong opinions help to sell papers, which means that the writers do their best to present a logical argument rather than neutral facts. That structure makes them ideal to analyse in the same way as you would a verbal reasoning passage.

Try reading an article and then summarising the information. Keep shrinking down your summary until you've removed all irrelevant fluff and meaningless words tugging at the heart or purse strings (depending on the columnist's political position). Half the time you'll find conflicting conclusions, which says more about the confused thinking of some columnists rather than your verbal reasoning ability.

You need to be able to summarise information quickly, stripping the verbose flesh away from the logical bones of a fat passage of purple prose. If you can do this task quickly, you'll probably find the UKCAT verbal reasoning subtest surprisingly simple.

The ability to rapidly extract information from a wide range of sources helps you formulate opinions for yourself and think widely about the world and its problems. This trait is a useful one for any human being to have and gives you an unusually lucid and perceptive perspective on life.

Working Efficiently on Test Day

Test day can be unnerving, and you can easily lose concentration and start to panic. Add in the time pressure and you may end up throwing away opportunities.

Try to follow the tips below to keep you focused, improve your accuracy and reduce the chances of spending too long on any one question in the verbal reasoning test:

✔ Read the passage quickly but carefully.

✔ Avoid skipping sentences or guessing how they finish.

✔ Each paragraph of a well-composed passage tends to make an individual point. Try to distil the essential meaning of each paragraph to help you simplify the text in your mind.

✔ Don't skim read because it can force unwarranted assumptions. You unconsciously draw on your external knowledge to mentally fill in the gaps and ignore what's actually written down.

✔ Don't get hung up on things that you know are wrong. The text is designed not to be factually correct but to test your verbal reasoning ability.

✔ Don't get angry or irritated with an opinion expressed in the passage. Put your own opinion to one side, stay cool and just answer the questions.

The easiest way to understand how these strategies work is to practise some questions, see how the answers are derived and discover how easily you make mistakes if you lose concentration.

Practising Verbal Reasoning

In this section, you'll get eleven practice passages, each with four questions, just like in the UKCAT. The best way to use this section is to read each passage and then attempt to determine the truthfulness of the four statements that follow the passage. We include worked-through answers following each passage – try to avoid looking at the answers until you come up with your own set of answers.

Don't be discouraged if you make mistakes. The whole point of this book is to prepare you for the actual test. Making a few mistakes now means that you're less likely to make the same mistakes on test day.

Avoid rushing through this section. We include full sample tests for you to do under mock exam conditions in Part III. For now, concentrate on understanding the answers and doing the best you can, even if you take a little more time than you will have in the real thing. Speed comes with practice and with confidence in the technique.

Passage 1

The Egyptian with the Evil Eye
(Adapted from *The Last Days of Pompeii*, by Edward Bulwer-Lytton)

As Clodius was about to reply, a slow and stately step approached them, and at the sound it made amongst the pebbles, each turned, and each recognised the newcomer.

except

He saw a man who had scarcely reached his fortieth year, of tall stature, and of a thin but nervous and sinewy frame. His skin, dark and bronzed, betrayed his Eastern origin; and his features had something Greek in their outline (especially in the chin, the lip, and the brow), save that the nose was somewhat raised and aquiline; and the bones, hard and visible, forbade that fleshy and waving contour which on the Grecian physiognomy preserved even in manhood the round and beautiful curves of youth. His eyes, large and black as the deepest night, shone with no varying and uncertain lustre. A deep, thoughtful, and half-melancholy calm seemed unalterably fixed in their majestic and commanding gaze. His step and mien were peculiarly sedate and lofty, and something foreign in the fashion and the sober hues of his sweeping garments added to the impressive effect of his quiet countenance and stately form. Each of the young men, in saluting the newcomer, made mechanically, and with care to conceal it from him, a slight gesture or sign with their fingers; for Arbaces, the Egyptian, was supposed to possess the fatal gift of the evil eye.

A – True   **B – False**   **C – Can't tell**

Statement 1: Clodius judged that Arbaces seemed calm and thoughtful.   *A*

Statement 2: Clodius had been waiting for Arbaces.   *C*

Statement 3: Arbaces's aquiline nose was typically Greek in physiognomy.   *B*

Statement 4: Arbaces possessed the gift of the evil eye.   *C*

Answer 1
A – True

The author reports that, to Clodius, Arbaces seemed to have 'A deep, thoughtful, and half-melancholy calm . . .' Although you can't tell whether Arbaces did indeed feel calm and thoughtful, Clodius perceived him to be so.

Purple prose

This passage is taken from *The Last Days of Pompeii* by Edward Bulwer-Lytton, a 19th-century author. Despite coining the phrases 'the great unwashed' and 'the pen is mightier than the sword', Edward Bulwer-Lytton is best remembered for the novel opening 'It was a dark and stormy night . . .' His memory is honoured by an annual contest for the kind of terrible writing found in the passage.

Answer 2

C – Can't tell

The passage contains insufficient information to let you decide whether Clodius expected to meet Arbaces at that time.

Answer 3

B – False

The text is written in a flowery and archaic style, making it hard to extract the relevant information. However, the author says that Arbaces's features '. . . had something Greek in their outline . . . save that the nose was . . . aquiline'. The 'save' means that the aquiline (eagle-like) aspect of Arbaces's nose wasn't typically Greek. The statement is therefore false.

Answer 4

C – Can't tell

Although Clodius and his unnamed companion made superstitious hand gestures to ward off the evil eye, and believed that Arbaces possessed the ability to cast that spell, this belief wass only their opinion. Statement 4 says that Arbaces possessed the gift of the evil eye, which you can't verify or deny based on the information in the passage. Note the difference between this answer and the answer for Statement 1. Statement 1 asks only about Clodius's belief, which you can verify from the passage, instead of making an absolute statement about Arbaces in the way Statement 4 does.

Passage 2

Creative Thinking and Schizophrenia
(Adapted from *The Meaning of Madness*, by Neel Burton)

At Vanderbilt University, Folley and Park conducted two experiments to compare the creative thinking processes of schizophrenia sufferers, 'schizotypes' (people with traits of schizophrenia), and normal control subjects.

In the first experiment, subjects were asked to make up new functions for household objects. While the schizophrenia-sufferers and normal control subjects performed similarly to one another, the schizotypes performed better than either.

In the second experiment, subjects were once again asked to make up new functions for household objects as well as to perform a basic control task while the activity in the prefrontal lobes was monitored by a brain scanning technique called near-infrared optical spectroscopy. While all three groups used both brain hemispheres for creative tasks, the right hemispheres of schizotypes showed hugely increased activation compared to the schizophrenia sufferers and normal controls.

For Folley and Park, these results support their idea that increased use of the right hemisphere and thus increased communication between the brain hemispheres may be related to enhanced creativity in psychosis-prone populations.

A – True   **B – False**   **C – Can't tell**

Statement 5: Folley and Park initially assumed that normal controls would perform best in their experiments.

Statement 6: The results of the first experiment were statistically significant.

Statement 7: In the second experiment, the right hemispheres of people with schizophrenia showed increased activation compared with normal controls.

Statement 8: The experiments do not demonstrate that increased communication between the brain hemispheres is related to enhanced creativity in psychosis-prone populations.

Answer 5
B – False

The last paragraph of the passage states that *for Folley and Park,* the results of the experiments support *their* idea that increased use of the right hemisphere and thus increased communication between the brain hemispheres may be related to *enhanced* creativity in psychosis-prone populations.

So, they didn't originally assume that normal controls would perform best. They assumed that the psychosis-prone populations would perform better than the controls.

You don't need to know whether Folley and Park's initial assumption was that schizotypes would outperform schizophrenics or not (and, indeed, you can't logically derive this information from the text). You need to know only that Folley and Park thought normal controls wouldn't have been expected to perform best out of the three groups.

The statement requires you to separate out the descriptive portions of the passage from those where the author describes Folley and Park's own position.

Answer 6
C – Can't tell

The text states that the schizotypes performed better than the people with schizophrenia and normal control subjects. However, the text doesn't specify how much better, the sample size, or any derived statistics. Statements regarding significance are therefore impossible to verify or disprove.

Answer 7
C – Can't tell

The passage says that the right hemispheres of the schizotypes showed hugely increased activation compared with the people with schizophrenia and normal controls. However, the text doesn't specify which of the people with schizophrenia and normal controls showed higher activation.

Although the answer to this question would almost certainly be present in the full results of the experiment, the answer isn't available in the text provided.

Answer 8
A – True

The text says that, even for Folley and Park, the results *support the idea* that increased use of the right hemisphere and thus increased communication between the brain hemispheres may be related to enhanced creativity in psychosis-prone populations.

This question is a reminder to be careful not to over-interpret the passage.

If the experiment's results didn't provide even the experimenters with enough confidence to assert this statement's veracity and to merely couch as 'supporting' the idea, then you certainly can't draw such a firm conclusion solely from the information provided in the passage.

You may be tempted to assume that the experiment's results are valid and universal, but because the passage doesn't imply that they are, you can't make this assumption.

Passage 3

Personality Disorders: Too Much of A Good Thing?
(Adapted from *The Meaning of Madness*, by Neel Burton)

While personality disorders can lead to distress and impairment, they can also enable a person to achieve very highly within certain fields. In 2005, BJ Board and KF Fritzon at the University of Surrey found that high-level British executives were more likely to have one of three personality disorders compared to criminal psychiatric patients at the high security Broadmoor Hospital. These disorders were histrionic personality disorder, narcissistic personality disorder, and anankastic personality disorder.

It is certainly possible to envisage that people could benefit from certain strongly ingrained and potentially maladaptive personality traits. For example, people with histrionic personality disorder may be adept at charming and manipulating others and therefore at building and exercising business relationships. People with narcissistic personality disorder may be highly ambitious, confident, and self-focused and able to exploit people and situations to their best advantage. People with anankastic personality disorder may get quite far up the corporate ladder simply by being so devoted to work and productivity.

This suggests that a personality disorder might be seen as 'too much of a good thing' or 'a good thing out of control'. In their study, Board and Fritzon described the executives with a personality disorder as 'successful psychopaths' and the criminals as 'unsuccessful psychopaths', and it may be that creative visionaries and disturbed psychopaths have more in common than first meets the eye. As the American psychologist and philosopher William James put it, 'When a superior intellect and a psychopathic temperament coalesce . . . in the same individual, we have the best possible condition for the kind of effective genius that gets into the biographical dictionaries.'

A – True   **B – False**   **C – Can't tell**

Statement 9: In 2005, Board and Fritzon found that high-level British executives are more likely to have a personality disorder than criminal psychiatric patients at the high-security Broadmoor Hospital.

Statement 10: People can benefit from having certain strongly ingrained and potentially maladaptive personality traits.

Statement 11: All ingrained and potentially maladaptive personality traits can be beneficial.

Statement 12: The author suggests that whether a person with a personality disorder becomes a 'successful psychopath' or an 'unsuccessful psychopath' is a function of his or her level of intelligence.

Answer 9

B – False

Board and Fritzon found that high-level British executives were more likely to have one of three personality disorders compared with criminal psychiatric patients at the high-security Broadmoor Hospital.

It's logically possible for the criminal population to have higher levels of other personality disorders not reviewed in this study, and therefore to have a higher level of personality disorder overall.

Answer 10

A – True

The text says that although personality disorders can lead to distress and impairment, they can also enable a person to achieve highly within certain fields.

Answer 11

C – Can't tell

You can't conclude this statement from the passage, which is both hypothetical and partial in this regard: 'It is certainly possible to envisage that people could benefit from certain strongly ingrained and potentially maladaptive personality traits.'

Answer 12

A – True

The author quotes William James in saying that 'When a superior intellect and a psychopathic temperament coalesce . . . in the same individual, we have the best possible condition for the kind of effective genius that gets into the biographical dictionaries.'

Passage 4

Antidepressant Efficacy
(Adapted from *The Meaning of Madness*, by Neel Burton)

Doctors often tell people starting on an SSRI antidepressant that they have a 55 to 70 per cent chance of responding to their medication. However, a recent paper by Turner *et al.* suggested that the effectiveness of SSRIs has been exaggerated as a result of a bias in the publication of research studies. Of the 74 total studies registered with the United States Food and Drug Administration (FDA), 37 of 38 studies with positive results were published in academic journals. In contrast, only 14 of 36 studies with negative results were published in academic journals, and 11 of these were published in such a way that they conveyed a positive outcome.

Another recent paper by Kirsch *et al.* combined 35 studies submitted to the FDA before the licensing of four antidepressants, of which there were two SSRIs: fluoxetine and paroxetine. The authors found that, while the antidepressants performed better than a placebo, the effect size was very small for all but very severe cases of depression. Furthermore, the authors attributed this increased effect size in very severe cases of depression not to an increase in the effect of the antidepressants, but to a decrease in their placebo effect.

A – True   **B – False**   **C – Can't tell**

Statement 13: The first paper found that although 94 per cent of published studies conveyed a positive outcome, only 51 per cent of all studies actually demonstrated a positive outcome.

Statement 14: Taken together, the papers raise concerns not only about the effectiveness of SSRIs but also about the effectiveness of antidepressants generally.

Statement 15: The authors believe that placebo drugs can have antidepressant effects.

Statement 16: As the efficacy of SSRIs has been greatly exaggerated, their cost–benefit urgently needs to be re-evaluated.

Answer 13
A – True

According to the text, Kirsch *et al.* found that 37 of the published studies demonstrated a positive result, and a further 11 published studies with negative results but were published in a way that conveyed a positive result, leaving only three published studies with negative results and without conveying a positive result.

There were a total of 51 published studies and 74 total registered studies. The percentage of published studies to convey a positive outcome is [(37 + 11)/51] × 100 = 94 per cent.

The percentage of all studies to demonstrate a positive outcome is (38/74) × 100 = 51 per cent.

Answer 14
A – True

The second paper by Kirsch *et al.* combined 35 studies submitted to the FDA before the licensing of four antidepressants, of which only two were SSRIs.

Answer 15
A – True

Kirsch *et al.* state that 'the antidepressants performed better than a placebo', but taken alone this statement may still mean the placebo has no antidepressant effect. However, the authors go on to say that they 'attributed this increased effect size (of antidepressants) in particularly severe cases of depression not to an increase in the effect of the antidepressants, but to a decrease in their placebo effect.'

This means that the placebo alone must be having an antidepressant effect.

The answer is hidden in the grammar of the statement.

Answer 16
C – Can't tell

This statement seems right, but you can't infer it from the text. For example, the papers may be flawed or otherwise misleading. Also, no information regarding cost is provided . . . perhaps all these medications are free!

Passage 5

Nenikekamen!
(Adapted from *Plato's Shadow*, by Dr Neel Burton)

In 490 BC, the Persian army landed at Marathon with the intention of invading Athens and mainland Greece. A runner called Pheidippides ran the 240km from Athens to Sparta to summon help, but the Spartans refused to budge. The Persians set camp at the bay of Marathon with a large marsh behind them for defence, and detached a contingent by ship to Athens. The Athenians needed not only to defeat the Persians at Marathon but also to rush back to Athens to defend their city – an almost impossible task.

As the Persian army advanced, the Athenian general Miltiades ordered his vastly outnumbered troops to converge onto the centre of the Persian infantry, which miraculously began to crumble. Instead of pursuing the fleeing Persians, the Athenians marched back to Athens, arriving just in time to put off an attack on their city.

The Athenians had sent Pheidippides ahead of them to announce their victory at Marathon. Pheidippides ran the 40 km from Marathon to Athens, breathed 'nenikekamen' ('we have won'), and died on the very spot.

A – True   **B – False**   **C – Can't tell**

Statement 17: Pheidippides had never run over a greater distance than that which separates Marathon from Athens.

Statement 18: When Pheidippides arrived in Sparta with news of the Persian landing, the Spartans refused to budge because it was the festival of Carneia, a sacrosanct period of peace to honour the god Apollo. Pheidippides was informed that the Spartan army couldn't march to war until the full moon rose.

Statement 19: At Marathon, the Persians strengthened their position by setting up camp with a large marsh behind them.

Statement 20: Had the Athenians pursued the fleeing Persians, Athens would've been destroyed.

Answer 17
B – False

In the first paragraph, the text says that when the Persian army landed at Marathon, Pheidippides ran 240 km from Athens to Sparta to summon help. Then in the last paragraph, the text says that the distance from Marathon to Athens is 40 km.

Because modern marathon races are based on the distance between Marathon and Athens, you may have the understandable misconception that 40 km is the longest distance that Pheidippides had ever completed. However, the passage points out that the run from Marathon to Athens was the second, considerably shorter leg of a much greater journey.

Answer 18
C – Can't tell

This statement happens to be true, but you can't infer it from the text.

Never use your outside knowledge to determine whether a statement is true.

Answer 19
A – True

The text clearly says that the Persians set up camp at the bay of Marathon with a large marsh behind them for defence, thus strengthening their position.

Answer 20

C – Can't tell

The text does say that, instead of pursuing the fleeing Persians, the Athenians marched back to Athens and arrived just in time to put off an attack on their city.

However, the attack may not have been successful, or the city may not have been destroyed, or fewer men may have been sufficient to put off the attack. Therefore, based solely on the information in the passage, you can't tell whether the statement is true.

Passage 6

What is the Supreme Good?
(Adapted from *The Art of Failure*, by Neel Burton)

In trying to think about what our purpose or meaning might be, a good place to start is with Aristotle's *Nicomachean Ethics,* which is named for or after Aristotle's son Nicomachus. In the *Nicomachean Ethics,* Aristotle tries to discover 'the supreme good for man', that is, the best way for man to lead his life and to give it purpose and meaning.

For Aristotle, a thing is best understood by looking at its end, goal, or purpose (*telos*). For example, the goal of a knife is to cut, and it is by grasping this that one best understands what a knife is; the goal of medicine is good health, and it is by grasping this that one best understands what medicine is (or should be).

If one does this for some time, it soon becomes clear that some goals are subordinate to other goals, which are themselves subordinate to yet other goals. For example, a medical student's goal may be to qualify as a doctor, but this goal is subordinate to his goal to heal the sick, which is itself subordinate to his goal to earn a living by doing something useful. This could go on and on, but unless the medical student has a goal that is an end-in-itself, nothing that he does is actually worth doing. What, asks Aristotle, is this goal that is not a means to an end but an end-in-itself? This Supreme Good, says Aristotle, is happiness (*eudaimonia*).

A – True   **B – False**   **C – Can't tell**

Statement 21: According to Aristotle, all things are best understood by looking at their end, goal, or purpose (*telos*).

Statement 22: According to Aristotle, the goal of medicine is good health, and the goal of good health is, ultimately, happiness.

Statement 23: The author of the passage implicitly agrees with Aristotle.

Statement 24: For Aristotle, the end ultimately justifies the means.

Answer 21
A – True

The text states that 'For Aristotle, a thing is best understood by looking at its end, goal, or purpose (*telos*).' As the statement is not otherwise modified or qualified within the passage, you're logically justified in assuming that the statement is an absolute applying to all things.

Answer 22
A – True

In the second paragraph, the text says that, according to Aristotle, the goal of medicine is good health.

In the third paragraph, the text implies that, according to Aristotle, happiness is, or should be, the ultimate goal of all human activity.

Answer 23
A – True

The author begins by saying that, in trying to think about what our purpose or meaning may be, a good place to start is with Aristotle's *Nicomachean Ethics*.

The author tends to speak for Aristotle.

Answer 24
C – Can't tell

You can't infer this from the text. For example, there may be a higher principle than the Supreme Good for humans.

Passage 7

Groupthink
(Adapted from *The Art of Failure*, by Neel Burton)

The desire to conform can lead to error, as has been demonstrated by the Asch Experiment, and even to evil, as has been demonstrated by the Milgram experiment. A phenomenon that is related to conformism is 'groupthink'. Groupthink arises when the members of a group seek to minimise conflict by failing to critically test, analyse, and evaluate the ideas that are put to them as a group. As a result, the decisions reached by the group are hasty and irrational, and more unsound than if they had been taken by either member of the group alone. Even married couples can fall into groupthink, for example, when they decide to take their holidays in places that neither spouse wanted, but thought that the other wanted. Groupthink principally arises from the fear of being criticised, the fear of upsetting the group, and the hubristic sense of invulnerability that comes from being in a group. The 20th century philosopher Ludwig Wittgenstein once remarked that 'it is a good thing that I did not let myself be influenced.' In a similar vein, the 18th century historian Edward Gibbon wrote that '. . . solitude is the school of genius . . . and the uniformity of a work denotes the hand of a single artist.'

A – True   **B – False**   **C – Can't tell**

Statement 25: In the presence of groupthink, better decisions will be taken by any member of the group alone.

Statement 26: The phenomenon of groupthink is particularly marked in large groups.

Statement 27: The phenomenon of groupthink arises when the members of a group seek to avoid isolation and rejection by failing to critically test, analyse and evaluate the ideas that are put to them as a group.

Statement 28: The phenomenon of groupthink is common.

Answer 25
A – True

The text clearly states that when groupthink arises, the decisions reached by the group are hasty, irrational and more unsound than if taken by a member of the group alone.

Answer 26
C – Can't tell

However likely this statement may seem, we can't logically infer this from the text. In fact, the text tells of groupthink being significant within a group of just two people.

Don't use your own life experience: Rely solely on the information provided in the passage.

Answer 27
B – False

The text says only that groupthink arises when the members of a group seek to *minimise conflict* by failing to critically test, analyse and evaluate the ideas put to them as a group.

The group members may well do this to avoid isolation and rejection, but they may also do it for a number of other reasons.

Answer 28
C – Can't tell

This statement feels intuitively correct, but you can't infer it from the text.

Passage 8

Grapes and Lemonade
(Adapted from *The Art of Failure*, by Neel Burton)

A person's beliefs, attitudes, and values (henceforth, 'beliefs') are stored in his brain in the form of nerve cell pathways. Over time and with frequent use, these neural pathways become increasingly worn in, such that it becomes increasingly difficult to alter them, and so to alter the beliefs that they correspond to.

If these beliefs are successfully challenged, the person begins to suffer from 'cognitive dissonance', which is the psychological discomfort that results from holding two or more inconsistent or contradictory beliefs at the same time.

To reduce this cognitive dissonance, the person may either (1) adapt his old beliefs, which is difficult, or (2) maintain the status quo by justifying or 'rationalising' his new beliefs, which is not so difficult and therefore more common. The ego defence of rationalisation involves the use of feeble but seemingly plausible arguments either to justify one's beliefs ('sour grapes') or to make them seem not so bad after all ('sweet lemons') . . . Human beings are not rational, but rationalising animals.

A – True   **B – False**   **C – Can't tell**

Statement 29: Cognitive dissonance can be helpful in that it can spur us on to alter our beliefs in the face of increasing evidence.

Statement 30: The ego defence of rationalisation can be used to reduce cognitive dissonance.

Statement 31: An example of 'sweet lemons' is the student who fails her exams and then blames the examiners for being biased.

Statement 32: Several ego defence mechanisms can serve to reduce cognitive dissonance.

Answer 29
A – True

You can infer so much from the text, which states that cognitive dissonance can be reduced by adapting (changing) one's old beliefs. This isn't an intuitive leap requiring assumptions or outside information but a direct and unambiguous logical corollary of the information provided in the passage.

This example highlights the subtleties of some of the harder questions of the verbal reasoning subtest.

Answer 30
A – True

The text clearly states that to reduce cognitive dissonance, a person may either adapt her old beliefs or maintain the status quo by justifying or 'rationalising' her new beliefs.

Answer 31
B – False

This is in fact 'sour grapes', the use of feeble but seemingly plausible arguments to justify one's new beliefs (in this case, the belief that 'I failed my exams').

Answer 32
C – Can't tell

Several ego defence mechanisms can serve to reduce cognitive dissonance, but you can't infer this from the text.

Note the difference in how this answer is reached compared with Answer 29. You can answer Question 32 as 'true' only by drawing on outside knowledge, but you can answer Question 29 as 'true' based purely on the information in the passage and without any outside knowledge.

Passage 9

The Speckled Band
(Adapted from the eponymous short story by Sir Arthur Conan-Doyle)

The little which I had yet to learn of the case was told me by Sherlock Holmes as we travelled back next day.

'I had,' said he, 'come to an entirely erroneous conclusion which shows, my dear Watson, how dangerous it always is to reason from insufficient data. The presence of the gypsies, and the use of the word *band,* which was used by the poor girl, no doubt, to explain the appearance which she had caught a hurried glimpse of by the light of her match, were sufficient to put me upon an entirely wrong scent.'

'I can only claim the merit that I instantly reconsidered my position when, however, it became clear to me that whatever danger threatened an occupant of the room could not come either from the window or the door. My attention was speedily drawn, as I have already remarked to you, to this ventilator, and to the bell-rope which hung down to the bed. The discovery that this was a dummy, and that the bed was clamped to the floor, instantly gave rise to the suspicion that the rope was there as a bridge for something passing through the hole and coming to the bed. The idea of a snake instantly occurred to me, and when I coupled it with my knowledge that Dr Grimesby Roylott was furnished with a supply of creatures from India, I felt that I was probably on the right track . . .'

A – True   **B – False**   **C – Can't tell**

Statement 33: Trying to reason from insufficient data is always dangerous.

Statement 34: Holmes deduced that gypsies couldn't be involved because it was impossible for a dangerous intruder to enter via the window or door.

Statement 35: Dr Grimesby Roylott had travelled to India.

Statement 36: Holmes could've summoned help by pulling the bell-rope to call for servants.

Answer 33
C – Can't tell

This statement is challenging to answer correctly. First, it's a brave reader who goes up against Sherlock Holmes in a battle of logic!

More confusingly, on a meta-level, you need to determine the truth of a fundamental axiom upon which the entire verbal reasoning subtest is based. That is, you need to use the very principle of the axiom itself to answer whether it is true or not. In fact, the passage contains insufficient data for you to decide whether the universal axiom presented in the statement is true or false. Therefore the answer is 'can't tell'.

Always separate out your external sources of knowledge from the information provided in the passage, and use only the latter to answer the questions.

Answer 34

A – True

In the second paragraph, Holmes admits to having initially been on the wrong scent and tangentially mentions the involvement of gypsies as being part of this mistake. At the start of the third paragraph, Holmes says he reconsidered this belief when he realised whatever danger threatened the occupant of the room couldn't have entered via the window or door. Putting these two elements together means that Holmes excluded the involvement of gypsies on the basis of it being impossible for a dangerous intruder to enter the room through the window or door.

Answer 35

C – Can't tell

The passage says that Dr Grimesby Roylott had a supply of snakes from India but makes no comment as to whether he'd personally visited that country.

Answer 36

B – False

The passage states that the bell-rope was a dummy. Therefore, Holmes couldn't have used the rope to summon servants.

Passage 10

Success
(Adapted from The Art of Failure, by Neel Burton)

Nothing illustrates the emptiness of society's conception of "success" better than Leo Tolstoy's novella of 1886, *The Life of Ivan Ilyich*, which is, among other things, an acerbic attack on the artificiality and limitations of the middle classes.

The novella begins with the death of a judge, Ivan Ilyich, and the gathering of a number of people including other judges, family members, and acquaintances to mark his passing. As these people have not yet come to terms with the possibility of their own death, they are unable to understand or empathise with Ivan's. Instead they begin to consider the various advantages of money or promotion that Ivan's passing is likely to mean for them.

The novella then goes back in time 30 years to depict Ivan in his prime. He leads a carefree existence that is "most simple and ordinary, and therefore most terrible". He devotes most of his effort to climbing the social ladder and "doing everything properly".

After later suffering a stroke and being informed it will be fatal, he considers on his life and finds nothing for comfort except the friendship and sympathy of a peasant boy.

A – True   **B – False**   **C – Can't tell**

Statement 37: It is impossible to be happy by pursuing the conventional definition of success.

Statement 38: Ivan Ilyich suffered a fatal stroke 30 years before the novel begins.

Statement 39: The author suggests that Tolstoy uses his work to criticise aspects of the middle classes.

Statement 40: In modern society, people tend to have mid-life crises of a similar existential nature to Ilyich's deathbed revelations.

Answer 37
C – Can't tell

You can't infer this from the text. We are told that Ivan doesn't find comfort in his conventionally successful life, but we cannot definitively extrapolate this to the entire population. While the opening paragraph describes Ivan's life as an illustration of the emptiness of society's definition of success, this cannot be used to absolutely declare that it is not possible to be happy by aiming to achieve it.

Answer 38
B – False

The story opens at Ivan's funeral, and then flashbacks to a time 30 years prior. We are not told when the stroke took place, only that it was later than the 30 year period. Of course, intuitively, one would surmise that it was very close to the timeframe of his funeral, but we cannot logically be certain of this. However, it being later than the 30 year timeframe is sufficient to prove the statement false.

Answer 39

A – True

The opening paragraph has the author describing one of Tolstoy's novellas as "an acerbic attack on the artificiality and limitations of the middle classes".

Answer 40

C – Can't tell

This seems intuitively correct, if you agree with the perspective of the passage author, but cannot be conclusively proven from the text.

Passage 11

Concerning Liberality and Meanness
(Adapted from *The Prince*, by Nicolo Machiavelli)

I say that it would be well to be reputed liberal. Nevertheless, liberality exercised in a way that does not bring you the reputation for it, injures you; for if one exercises it honestly and as it should be exercised, it may not become known, and you will not avoid the reproach of its opposite.

Therefore, anyone wishing to maintain among men the name of liberal is obliged to avoid no attribute of magnificence; so that a prince thus inclined will consume in such acts all his property, and will be compelled in the end, if he wish to maintain the name of liberal, to unduly weigh down his people, and tax them and do everything he can to get money.

This will soon make him odious to his subjects, and becoming poor he will be little valued by any one; thus, with his liberality, having offended many and rewarded few, he is affected by the very first trouble and imperilled by whatever may be the first danger; recognising this himself, and wishing to draw back from it, he runs at once into the reproach of being miserly.

There is nothing wastes so rapidly as liberality, for even whilst you exercise it you lose the power to do so, and so become either poor or despised, or else, in avoiding poverty, rapacious and hated. And a prince should guard himself, above all things, against being despised and hated; and liberality leads you to both. Therefore, it is wiser to have a reputation for meanness, which brings reproach without hatred, than to be compelled through seeking a reputation for liberality to incur a name for rapacity which begets reproach with hatred.

A – True   B – False   C – Can't tell

Statement 41: According to the author, liberality, if done as it should be, doesn't necessarily result in a person being known for his liberality.

Statement 42: The author believes that long-term liberality in a prince means that he spends more money than he has, resulting in tax increases on his population to continue his spending.

Statement 43: The conclusion of the passage is that a reputation for miserliness is more damaging to a prince than a reputation for generosity.

Statement 44: The principles outlined in the passage apply to modern democratic governments.

Answer 41
A – True

The passage is quite dense, with many subordinate clauses, which makes it challenging to read and to extract information. The first paragraph includes the lengthy sentence 'Nevertheless, liberality exercised in a way that does not bring you the reputation for it, injures you; for if one exercises it honestly and as it should be exercised, it may not become known, and you will not avoid the reproach of its opposite.'

Removing clauses irrelevant to the statement under scrutiny, you can reduce this statement to 'Liberality, if one exercises it honestly as it should be, may not become known.' Therefore the statement is true.

Although you don't need to understand the term 'liberality' to answer the question, you may want to understand that the term, as used in the context in the passage, refers to spending money in large quantities on many different projects, from public buildings and works, to charity, to having a large staff.

Answer 42
A – True

The relevant information is in the second paragraph: '. . . anyone wishing to maintain among men the name of liberal is obliged to avoid no attribute of magnificence; so that a prince thus inclined will consume in such acts all his property, and will be compelled in the end, if he wish to maintain the name of liberal, to unduly weigh down his people, and tax them, and do everything he can to get money.'

You can simplify this information logically to 'Anyone trying to maintain a liberal reputation is inclined to consume all his property, and to tax his people to get money.' You can now see easily that the statement is true.

Princely behaviour

Nicolo Machiavelli wrote *The Prince* during the early part of the 16th century. Machiavelli dedicated the text to a member of the ruling Florentine Medici family. To their detractors, the behaviour of the Medici became a byword for ruthlessness and corruption. To their advocates, the Medici were successful rulers who expanded the power of the states they governed and sponsored much of the cultural efflorescence of the Italian Renaissance.

Machiavelli's work tends to split observers in a similar way. Some view his writing as a triumph of realism and practicality over grandiose ambition, and thus a model for prudent government. Others dislike the cynicism underlying much of the work and the lack of a consistent ethical direction to its advice.

The Prince is still a popular work and highlights many of the tensions inherent in any governing system, including democracies.

Answer 43
B – False

The passage concludes the opposite. The passage suggests that because of the need to have onerous tax rises to maintain high levels of expenditure, liberality eventually results in people hating the prince and considering him wrong. Being miserly also results in people considering the prince wrong, but because tax rises have been avoided the people don't hate the prince as well.

Therefore being liberal causes more damage to the prince's reputation than being miserly.

Answer 44
C – Can't tell

The passage, unsurprisingly for one written during the Italian Renaissance, draws no parallels with modern democratic government. Although you can theorise that the same basic principles of wise economic management apply to the popularity of an elected government as much as they did to Florentine nobility, you can't state this for certain based solely on the information provided in the passage.

Chapter 5

Making Things Add Up: The Quantitative Reasoning Subtest

. . . .

In This Chapter

▶ Understanding what the quantitative reasoning subtest looks for

▶ Exploring strategies to answer quantitative reasoning questions quickly and correctly

▶ Practising quantitative reasoning questions

. . . .

*I*f you plan to apply for medical or dental school, you've almost certainly already got a good GCSE in maths. The quantitative reasoning subtest in the UKCAT doesn't draw on any skills beyond GCSE maths, so with a bit of practice you should do really well in this test.

At first glance you may think that the ability to comfortably manipulate numbers has little to do with medicine or dentistry, but maths crops up in all sorts of clinical nooks and crannies. Consider a doctor on his ward round, seeing patients. His junior doctor updates him on a particularly unwell patient with a serious infection, reeling off a string of blood test results. The doctor realises that not only do the patient's lab results remain outside the normal range, but also the results are worse than the day before. This deduction is a basic mathematical operation.

The doctor decides to switch the patient's antibiotic from an oral tablet to an intravenous infusion, knowing that this infusion is more likely to treat the infection. The antibiotic he wants to prescribe is potentially toxic in excess. He double-checks the dose in his formulary and sees that he should base the dose on the patient's weight. The doctor looks up the weight on the patient's weight chart, calculates the required total dose and writes that up on the patient's drug chart.

This example is maths at work and saving lives.

The quantitative reasoning subtest is designed to assess how you solve numerical problems, some of which aren't dissimilar to the problems the doctor described above has to solve.

In this chapter, we show you everything you need to score highly in the UKCAT quantitative reasoning subtest. We include an explanation of the types of questions found in the quantitative reasoning subtest, some useful test strategies, and plenty of practice questions, with answers and fully worked-through explanations.

Finding Out the Format of the Quantitative Reasoning Subtest

The UKCAT quantitative reasoning subtest consists of nine numerical presentations. After each presentation comes four questions based on the content within the presentation, giving a total of 36 questions. You have 23 minutes to complete the subtest.

In the subtest, data is presented in the form of tables, charts and graphs. You have to be able to rapidly identify relevant information from the presentation, and then manipulate that information appropriately to answer the question.

The testers are looking for basic mathematical capabilities. They want to see that you:

- ✔ Can perform simple mathematical operations.
- ✔ Understand proportions, percentages and ratios.
- ✔ Apply different kinds of average.
- ✔ Work comfortably with fractions and decimals.
- ✔ Can convert from one measurement system to another.
- ✔ Can solve basic equations.

The UKCAT quantitative reasoning subtest focuses on using numbers to solve problems instead of raw numerical facility. The subtest is checking that you can determine what numbers can reveal (and hide!), not whether you can number-crunch like a computer.

Most people find that, compared with the other sections of UKCAT, the quantitative reasoning subtest is intellectually simpler yet harder to complete within the time limit. Although the subtest is less conceptually difficult, try to remain focused throughout the subtest and don't let yourself make silly mathematical errors.

Since its most recent overhaul, the UKCAT prohibits the use of handheld calculators. The software used to administer the test includes an on-screen calculator with basic functionality. You can access this calculator with the click of an icon and let it run in the background as you move from one question to another. Many people find on-screen calculators harder to use than their more familiar handheld devices. To improve your familiarity with the on-screen calculator, try practising with the calculator program featured on most Windows PCs, and then do the practice tests on the UKCAT website to familiarise yourself with the real thing.

Preparing for Success in the Quantitative Reasoning Subtest

To do well in the quantitative reasoning subtest, you need to be familiar with some basic mathematical operations, which you may already know from GCSE level mathematics:

- Addition, subtraction, multiplication and division
- Percentages, ratios and fractions
- Speed, distance and time calculations
- Working with money
- Areas and volumes
- Graphs and charts

If you feel rusty working with these simple operations, first have a look through your GCSE maths books again. Then get yourself up to speed by doing a lot of practice UKCAT questions.

Working Well on Test Day

Test day can be unnerving, making it easy to lose concentration and panic. Add in the time pressure and you may throw away scoring opportunities.

To help keep you focused, improve your error rate, and reduce your chances of spending too long on one question in the quantitative reasoning subtest, try to follow the tips below:

- ✔ Try not to be intimidated by presentations on topics you know nothing about. Remember the testers are looking to see how well you can manipulate numerical information, not whether you're familiar with the topic of the presentation.

- ✔ Practise using the on-screen calculator before test day. Also, beware of typos when you use the on-screen calculator. On the day itself, try to leave yourself time to double-check the more complicated calculations.

- ✔ Don't overcomplicate the questions. The questions require the use of fairly basic mathematical operations. If you have to draw on advanced mathematics in your attempts to solve the problem, you're almost certainly overcomplicating things and heading down the wrong track.

- ✔ If you're already comfortable working with maths, don't be overconfident in the subtest. Read each question carefully and work steadily to avoid making careless errors. Vital information can easily be misinterpreted or missed entirely.

- ✔ Don't relax too much. Doing so leads to avoidable careless errors in a subtest you can otherwise score highly on.

- ✔ Don't spend too much time on a question you can't solve. Move on to the next question and keep your cool.

The easiest way to understand these strategies is to practise questions, see how the answers are derived, and see how you can make mistakes if you lose concentration.

Practising Quantitative Reasoning

We suggest that you use this section to practise your quantitative reasoning skills. Concentrate on moving swiftly through the questions, avoiding careless and preventable errors. The content isn't mathematically challenging, provided you stay alert.

Don't be discouraged if you make a few mistakes. The whole point of this book is to prepare you for the actual test. Making a few mistakes now means you're less likely to make the same mistakes on test day.

Avoid rushing through this section. We include full sample tests for you to do under mock exam conditions in Part III. For now, concentrate on understanding the answers and doing the best you can, even if you take a little longer than you have in the real thing. Speed comes with practice and with confidence in the technique.

Numerical presentation 1

EU debt

The number of countries per group is shown in Figure 5-1.

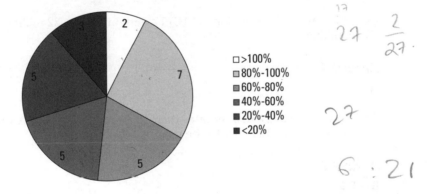

EU Countries Debt Burdens, expressed as a percentage of GDP and grouped by ranges

□ >100%
▨ 80%-100%
▩ 60%-80%
▦ 40%-60%
▪ 20%-40%
■ <20%

Figure 5-1:
EU debt bur-
dens as a
percentage
of GDP.

Item 1:

To the nearest whole number, what percentage of countries has a debt greater than 100% of GDP?

(A) 7%   (B) 19%   (C) 26%   (D) 33%   (E) 93%

Item 2:

What is the ratio of the number of countries with a debt burden greater than 80% of GDP to the rest of the countries?

(A) 2:25   (B) 1:2   (C) 1:3   (D) 8:27   (E) 1:9

Item 3:

The countries with debts between 80% and 100% of GDP pass aggressive austerity budgets, and as a result, three of them reduce their debts to between 60% and 80% of GDP. Assuming that all the other countries in the EU remain the same, what is the new ratio of countries with a debt burden greater than 80% of GDP to the rest of the countries?

9:18

12:. 15.

(A) 2:25   (B) 5:22   (C) 1:3   (D) 6:21   (E) 4:23

Item 4:

The EU countries in this survey account for a total of 500 million people. If the two countries with debts in excess of 100% of GDP account for 16% of that population, how many people live in each of the other countries, assuming that they're evenly distributed across the rest of the EU? Round your answer to the nearest whole million.

(A) 6 million   (B) 8 million   (C) 17 million   (D) 22 million
(E) 40 million

Answer 1
A 7%

Two countries have a debt greater than 100% of GDP. The survey includes 27 countries. $(2/17) \times 100 = 7\%$ to the nearest whole number.

Answer 2
B – 1:2

Nine countries have a debt greater than 80%. The survey includes 27 countries; therefore, 18 other countries are in the EU. The ratio is 9:18, which simplifies to 1:2.

Answer 3
D – 6:21

Seven countries are in the range of 80 to 100%. If three of these countries succeed in moving into the range of 60 to 80% as a result of their austerity measures, four countries remain in the range of 60 to 80%. Including the two countries with debts above 100%, a total of six countries now have debts greater than 80%. As the total number of countries is 27, the ratio of countries with debts above 80% to those below is 6:21.

6:21

2:

22/2

Answer 4

C – 17 million

The total population is 500 million. The two countries with debts above 100% of GDP account for 16% of the population, which in terms of millions of people is 500 million $\times$ (16 ÷ 100) = 80 million. Therefore, the remaining 25 countries account for (500 – 80) = 420 million people.

You're told that the remaining population is distributed evenly across those 25 countries, so the number of people in each country is 420 ÷ 25 million = 17 million, to the nearest whole number.

Numerical presentation 2

Mental Health Act Assessments

Table 5-1	Distribution of Mental Health Act Assessments in 2010
Month	**Assessments**
January	132
February	85
March	88
April	101
May	95
June	110
July	123
August	117
September	78
October	92
November	167
December	286

Item 5:

How many assessments took place in the first three months of the year?

(A) 132   (B) 217   (C) 305   (D) 318   (E) 406

Item 6:

By the end of which month had 50% of the assessments taken place?

(A) May   (B) June   (C) July   (D) August   (E) September

Item 7:

What percentage of assessments, to the nearest whole number, took place in the last three months of the year?

(A) 13%   (B) 21%   (C) 25%   (D) 31%   (E) 37%

Item 8:

The monitoring exercise was repeated a year later. There were the following changes in the numbers of assessments: May (+15), June (–6), July (+7), August (–11). In calculating the revised totals, what's the new ratio of assessments in May and June to those in July and August?

(A) 1:1   (B) 113:129   (C) 41:48   (D) 107:118   (E) 52:65

Answer 5
C – 305

This test is a straightforward check of your ability to extract the relevant data from the table and then add the data together to find the total. The relevant data for the answer is included in Table 5-2.

Table 5-2	Assessments in the First Three Months
Month	**Assessments**
January	132
February	85
March	88

The sum of 132, 85 and 88 is 305.

Answer 6
D – August

This problem is a two-step operation. First you need to find 50% of the total number of assessments. The total is 1,474 (calculated by adding up each of the individual data points). The 50% mark is therefore 737 assessments.

Then work your way down the table, adding up the assessments as you go, until you go past 737. This point occurs after you pass August, so the answer is D.

Answer 7
E – 37%

First you need to find the total number of assessments that took place in the last three months of the year. Take a look at the relevant information in Table 5-3.

Table 5-3	Assessments in the Last Three Months
Month	*Assessments*
October	92
November	167
December	286

92 + 167 + 286 = 545.

As the total number of assessments is 1,474 (which you calculated for Item 6), the percentage is 545 ÷ 1,474 × 100 = 37% to the nearest whole number.

Answer 8
D – 107:118

You've been given the change in data compared with the earlier year. You can quickly determine the new totals, outlined in Table 5-4.

Table 5-4	New Distribution of Assessments in 2011
Month	*Assessments*
May	95 + 15 = 110
June	110 − 6 = 104
July	123 + 7 = 130
August	117 − 11 = 106

To work out the ratio between the months of May and June and July and August, you need to add up the relevant data points:

May + June = 110 + 104 = 214

July + August = 130 + 106 = 236

The ratio 214:236 simplifies to 107:118.

Numerical presentation 3

Medal Winning Performances

Table 5-5	2008 Olympic Gold Medals per Million Population				
Belarus	0.41	Slovenia	0.50	Spain	0.12
Jamaica	2.16	Great Britain	0.31	Italy	0.14
Portugal	0.09	Bahrain	1.41	Latvia	0.44
India	<0.01	Netherlands	0.42	Russia	0.16
Australia	0.69	Denmark	0.37	New Zealand	0.73
United States	0.12	Mongolia	0.68	Japan	0.07
Georgia	0.65	France	0.11	Norway	0.65

Mike, a football fan, decides to stratify the countries in Table 5-5 into a league table of performance, shown in Table 5-6.

Table 5-6	Country League Table	
League		**Number of Countries**
Premiership (>1 gold per million)		2
Championship (0.7–0.99 gold per million)	0.7 .	1
League One (0.5–0.69 gold per million)		4
League Two (0.25–0.49 gold per million)	0.31	5
Conference (<0.25 gold per million)		8

Item 9:

What's wrong with Mike's table?

> A – One too many in the Premiership
>
> B – One too few in League One
>
> C – One too few in League Two
>
> D – One too many in the Conference
>
> E – One too few in the Premiership

Item 10:

Great Britain has a population of 61.3 million. New Zealand has a population of 4.15 million. How many more gold medals did Great Britain win than New Zealand? Round your answer to the nearest whole medal.

(A) 1   (B) 2   (C) 16   (D) 25   (E) 43

Item 11:

Mike is asked to calculate the modal average gold medal per million. Which of the following would he do?

> A – Find the gold medal per million figure that occurs most frequently
>
> B – Add up all the gold medal per million figures and divide by 21
>
> C – Add up all the gold medal per million figures and divide by 2
>
> D – Rearrange the numbers into numerical order and find the tenth number
>
> E – Rearrange the numbers into numerical order, find the tenth and eleventh numbers, add them up and divide by 2

Item 12:

How many more gold medals would Great Britain have to win to achieve Championship status? (You may continue to assume that Great Britain has a population of 61.3 million.)

(A) 12   (B) 24   (C) 31   (D) 43   (E) 61

Answer 9

B – One too few in League One

The relevant League One countries are highlighted in bold in Table 5-7. Five countries are highlighted, but only four countries are counted in Table 5-6. Answering this question requires that you do the same task Mike attempted and check your totals against his as you go.

Table 5-7		League One Countries			
Belarus	0.41	**Slovenia**	**0.50**	Spain	0.12
Jamaica	2.16	Great Britain	0.31	Italy	0.14
Portugal	0.09	Bahrain	1.41	Latvia	0.44
India	<0.01	Netherlands	0.42	Russia	0.16
Australia	**0.69**	Denmark	0.37	New Zealand	0.73
United States	0.12	**Mongolia**	**0.68**	Japan	0.07
Georgia	**0.65**	France	0.11	**Norway**	**0.65**

Answer 10

C – 16

This question involves a multistage calculation. The data in Table 5-6 shows gold medals per country per million population. Before calculating the difference, you have to convert these standardised figures back into absolute numbers of gold medals won by Great Britain and New Zealand by multiplying each figure by its population:

Number of gold medals won by Great Britain = 0.31 × 61.3 = 19 medals, to the nearest whole number.

Number of gold medals won by New Zealand = 0.73 × 4.15 = 3 medals, again, to the nearest whole number.

Then you subtract the British total from the New Zealand total = 19 – 3 = 16.

Answer 11

A – Find the gold medal per million figure that occurs most frequently

This question checks that you understand the term 'modal average'.

Answer 12

B – 24

To be in the Championship, Great Britain needs a minimum gold medal per million of 0.7. As its population size is 61.3, Great Britain needs to win 61.3 0.7 = 43 medals (rounding up to the nearest whole gold medal). You've already calculated that Great Britain won 19 medals, so it needs to win (43 – 19) = 24 more gold medals.

Numerical presentation 4

\\| / /

Table 5-8		UKCAT Scores of Medical School Applicants		
2,250	2,650	3,200	2,900	1,900
2,300	2,750	2,400	3,050	2,400
3,050	2,150	2,800	3,100	2,900
2,550	2,700	2,450	2,600	3,300

9/20

Item 13:

Any applicant scoring 2,750 or greater was shortlisted for an interview. What percentage of applicants weren't called for an interview?

(A) 35%   (B) 40%   (C) 45%   (D) 55%   (E) 60%

Item 14:

Based solely on the numbers in the table, what were any given applicant's odds of getting an interview? Round your answer to two decimal places.

(A) 0.67   (B) 0.82   (C) 1.22   (D) 1.5   (E) 0.43

Item 15:

What proportion of applicants, expressed as a fraction, would have been interviewed if the cut-off score had been 3,000?

(A) ⅕   (B) ¼   (C) ³⁄₁₀   (D) ¹⁄₂₀   (E) ¾

Item 16:

What's the average UKCAT score of the interviewed candidates in the scenario outlined in Item 15?

(A) 3,140   (B) 3,160   (C) 3,180   (D) 3,200   (E) 3,240

Answer 13
D – 55%

Nine applicants have a score of 2,750 or greater. As the table shows scores for a total of 20 total candidates, (20 – 9) = 11 candidates were not selected for interview. Expressed as a percentage, this calculation is (11 ÷ 20) × 100 = 55%.

Answer 14
B – 0.82

Odds are expressed as the number of chances of an event happening compared with the number of chances of the same event not happening. The question lists 9 interviewed candidates and 11 non-interviewed candidates, so the odds of being interviewed are 9:11, or $\frac{9}{11}$, or in decimal form 0.82.

Answer 15
B – ¼

Only 5 applicants out of a total of 20 have scores of 3,000 or above. Expressed as a fraction, this calculation is 5 ÷ 20 = ¼.

Answer 16
A – 3,140

This question is a straightforward test of your ability to calculate an arithmetic mean, in this case of the five candidates with scores of 3,000 or above: (3,200 + 3,050 + 3,050 + 3,100 + 3,300) ÷ 5 = 3,140.

Numerical presentation 5

Items 17–20 relate to faster-than-light (FTL) space travel.

Distance in space is measured in light-years (lt-yr). One lt-yr is the distance covered by an object travelling at c, the speed of light, in 1 year.

FTL speeds are measured by warp factor. Warp factor is expressed as a multiple of c. Thus, Warp1 = c, Warp2 = $2c$, Warp3 = $3c$, Warp4 = $4c$ and so on.

You may assume that 1 year = 365 days.

Item 17:

A spaceship leaves Earth in order to travel to the Alpha Centauri star system, 4.25 lt-yr away. Assuming travel at Warp5, how many days does it take to arrive at Alpha Centauri? Please express your answer in Earth days, and you may ignore any potential relativistic effects of FTL travel.

(A) 292.00   (B) 306.60   (C) 310.25   (D) 328.50   (E) 332.15

Item 18:

The spaceship's warp drive requires frequent repairs. On its journey to Alpha Centauri, it first breaks down after travelling 180 days at Warp6, and then again after 50 days at Warp4, before completing the rest of the journey at Warp7. How long did the last leg of the journey take, rounding to the nearest whole day?

(A) 18   (B) 22   (C) 25   (D) 33   (E) 39

Item 19:

The spaceship runs on dilithium crystals and it takes 3 dilithium crystals to travel a light year. The spaceship is on a journey from Earth to a distant star system. The spaceship is currently 30% of the way from Earth to that distant system, and it has 21 further light years to travel before it reaches it. Before starting any journey, the ship's engineer always orders 10% extra dilithium crystals than the minimum needed for the trip. Assuming that the spaceship intends on returning to Earth, how many crystals did the engineer order before leaving Earth?

(A) 42   (B) 90   (C) 99   (D) 180   (E) 198

Item 20:

A wormhole is discovered between Earth and Alpha Centauri, which shortens the overall distance that needs to be travelled by a total 2 lt-yr. Travel through the wormhole is instantaneous. If a spaceship travels the 0.5 lt-yr to the wormhole at Warp2, and then travels at Warp5 from the wormhole to Alpha Centauri, how long is the total journey using the wormhole, expressed in days?

(A) 200.75   (B) 219.00   (C) 280.25   (D) 310.25   (E) 365.00

These questions involve topics that are partly the realm of science-fiction and partly the realm of quantum physics. The mathematics you're required to do in order to answer the questions, however, are straightforward. Don't be fazed by unusual topics – just focus on the maths!

The key thing to realise for this set of questions is that if distance is expressed in light-years (with 1 lt-yr being the distance covered by light in a year) and warp speeds are multiples of the speed of light, then dividing any distance in light-years by a warp speed gives you an answer in years. So, the time for any journey (in years) can be found by dividing light-years by warp factor. All the information required to work this out is within the question, with no mathematics more complicated than GCSE level knowledge and no knowledge of physics required.

Answer 17

C – 310.25

The distance to Alpha Centauri is 4.25 lt-yr. The spaceship is travelling at Warp5, which is $5c$. In 1 year, the spaceship will cover 5 lt-yr (because c is the speed of light).

Time = distance ÷ speed = 4.25 ÷ 5 = 0.85 years

As a year has 365 days, the spaceship takes $(0.85 \times 365) = 310.25$ days to reach Alpha Centauri.

Answer 18

E – 39

This question involves a fairly complicated multistage calculation. You know that the total distance to be travelled is 4.25 lt-yr. To calculate how long the last leg took, you need to calculate the distance left to travel during that leg. You know the speed the spaceship travelled at, so you can work out how long the final leg took.

To calculate the distance of the final leg, you work out the distances of the first two legs, add them together, and then subtract them from the total journey distance. You already know the speed of the first two legs and the time in days (which you can easily convert to time in years). You need to use the equation distance = speed × time:

First leg: $6c \times (180 \div 365) = 2.96$ lt-yr

Second leg: $4c \times (50 \div 365) = 0.55$ lt-yr

Distance of third leg = 4.25 − 2.96 − 0.55 = 0.74 lt-yr

The time in days to cover the third leg = distance ÷ speed = $(0.74 \div 7c) \times 365$ = 39 days (multiplying by 365 to convert from years into days, and then rounding to the nearest whole day).

Answer 19

E – 198

The spaceship has 21 lt-yr left to travel to its destination and has already travelled 30% of the trip to the star system. This means that the 21 lt-yr represents 70% of the total distance between Earth and the destination. The total distance is $(100 \div 70) \times 21$ = 30 lt-yr.

As the spaceship plans a return journey, the total distance is 30×2 = 60 lt-yr.

At a consumption rate of 3 crystals per lt-yr, the minimum number of crystals required is 60×3 = 180 crystals. Adding in the engineer's 10% safety buffer gives: $(110 \div 100) \times 180$ = 198 crystals.

Answer 20

B – 219

The original distance from Earth to Alpha Centauri is 4.25 lt-yr. The wormhole shortens travel by 2 lt-yr, so the new total distance is 2.25 lt-yr.

The journey to the wormhole is 0.5 lt-yr, so the journey from the wormhole is $(2.25 - 0.5)$ = 1.75 lt-yr.

Time to reach the wormhole = distance ÷ speed = $0.5 \div 2$ = 0.25 years

Time from the wormhole to Alpha Centauri = distance ÷ speed = $1.75 \div 5$ = 0.35 years

The total journey time is $0.25 + 0.35$ = 0.6 years. Converting into days, this calculation is 0.6×365 = 219 days.

Numerical presentation 6

Governing Ruritania

The bars in Figure 5-2 respectively represent the Monarchist Party, the Rupertist Party, the Maubanite Party and those voting for other parties.

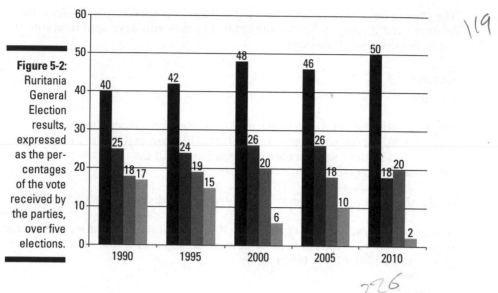

Figure 5-2:
Ruritania
General
Election
results,
expressed
as the per-
centages
of the vote
received by
the parties,
over five
elections.

19

226

Item 21:

In 2005, what is the ratio of Rupertist votes to votes for all other parties?

(A) 1:5   (B) 1:4   (C) 13:50   (D) 13:37   (E) 37:13

Item 22:

Which of the following statements is supported by the information in the chart?

A – The percentage of Rupertist votes is increasing over time.

B – The percentage of Maubanite votes is increasing over time.

C – The percentage vote for the Rupertists in 2005 is similar to that for the Maubanites in 1995.

D – The percentage of Monarchist votes has been increasing at the expense of Maubanites votes.

E – The percentage of Monarchist votes has been increasing at the expense of Rupertist and other votes.

50% = 6.32.

Item 23:

In 2010, 6.32 million people voted Monarchist. How many people voted Rupertist?

(A) 9.50 million   (B) 6.32 million   (C) 3.60 million   (D) 2.72 million
(E) 2.28 million

Item 24:

What is the percentage range for all parties/groupings across the five elections?

(A) 6%   (B) 10%   (C) 28%   (D) 48%   (E) 50%

24.
26:

Answer 21

D – 13:37

26% voted Rupertist and 74% voted for other parties. The ratio is 26:74, which simplifies to 13:37.

Answer 22

B – The percentage of Maubanite votes is increasing over time.

You can see this information relatively easily in the chart. The other options are contrary to the information provided or incomplete assumptions.

Answer 23

E – 2.28m

A total of 6.32 million people account for 50% of votes cast. Therefore, the total number of votes cast is $6.32 \times (100/50) = 12.64$ million.

Eighteen percent of votes cast were Rupertist votes. Therefore, the number of Rupertist votes is 12.64 million $\times 0.18 = 2.28$ million.

If you're more comfortable with maths, a quicker method is to calculate $18 \div 50 \times 6.32$, making use of the relative proportions of the Monarchist and Rupertist parties.

Answer 24

D – 48%

The range is the highest reading across the period minus the lowest reading across the period = 50% – 2% = 48%.

Numerical presentation 7

Managing the Money Managers

Table 5-9	Wormtongue Financial Management		
Portfolio Set-Up Charge: £500			
Annual management fee (deducted on the anniversary date of portfolio creation)	Portfolio value of less than £50,000 on anniversary date	Portfolio value between £50,000 and £249,999 on anniversary date	Portfolio value greater than £250,000 on anniversary date
Percentage of portfolio value	0.5%	0.3%	0.1%

Table 5-10	Thumbscrews Asset Management
Item	**Cost**
Portfolio set-up charge	Free
Annual management fee (deducted on the anniversary date of portfolio creation)	0.2% of portfolio value
Exit charge on money withdrawn from portfolio up to and including the first annual anniversary of set-up	0.08% of value of money withdrawn
Exit charge on money withdrawn from portfolio after first year	0.03% of value of money withdrawn

The questions in this section require some complicated calculations, although the mathematical operations involved are straightforward. The questions demonstrate how murky it can be to compare tariffs between different providers. Similar kinds of calculation are required in real life when comparing mobile phone bills, mortgage providers and energy companies.

Item 25:

Josefin is looking for a wealth manager. She has narrowed her options down to these two firms. She has a lump sum of £200,000 to invest immediately and also plans of invest an extra £50,000 annually on the anniversary date of the portfolio's creation, for a further two years, that is, there will be a total of two further payments into the portfolio.

These extra anniversary payments into the portfolio aren't included in the portfolio total when calculating fees owing on that same anniversary date, but do count toward future year totals.

Assuming that Josefin sticks to this schedule, how much will it cost her in overall fees and charges if she employs the services of Wormtongue Financial Management over her planned investment period (and not including any fees the portfolio attracts after the date of the final payment into the portfolio)?

You may assume that whatever funds are invested in the portfolio grow at 10% per year, and the annual management fees are deducted from her portfolio balance. Round your answer to the nearest penny.

(A) £956.27 (B) £1,456.27 (C) £1,457.00 (D) £1,700.00
(E) £1,968.02

Item 26:

How much would Josefin's portfolio be worth if she invests the same amounts over the same timeframe as in Item 25, but uses Thumbscrews Asset Management instead? Thumbscrews, like Wormtongue, generates a 10% annual growth rate.

(A) £241,516.00 (B) £295,922.97 (C) £296,516.00
(D) £345,922.97 (E) £380,515.27

Item 27:

Josefin chooses to use Thumbscrews, and follows her investment plan as already outlined. However, she decides to withdraw the entire amount of her portfolio on the third anniversary of its set-up, in order to buy a house. How much does she pay Thumbscrews in exit charges?

(A) £303.01 (B) £284.56 (C) £231.27 (D) £143.63 (E) £113.63

Item 28:

Which of the following statements is false?

A – If Josefin had less than £50,000 to invest overall, she would be best off using Thumbscrews.

B – If Josefin had £1,000,000 to invest for one year, she would be best off using Thumbscrews.

C – If Josefin had £1,000,000 to invest for one year, she would be best off using Wormtongue.

D – If Josefin wants to minimise her upfront costs, regardless of later charges, she is best off using Thumbscrews.

E – Thumbscrews penalise early withdrawals.

Answer 25
B – £1,456.27

Wormtongue charges a portfolio set-up fee of £500, which must be added to any other charges. They also charge an annual management fee, which is based on a percentage of the total funds being managed, with a discounted rate for larger portfolios. Remember also that Josefin's fund grows in size by 10% every year due to the investments that Wormtongue makes with her money.

The fees for Josefin are shown in bold in the calculations below:

Portfolio creation: **£500** set-up fee

Year one anniversary portfolio value: £200,000 × 110 ÷ 100 = £220,000

Year one fee: £220,000 × 0.3% = **£660**

Year one balance: £220,000 – £660 = £219,340

Add Josefin's new £50,000 investment: £219,340 + £50,000 = £269,340

Year two anniversary portfolio balance: £269,340 × 110 ÷ 100 = £296,274

Year two fee: £296,274 × 0.1% = **£296.27**

Year two balance: £296,274 – £296.74 = £295,977.73

Add Josefin's new £50,000 investment = £295,977.73 + £50,000 = £345,977.73

The total fees are therefore £500 + £660 + £296.27 = **£1,456.27**

Answer 26
D – £345,922.97

The calculation can be broken down as follows:

> Portfolio creation: free
>
> Year one anniversary portfolio value: £200,000 × 110 ÷ 100 = £220,000
>
> Year one fee: £220,000 × 0.2% = £440
>
> Year one balance: £220,000 – £440 = £219,560
>
> Add Josefin's new £50,000 investment: £219,560 + £50,000 = £269,560
>
> Year two anniversary portfolio value = £269,560 × 110 ÷ 100 = £296,516
>
> Year two fee: £296,516 × 0.2% = £593.03
>
> Year two balance: £296,516 – £593.03 = £295,922.97
>
> Add Josefin's new £50,000 investment: £295,922.97 + £50,000 = £345,922.97

Despite the different fee structures between the two companies, the fund grows to pretty much the same size with both firms. This kind of thing often happens in real life too.

Answer 27
E – £113.63

Extending the calculation from Answer 26:

> Year three anniversary portfolio value = £345,022.97 × 110 – 100 = £379,525.27
>
> Year three fee: £379,525.27 × 0.2% = £759.05
>
> Year three balance: £379,525.27 – £759.05 = £378,766.22
>
> Exit charge = £378,766.22 × 0.03% = £113.63

Answer 28
B – If Josefin had £1,000,000 to invest for one year, she would be best off using Thumbscrews.

You can solve this question by working through all the options. Answer B is clearly false, because Wormtongue charge 0.1% per annum for large portfolios compared with Thumbscrews' 0.2% flat rate. Even the £500 set-up fee that Wormtongue charges cannot possibly outweigh the percentage difference for such a large balance, even without considering the percentage-based exit charge Thumbscrews add too.

Numerical presentation 8

Death and Taxes

Table 5-11	Causes of Death in 2009 (in Thousands)	
Cause of death	**Men**	**Women**
Circulatory disease	78	82
Cancer	74	66
Respiratory disease	32	36
Digestive disease	12	13
Neurological disease	8	9
Mental disorder	6	12
Genitourinary disease	5	7
Endocrine disease	3	4
Infectious disease	2	3

Item 29: What is the average number of deaths, in thousands and to the nearest thousand, across all the causes of death in men?

(A) 78   (B) 32   (C) 44   (D) 24   (E) 22

Item 30: Find the difference between men's and women's deaths due to digestive disease or mental disorder and express this difference as a percentage of men's death from those conditions.

(A) 8.3%   (B) 28%   (C) 33.3%   (D) 38.9%   (E) 50.0%

Item 31:

What's the difference, in thousands of deaths, between the fifth most common cause of death for men and the fifth most common cause of death for women?

(A) 0   (B) 1   (C) 4   (D) 8   (E) 10

Item 32:

Which of the following statements is true?

A – Men more commonly die of mental disorder than women.

B – More women die of circulatory disease than men.

C – More women die of cancer than men.

D – Infectious disease is the least common cause of death in men, but only the second-least common in women.

E – More people die of respiratory disease than women die from circulatory disease.

Answer 29

D – 24

This question is a straightforward test of your ability to work out the arithmetic mean of all the data points in the 'Men' column. The sum is (78 + 74 + 32 + 12 + 8 + 6 + 5 + 3 + 2) = 220. The mean is 220 ÷ 9 = 24.4 to one decimal place, or 24 to the nearest thousand.

Answer 30

D – 38.9%

A total of (12 + 6) = 18 thousand men died from digestive and mental disorders combined. A total of (13 + 12) = 25 thousand women died from the two causes combined. So (25 – 18) = 7 thousand more women died than men.

Expressed as a percentage compared with the number of men that died, the answer is (7 ÷ 18) × 100 = 38.9%.

Answer 31

C – 4

The fifth most common cause of death in men is neurological disease, with 8,000 deaths. The fifth most common cause of death in women is mental disorder, with 12,000. The difference is 4,000 deaths, or 4 if expressed in thousands.

This question tests your ability to note that although the table is sorted by frequency of death in men, women's causes of death don't share the same order, so the fifth most common cause of death in men is different from that in women.

Answer 32

B – More women die of circulatory disease than men.

This question is relatively straightforward. You can find the answer simply by testing each statement's truth against the data in the table.

Numerical presentation 9

Changing Rooms

Mr Wickes has decided to convert his regular master bathroom into a wet room. This decision means the entire floor and walls have to be waterproofed, and then tiled up to the ceiling, and a central drain fitted to the floor.

For the purposes of this question, the bathroom can be considered to have a simple cuboidal structure, as pictured in Figure 5-3.

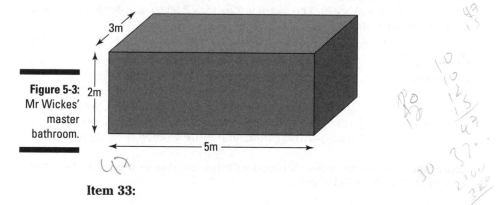

Figure 5-3: Mr Wickes' master bathroom.

3m
2m
5m

Item 33:

Waterproofing costs £8 per 0.75 square metres to be covered. Travertine tiles cost £70 per square metre. How much will it cost, in terms of materials, to waterproof and tile the new wet room, to the nearest hundred pounds?

(A) £1,100   (B) £2,600   (C) £3,300   (D) £3,800   (E) £4,200

Item 34:

Waterproofing takes 10 minutes per square metre, and tiling takes 2 hours per square metre. How long would it take to complete the job, to the nearest hour?

(A) 64 hours   (B) 94 hours   (C) 102 hours   (D) 104 hours
(E) 124 hours

Item 35:

Mr Wickes breaks the habit of a lifetime and decides not to do the job himself. Instead, he hires a professional tiler who charges £12 an hour, as well as charging Mr Wickes the full market rate for the materials required. Assuming the tiler can access the materials at a 20% trade discount, how much profit does he make from the job, to the nearest hundred pounds?

(A) £1,200   (B) £2,000   (C) £3,600   (D) £4,300   (E) £5,000

Item 36:

Mr Wickes decides to buy a new shower system to go in his wet room. He goes for a thermostatic body jet shower mixer which costs £400. It uses approximately 12 litres of water per minute. Mr Wickes' water company charges £2 per cubic metre of water used. Assuming Mr Wickes uses his new shower for 15 minutes per day, how much does the shower cost Mr Wickes annually, over a 5-year period, evenly amortising the capital cost of the shower system over that timeframe? You need not consider any of the other wet room costs, and you may ignore any effect leap years may have in calculating your answer.

(A) £131.40   (B) £211.40   (C) £631.40   (D) £657.00   (E) £1,057.00

Answer 33
D – £3,800

First you need to calculate the area to be waterproofed and tiled. This area consists of the four walls and the floor:

Wall area = $[2 \times (2 \times 5)] + [2 \times (2 \times 3)] = 20 + 12 = 32$ square metres

Floor area = $3 \times 5 = 15$ square metres

Total area = $32 + 15 = 47$ square metres to be waterproofed and tiled

Waterproofing costs = $(47 \div 0.75) \times 8 = £501.33$

Tiling costs = $47 \times 70 = £3,290$

The total cost is £501.33 + £3,290 = £3,791.33, or £3,800 to the nearest hundred.

You need to tile the floor but not the ceiling. Also, don't forget to include the waterproofing costs in your answer.

Answer 34
C – 102 hours

From Answer 33 you already know the area to be worked on – 47 square metres. If waterproofing takes 10 minutes per square metre, waterproofing takes $(47 \times 10) \div 60 = 7.83$ hours to two decimal places. Tiling takes 2 hours per square metre, for a total of $47 \times 2 = 94$ hours.

The total time is approximately (as above answer is inexact) $7.83 + 94 = 101.83$, or 102 hours to the nearest hour.

Answer 35
B – £2,000

From Answer 34 you already know that the job takes 102 hours, which at £12 per hour comes to a labour charge of £1,224. You already know that the materials cost £3,800, but the tiler buys them at a 20% discount, so he makes a further profit of $£3,800 \times 0.2 = £760$ on materials.

The tiler therefore makes a total profit of $£1,224 + £760 = £1,984$, or £2000 to the nearest hundred.

Incidentally, the figures in this question aren't entirely unrealistic, which means that if the tiler has enough work to keep him busy full-time, he can earn well north of £40,000 a year, and possibly significantly more in better economic times, when he can charge somewhere in the region of £20 per hour. Of course, he still has to cover any other business expenses and pay his taxes after this!

Answer 36
B – £211.40

The shower uses 12 litres per minute and runs for 15 minutes per day, 365 days per year. The total annual water usage is therefore $12 \times 15 \times 365 = 65,700$ litres, or 65.7 cubic metres. At a cost of £2 per cubic metre, the annual cost of water is $65.7 \times £2 = £131.4$.

The shower itself costs £400, which you have to amortise over a 5-year period. Each year, therefore, costs the equivalent of $£400 \div 5 = £80$. Adding this amount to the water costs $£131.4 + £80 = £211.40$.

Chapter 6

Looking at Pretty Patterns: The Abstract Reasoning Subtest

*T*he abstract reasoning subtest is odd.

We can think of no other way to describe this subtest. In the test, you look at groups of strange pictures and identify how the pictures are related to each other. You then work out which group the next item in the list belongs to.

The abstract reasoning subtest assesses how you infer relationships from the patterns of abstract shapes. The patterns may include irrelevant and distracting material, which the examiners include as *red herrings,* sometimes leading you to give the wrong answer.

Many students find this section of the UKCAT the most intimidating. Whereas the verbal and quantitative reasoning subtests deal with familiar concepts, the abstract reasoning subtest is . . . well . . . abstract.

To understand why a test for prospective doctors and dentists includes something so abstract, consider a dentist about to see a patient in her clinic.

As the patient relates his medical history, the dentist part-listens and part-thinks. She looks ahead, formulating hypotheses as to what may be wrong with the patient and deciding what questions she needs to ask to prove or disprove her hypotheses. Working in this way keeps the consultation brief but productive, and lets the dentist concentrate on helping the patient understand what's going on rather than pestering him with endless questions.

The dentist's way of working feels instinctive to her, but it's actually the product of a lot of training, accumulation of knowledge – and *pattern-recognition*. That's her ability to identify thematic similarities between the patient in the chair at the time of the consultation and the symptoms of patients she's seen in the past. Those similarities help her form an idea of what the patient is suffering from, even before looking in his mouth. As the patient divulges more information, the dentist slots the data into her overall impression, narrowing down onto the correct diagnosis.

Training has helped the dentist in this task, but the job's much easier if she's naturally talented at this sort of thing. The UKCAT abstract reasoning subtest measures this natural ability.

To be successful in this subtest, you need to demonstrate a scientific approach to recognising patterns. You need to rapidly create hypotheses, test them against the available information, and use the results to generate answers.

In this chapter, we offer you all you need to score highly in the UKCAT abstract reasoning subtest. We include an explanation of the types of question found in the subtest, some useful test strategies and plenty of practice questions, with answers and fully worked-through explanations.

Figuring Out the Format of the Abstract Reasoning Subtest

In this subtest, you see two sets of shapes, labelled Set A and Set B. The shapes in Set A all have something in common about their patterns. Likewise, all the shapes in Set B have something in common about their patterns. The two sets of shapes aren't related to each other in any way. For each pair of sets, you then see five test shapes. Your task is to decide whether each test shape belongs to Set A, Set B, or neither.

The subtest contains 13 set pairs, with 5 test items each, giving a total of 65 questions. You've just 16 minutes to complete the subtest.

To answer 65 questions in 16 minutes, you need to work at a fast rate of 4 questions a minute.

Working Out Patterns in the Abstract Reasoning Subtest

You rarely notice the pattern similarity within each set instantly. To speed up your work rate, we suggest that you use an efficient common approach to identifying the pattern similarity within each set.

With practice, you discover your own best approach to answering questions in the abstract reasoning subtest, but for now try working through the following list of ideas to focus quickly on the commonality within each set:

- ✔ Shape of components
- ✔ Number of corners on each component
- ✔ Type of edges on each component
- ✔ Colour of each component
- ✔ Number of components
- ✔ Orientation of components
- ✔ Consistent (or consistently evolving) position of one component relative to the others
- ✔ Size of components

By applying this list of possible similarities to each set, you can quickly generate potential hypotheses about the set. You can then test each hypothesis in turn, accepting or discarding hypotheses as applicable.

The list above isn't exhaustive, and sometimes more than one rule applies, making the question more complicated. But our suggestions are a good starting point and may get you out of trouble if you're stuck on a question.

The more abstract reasoning questions you practise, the easier you'll find the abstract reasoning subtest.

Coping with the Abstract Reasoning Subtest on Test Day

The abstract reasoning subtest is intimidating, and many candidates panic and give up too quickly. This is understandable because you need to answer four questions a minute to complete the subtest. Try using the tips below to help you keep your cool:

- **Don't be intimidated by a set you can't solve instantly.** Consider the list of basic commonalities and work your way through each possibility. If none of the possibilities fits the set of shapes, move on to the next question. You can always come back to a set later on. By keeping moving, you maximise your scoring opportunities.

- **Remember that you've more time than you think.** The time-consuming portion of the subtest is identifying the commonality in the first place – try to think in terms of time per set rather than time per question. After you spot the commonality in a set, working through each test shape and seeing which set it belongs to is usually quick and easy.

- **Accept that some of the sets are complex.** The sets toward the end of the subtest are particularly complicated, with multiple interacting features. Few people solve these questions correctly, so don't be surprised or worried if you can't manage these.

- **Be wary of red herrings.** Look out for features that appear to present the solution but aren't quite correct. Check your answer: If your answer's correct, you find no exceptions to the commonality rule within a set and you see a consistent difference between the sets.

- **If you feel that you've done badly in the subtest, take a few deep breaths and try to mentally set the test aside.** The UKCAT tests a range of different aptitudes and few people excel at all of them. Try to refocus on maximising your score on the next subtest instead.

The easiest way to understand how these strategies work in practice is to do some questions, see how the answers are derived, and see how easy the questions are when you spot the commonality quickly.

Practising Abstract Reasoning

In this section, we give you many questions to help you practise your abstract reasoning skills. We include 13 sets and 65 test shapes in total, just like in the real UKCAT test. Concentrate on moving swiftly through the questions.

Display 1

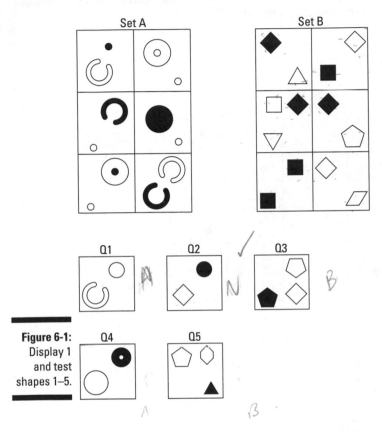

Figure 6-1:
Display 1
and test
shapes 1–5.

Answers

1. Set A; **2.** Neither set; **3.** Set B; **4.** Set A; **5.** Set B.

Explanation

All the shapes in Set A have curved edges. All the shapes in Set B have straight edges. The size, colour and orientation of the shapes demonstrate no commonality within the sets.

Test shapes 1 and 4 contain only shapes with curved edges and therefore fall into Set A. Test shapes 3 and 5 contain only shapes with straight edges and so fall into Set B. Test shape 2 contains shapes with both curved and straight edges and therefore doesn't go in either set.

Display 2

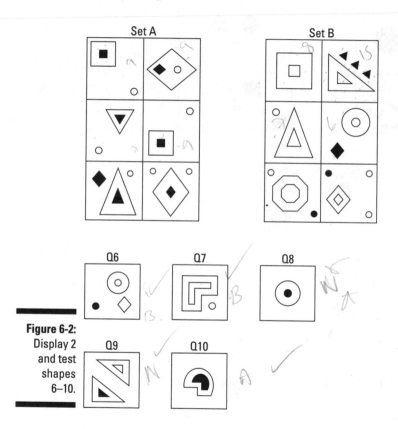

Figure 6-2: Display 2 and test shapes 6–10.

Answers

6. Set B; **7.** Set B; **8.** Set A; **9.** Neither set; **10.** Set A.

Explanation

All the examples in Set A contain a shape that's internally replicated with a shape of the opposite colour. For instance, the top-left item contains a large white square with a smaller black inner square, while the top-right item contains a large white rhombus with a smaller black inner rhombus.

All the examples in Set B contain a shape that's internally replicated with a shape of the same colour. For instance, the top-left item contains a large square with a smaller white inner square, while the top-right item contains a large white right-angled triangle with a smaller white right-angled triangle within it.

Apart from this, the placement and orientation of the large object within the box are irrelevant, and any other shapes featured in each item show no consistent features of commonality.

Test shapes 6 and 7 contain a large object that is replicated internally by a smaller black item, and so both fall within Set B. Test shapes 8 and 10 contain a large object that is internally replicated with a smaller white object, and so both fit in Set A. Test shape 9 has both types of internal replication and so falls into neither set.

Display 3

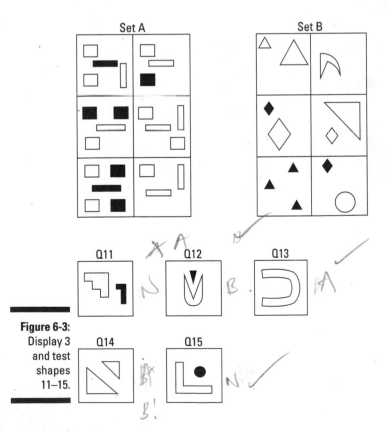

Figure 6-3: Display 3 and test shapes 11–15.

Answers

11. Set A; **12.** Set B; **13.** Set A; **14.** Set B; **15.** Neither set.

Explanation

All the examples in Set A contain items that have at least two right-angles each.

All the examples in Set B contain items that have at most one right-angle each. The exact nature of the overall shape, the colour and the orientation show no consistent features of commonality.

Test shapes 11 and 13 have only objects with at least two right-angles and so fit in Set A. Test shapes 12 and 14 have only objects with at most one right-angle each and so fall within Set B. Test shape 15 has one object with four right-angles but also a shape with no right-angles; therefore it can't be classified as Set A or Set B.

Display 4

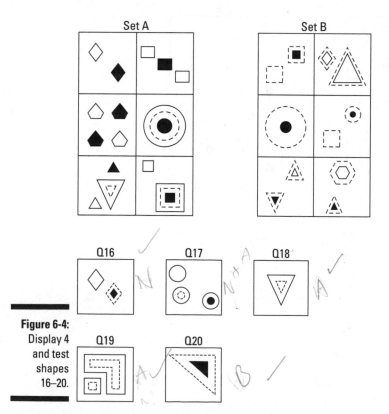

Figure 6-4:
Display 4
and test
shapes
16–20.

Answers

16. Neither set; **17.** Set A; **18.** Set A; **19.** Set A; **20.** Set B.

Explanation

All the objects in Set A have solid outer edges. All the objects in Set B have outer edges with interruptions. The exact nature of the overall shape, the colour and the orientation show no consistent features of commonality.

Test shapes 17, 18, and 19 have only objects with uninterrupted solid outer edges and so fall within Set A. Test shape 20 has an interrupted outline and so fits in Set B. As test shape 16 contains objects with both solid and interrupted outlines, it falls into neither set.

Display 5

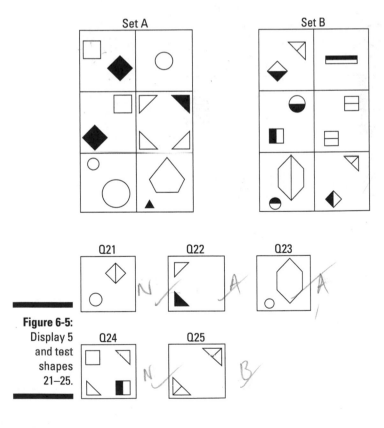

Figure 6-5:
Display 5 and test shapes 21–25.

Answers

21. Neither set; **22.** Set A; **23.** Set A; **24.** Neither set; **25.** Set B.

Explanation

All the objects in Set A have no internal subdivisions. All the objects in Set B have internal subdivisions. The exact nature of the overall shape, the colour of the shapes and subdivisions, and the orientation show no consistent features of commonality. Test shapes 22 and 23 have only objects without subdivisions and are therefore members of Set A. Test shape 25 contains only objects with subdivisions and is therefore a member of Set B. Test shapes 21 and 24 are mixes of objects with and without subdivisions and so can't be classified into either set.

Display 6

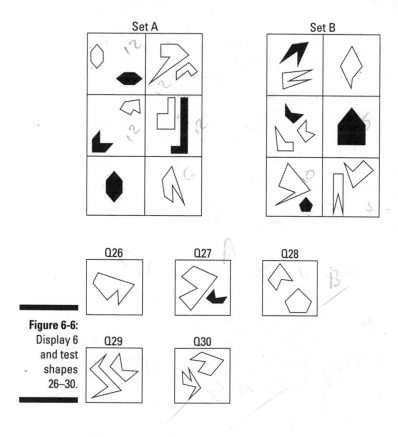

Figure 6-6:
Display 6 and test shapes 26–30.

Answers

26. Set A; **27.** Set A; **28.** Set B; **29.** Neither set; **30.** Neither set.

Explanation

All the objects in Set A are six-sided. All the objects in Set B are five-sided. The colour of the shapes and their orientations show no consistent features of commonality.

Test shapes 26 and 27 contain only six-sided objects and so fall within Set A. Test shape 28 contains only five-sided objects and so is in Set B. Test shapes 29 and 30 contain objects with various numbers of sides and so don't fall within either set.

Display 7

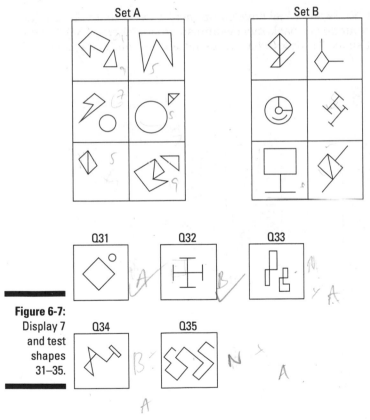

Figure 6-7: Display 7 and test shapes 31–35.

Answers

31. Set A; **32.** Set B; **33.** Set A; **34.** Set A; **35.** Set A.

Explanation

You can draw each of the component objects in Set A without lifting your pen off the paper or backtracking. You can't draw the component objects in Set B without lifting your pen off the paper or backtracking.

This commonality is harder to spot than the commonalities in some of the earlier questions, but it is not an uncommon point of difference between shapes in the UKCAT abstract reasoning test. Shapes with this commonality often contain lines that start and end in unusual places, such as the bottom-right and top-right shapes in Set B. Unusually placed lines such as these are often giveaways of shapes that you can't draw without lifting your pen or backtracking.

The colour and orientation of the shapes show no consistent features of commonality.

Test shapes 31, 33, 34 and 35 all have component objects that you can draw without lifting your pen or backtracking and so are members of Set A. You can't draw test shape 32 without backtracking, and so this shape is in Set B.

Display 8

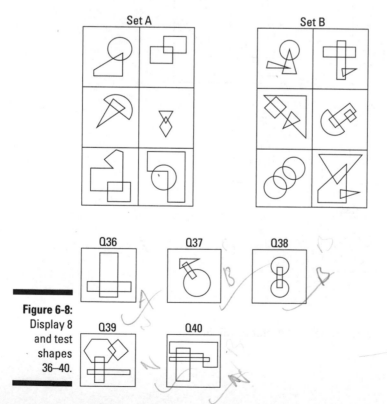

Figure 6-8:
Display 8 and test shapes 36–40.

Answers

36. Set A; **37.** Set B; **38.** Set B; **39.** Neither set; **40.** Neither set.

Explanation

Set A contains objects that form only one overlapping area. Set B contains objects that form two areas of overlap.

Whenever you see objects that intersect with each other, consider whether the number of overlapping areas, or the colour or shape of the overlapping area, forms a set commonality. In this set, the number of overlaps is a commonality.

Test shape 36 has one area of overlap and so falls within Set A. Test shapes 37 and 38 both contain two areas of overlap and so are members of Set B. Test shapes 39 and 40 both contain three areas of overlap and so fall into neither set.

Don't be tempted to overcomplicate the solution – this subtest is confusing enough already! You may argue that the Set B commonality is 'at least two areas of overlap' rather than simply 'two areas of overlap'. You may also argue that it is the number of shapes rather than the number of areas of overlap that matters. In potentially ambiguous cases, you must apply Occam's razor. This is the logical principle that if more than one solution can apply, the simplest solution is usually the correct one. This is used often in medical and dental fields to narrow down a broad differential diagnosis and best summarised by the truism: 'Common things are common.' Health professionals who jump to an obscure and rare diagnosis when faced with common symptoms are sometimes whimsically referred to as "hunting zebras". Horses are more common, at least in European and North American practice!

No object in Set B contains more than two areas of overlap, so the most logical commonality is 'two areas of overlap' rather than 'at least two areas of overlap'. And if elements are depicted as overlapping, whereas in most other parts of the Abstract Reasoning subtest they're found discretely, then it's wise to focus on the fact of their overlapping rather than just the number of elements in each shape.

Display 9

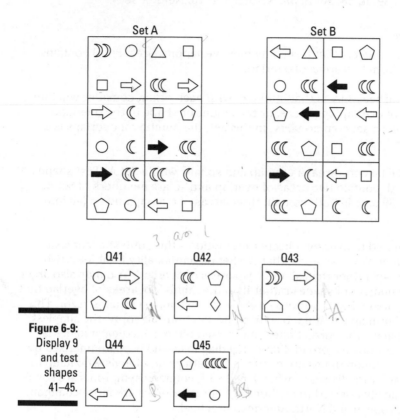

Figure 6-9:
Display 9
and test
shapes
41–45.

Answers

41. Neither set; **42.** Neither set; **43.** Set A; **44.** Set B; **45.** Set B.

Explanation

This question takes the abstract reasoning subtest to the next level. Instead of examining individual objects, you have to consider the relationship of one object to other objects within the same shape.

A clue that you need to head down this complicated route is if you see objects that point in one direction and then change direction between shapes. Objects such as arrows and triangles are classic examples. Also look for objects that appear consistently between shapes but change colour from one shape to the next.

In Set A, if you see exactly two crescent moons, the arrow points right. With any other number of moons, the arrow points left. In addition, if you see a pentagon, the arrow is black.

In Set B, if you see exactly two crescent moons, the arrow points left. With any other number of moons, the arrow points right. In addition, if you see a pentagon, the arrow is black.

The pentagon-related colour change doesn't let you differentiate between the two sets, but you can use the colour change to determine whether shapes fit into either set at all. The orientation of the arrow in response to the number of crescent moons is diagnostic.

Test shape 41 has two crescent moons and a right-pointing arrow; however, the shape has a pentagon but the arrow is white instead of black, and so it doesn't fit in either set. Test shape 42 has a similar issue, forcing it out of both sets.

Test shape 43 has two crescent moons and a right-pointing arrow. No pentagon means that the shape is correctly coloured white, so the shape falls into Set A. Test shapes 44 and 45 don't have two moons and have left-pointing arrows, fitting with Set B; you can confirm this by noticing the correct colour for their respective pentagon status.

Display 10

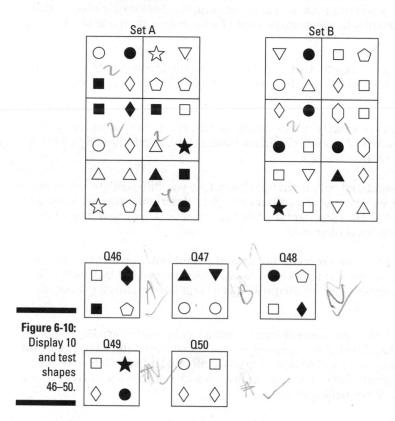

Figure 6-10:
Display 10
and test
shapes
46–50.

Answers

46. Set A; **47.** Set A; **48.** Neither set; **49.** Neither set; **50.** Set A.

Explanation

In comparison with the test shapes in Display 9, this set of questions is some-what more straightforward. Each of Set A's shapes has horizontally or verti-cally matching objects. Set B's shapes contain diagonally matching objects.

For instance, the middle-left shape of Set A has two diamonds in vertical alignment, and the bottom-right shape of Set A has two triangles in vertical alignment. In Set B, the top-right shape has two squares in diagonal alignment and the middle-right shape has the same alignment for two hexagons.

The colour of the objects and their number of sides are irrelevant.

Test shapes 46, 47 and 50 have horizontally or vertically aligned matching objects and so fall within Set A's constraints. Test shapes 48 and 49 have no matching shapes at all and so belong to neither set.

Display 11

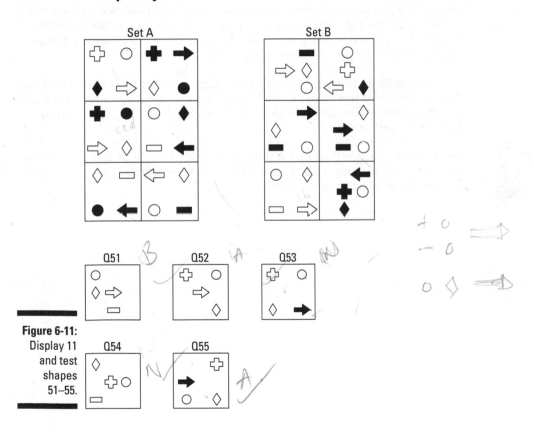

Figure 6-11:
Display 11
and test
shapes
51–55.

Answers

51. Set B; **52.** Set A; **53.** Neither set; **54.** Neither set; **55.** Set A.

Explanation

This difficult question has multiple interacting rules.

For Set A, if you see a plus sign, the arrow points right; if you see a minus sign, the arrow points left. Additionally, if you see a circle horizontally next to the plus or minus sign, the arrow is white; if you see no circle in horizontal alignment with the plus or minus sign, the arrow is black.

For Set B, if you see a plus sign, the arrow points left; if you see a minus sign, the arrow points right. Additionally, if you see a circle horizontally next to the plus or minus sign, the arrow is black; if you see no circle in horizontal alignment with the plus or minus sign, the arrow is white.

Test shapes 52 and 55 are Set A and Test shape 51 is Set B. Test shape 53 has the correct arrow direction for Set A but also the correct colour for Set B and so falls within neither set. Test shape 54 lacks an arrow altogether and so belongs to neither set.

Don't be discouraged if you think that you'll never be able to spot this sort of correlation on test day. This is an example of a seriously hard set of questions that few people can answer correctly.

Display 12

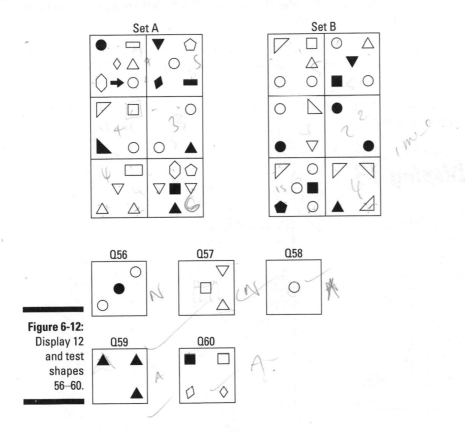

Figure 6-12:
Display 12 and test shapes 56–60.

Answers

56. Neither set; **57.** Neither set; **58.** Set A; **59.** Set A; **60.** Set A.

Explanation

Each shape within Set A contains the same number of objects as the object with the most edges within the shape, excluding the circles. For example, the top-left shape has an arrow with seven edges and seven objects; and the middle-right shape has a triangle (three edges) and three objects.

Each shape within Set B has one more shape than the object with the most edges within the shape. For example, the middle-right shape has a circle (1 continuous edge) and two objects; and the middle-left shape has a triangle (three sides) and four objects.

TIP

A good way to spot this sort of pattern is to notice that the number of objects in the shapes within a set varies dramatically. Then try to understand why the number changes.

Test shapes 58, 59 and 60 follow Set A's rules. Test shapes 56 and 57 follow neither set's rules.

Display 13

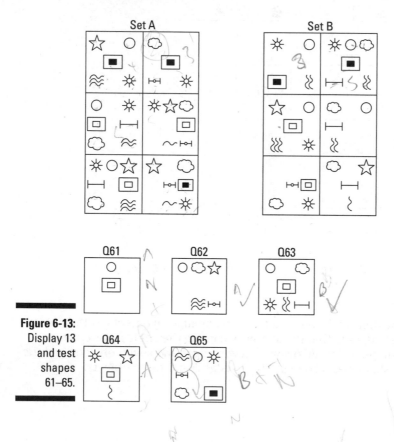

Figure 6-13:
Display 13 and test shapes 61–65.

Answers

61. Set A; **62.** Set A; **63.** Set B; **64.** Neither set; **65.** Neither set.

Explanation

Unless you're exceptionally adept at abstract reasoning, these test shapes are almost impossible to get correct, as three sets of rules are at play. As the rules don't interact, placing an object in Set A or Set B by guessing, and then working out whether you've guessed correctly, is the best thing to do. Excluding test shapes from both sets is much, much harder.

In Set A, if the sun symbol is at the top of the box, the big square has a white inner square. If the sun symbol is at the bottom of the box, the big square has a black inner square.

Also in Set A, if the star symbol is at the top of the box, you see one wavy line. If the moon symbol is at the top of the box, you see two wavy lines. If both the star and the moon symbols are at the top of the box, you see three wavy lines.

Finally, in Set A, if the cloud symbol is at the top of the box, the elongated 'H' (or gate) symbol has a circle on it (the gate is closed). If the cloud symbol is at the bottom of the box, the gate lacks the circle (the gate is open).

Set B inverts rules 1 and 3, but maintains rule 2. So, if the sun is up, the square has a black inner square; and if the cloud is up, the gate is open.

Test shapes 61 and 62 follow Set A's rules. Test shape 63 follows Set B's rules. Test shapes 64 and 65 mix the rules and therefore fall into neither set.

Chapter 7

Deciphering the Code: The Decision Analysis Subtest

● ●

In This Chapter

▶ Understanding what the decision analysis subtest looks for

▶ Exploring strategies to answer decision analysis questions quickly

▶ Practising decision analysis questions

● ●

*T*he decision analysis subtest is all about making judgement calls.

In this subtest, you have to use a code to unscramble coded phrases into English and to encode English phrases into the code.

At first glance, the concept is straightforward. The catch is that the code lacks the breadth you need to translate fully and explicitly to and from English. The code covers concepts rather than letters, so translation is as much an exercise in manipulating concepts as in looking up items in the code.

Playing around with concepts and manipulating their meaning requires a high level of decision-making ability – which is what the testers want to check that you have.

Imagine a consultant on call one evening. This consultant deals with GPs who phone to ask the on-call medical team at the hospital to see certain patients. The most junior member of the on-call team on any given day used to do this task, but nowadays more senior members of the team take on the job, because the task requires experience and judgement to make decisions.

A GP calls to say that he has a patient in his surgery with limb weakness. The GP is concerned that the patient may be having a stroke and wants to send him into hospital. The GP has done some initial history-taking and physical examination, but he lacks immediate access to the advanced diagnostic testing and treatments available at the hospital.

The consultant and the GP discuss the patient over the phone. The GP doesn't have all the data to know for sure whether the patient needs hospital treatment. The patient may be having a stroke – but on the other hand, he may have a less urgent complaint.

The consultant prioritises the urgency of the patient's symptoms using the conceptual framework he knows from his training and slotting the limited information the GP has supplied into that framework. Not accepting a seriously ill patient for review would be a serious error – but seeing patients with non-urgent complaints takes time away from more seriously ill patients.

Triaging requires quick decision-making skills. The UKCAT decision analysis subtest checks that you have the innate aptitude to make such decisions.

In this chapter, we explain the types of question found in the decision analysis subtest, suggest useful test strategies and include plenty of practice questions, with answers and fully worked-through explanations.

Decoding the Format of the Decision Analysis Subtest

In this subtest, you have to read a scenario and then answer 26 questions based on the scenario. You have 32 minutes to complete the subtest.

The scenario typically involves a brief paragraph of prose outlining the basic context of the scenario, followed by a table full of data. The questions are based around codes built from the data in the table.

Unlike questions in the other subtests, decision analysis questions have four or five response options, and more than one answer may be correct. The question states whether you need to select more than one answer.

Each of the questions in the decision analysis subtest is in the form of a coded message that you have to decode into English, or an English phrase that you have to encode. The code covers concepts and is not a simple letter-for-letter substitution, so your decisions about which symbols to use and what order to place them in may be ambiguous. You can also combine symbols to alter their meaning, which creates further complexity.

For example, suppose that you've a symbol for 'hot' and a symbol for 'earth'. Combining the two symbols may mean 'hot earth', but you can also use the combination to describe 'hot sand' or even 'lava'. The decision analysis subtest uses this inherent ambiguity to make the questions increasingly complex as the subtest progresses.

Unlike some of the other subtests in the UKCAT, this subtest rewards lateral thinking and an ability to apply judgement rather than pure logic to situations.

Preparing for Success in the Decision Analysis Subtest

The decision analysis subtest rewards good judgement, which generally comes with experience. As the subtest is basically a series of puzzles, doing similar puzzles can help you to build up a lot of experience quickly.

Any puzzle that stretches your ability to think and requires lateral thinking can help you with the decision analysis subtest. Riddles are one example, but the most accessible example is newspaper crosswords, especially the cryptic variety. Cryptic crosswords encourage you to think outside the box, drawing on common concepts and conventions, which you then apply to the clues. If you already enjoy cryptic crosswords, you'll probably find the decision analysis subtest right up your street.

If you're not a crossword fan, don't worry. Other ways to improve your ability in the decision analysis subtest include creative writing (which encourages the manipulation of ideas and words), simply thinking about how you make real-life decisions (what facts you use, how you combine the facts, and how much weight you give each fact), and practising the questions in this book.

A surprisingly effective way to practise for this subtest is to keep a diary. Human beings are constantly thinking and feeling lots of different things, but we rarely take time to understand why we think and feel those things. Developing insight into your emotions and actions requires you to place some sort of logical framework around those fleeting impulses. Doing so means translating – or decoding – emotional states into concepts, and then encoding those concepts into prose. Ordering the concepts into a narrative structure is the essence of good diary-keeping. Try to make your diary a developed explanation of what the day meant to you, rather than random 'blurtings'.

Making the Right Decisions on Test Day

The decision analysis subtest comes at the end of the UKCAT. By the time you get to this subtest, you probably already feel tired. Unfortunately, the decision analysis subtest requires you to be at your freshest and to think the most clearly.

Try to cleanse your mind before you start the decision analysis subtest and then use the tips we list below to refresh yourself before the subtest:

- ✓ **Relax for 10 seconds before you start the subtest.** You're under time pressure, but losing 10 seconds isn't the end of the world. Those 10 seconds of relaxation may be just the ticket to refresh yourself. Take a few deep breaths in and out, focus on slowing your breathing and try to imagine yourself in a happy and relaxed environment.

- ✓ **Don't be intimidated by the large amount of data at the start of the subtest.** You may see lots of unusual symbols, some of which are annoyingly similar to each other. Mentally acknowledge the information and then move on to the test questions.

- ✓ **Try to think in concepts, not words.** If you can consider that words and language are merely a human construct applied to underlying concepts, you may find the questions much easier. Your job is to fit a round peg into a square hole – just like in real life when you put your thoughts or feelings into words.

- ✓ **Accept that the questions are deliberately ambiguous.** Feeling some doubt about your answers is normal. Don't spend ages going over a question again and again. Keep moving methodically through the subtest – and remember that you've just over a minute per question.

- ✓ **Remember the UKCAT is over after you finish this subtest.** Try to summon up the strength to keep going for just a little longer.

The easiest way to understand how these strategies work in practice is to do some questions, see how the answers are derived, and discover how to deal with the complexity and ambiguity of some of the later questions.

Practising Decision Analysis

Working through this section is a good way to practise your decision analysis skills. We include 26 questions in total, just like in the real UKCAT test. Concentrate on thinking in terms of the concepts required by the translation and moving methodically through each question.

Don't be discouraged if you make some mistakes. The whole point of this book is to prepare you for the actual test. Making a few mistakes now means that you're less likely to make the same mistakes on test day.

Avoid rushing through this section. We include full sample tests for you to do under mock exam conditions in Part III. For now, concentrate on understanding the answers and doing the best you can, even if you take a little longer than you have in the real thing. Speed comes with practice and with confidence in the technique.

Scenario

The Symbolians

The Terran Star Navy has a primary mission of seeking out new alien civilisations. On a mission to a previously unexplored planet, they encounter a race without vocal cords. Instead, they 'speak' using a bio-luminescent patch on their face that is under a Symbolian's conscious control in such a way as to be able to form intricate glowing patterns that form symbols.

First contact with this alien species was difficult, as the Star Navy's Ubiquitous English Device can't translate the pictorial Symbolian language. However, the Star Navy crew has been able to work out some rudimentary translations of symbols through trial and error. Their primitive dictionary is shown in Table 7-1.

Table 7-1		The Symbolian Language	
Things	**Descriptors**	**Emotions**	**Times**
Spaceship = ⤝	Enlarge = ▶▶	Angry = ▓	Now = ▶
Planet = ●	Shrink = ◀◀	Calm = ▪▪	Later = ▼
Symbolian = ▓	Metal = 👌	Friendly = ♥	Never = ▶▶▶
Terran = ⚡	Wooden = ♥	Shy = ⊖	Maybe = _
House = 🏠	Hot = ①		
City = 🏙	Cold = ✚		
Farmland = 🔨			
Road = ▐			
Laser = ⟋			
Book = ▮			
Ground Car = 🚌			

Question 1: What is the best interpretation of the following Symbolian message?

▶▶ ! ⌷ ⤙, ①

[handwritten: enlarge, terran, metal, spaces?, hot]

[handwritten: CA]

A – The large Terran metal Spaceship is hot.

B – The large Terran Spaceship is made of metal.

C – The large Terran Spaceship is cold. *[handwritten: x]*

D – The Terran Spaceship got hot on landing.

E – The Terran Spaceship got larger as it heated up. *[circled]*

Question 2: What is the best interpretation of the following Symbolian message?

✳ ✤ ⤙, ✎ , ! ⤙

A – The Symbolian Spaceship and Terran Spaceship fired lasers at each other.

B – The Symbolian Spaceship fired at the hostile Terran Spaceship.

C – The Terran Spaceship fired at the Symbolian Spaceship.

D – The Symbolian Spaceship fired multiple lasers at the Terran Spaceship.

E – The hostile Symbolian Spaceship fired lasers at the Terran Spaceship. *[circled E]*

[handwritten: angry symbolian spaceship lazer]

Question 3: What is the best way to translate the following into Symbolian?

[handwritten: teerran]

The Terran driving the ground car ruthlessly crashed into the Symbolian.

[handwritten: space]

A. 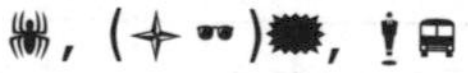 ✤, (✛ ⁚)✳, ! 🚌

B.  (✛ ⁚)!, 🚌✳, ✤

C.  ! 🚌, (✛ ⁚)✳, ✤ *[circled C]*

D. !, ✳, ✤

E.  (✛ ⁚)🚌, !, ✤

Question 4: What is the best interpretation of the following coded message?

[coded symbols] ~terran friendly late book symbolian house~

A – The Terran will steal the book from the Symbolian's house.

B – The Symbolian angrily took the book back from the Terran.

C – The Terran will give the book as a present to the Symbolian in his home.

D – The Terran spaceship teleports the book into the Symbolian's house.

E – The Terran's house contains a Symbolian book.

Question 5: What is the best interpretation of the following coded message?

[coded symbols] ~symbolian farmland now enlarge road city enlarg~

A – Symbolian farmland is increasingly being converted into road use as their cities expand.

B – Symbolian roads connect farming areas to cities.

C – Symbolian cities are getting smaller as farmland and road networks enlarge.

D – Symbolian farms are so profitable that they support the cities.

E – Farms and cities on Symbolia are both expanding as the road network improves.

Question 6: What is the best interpretation of the following coded message?

[coded symbols] ~terran spaceship later angry laser planet symbolian symbolian shy now house thank~

A – The spaceship urgently fired lasers at the Symbolian house.

B – The Symbolian base opened fire on the orbiting Terran spaceship.

C – The Symbolians ran out of their house, firing on the Terran spaceship.

D – The Terran Space Navy is threatening orbital bombardment should the Symbolian fugitives not immediately emerge from their hiding place.

E – The Symbolian High Command declared war on the Terran Space Navy.

Question 7: What is the best interpretation of the following coded message?

●ⓘ⠀⠀, ▼, ⬛⛰⛰, ◀◀, ♥

A – As a result of global nuclear war, the Symbolian civilisation collapsed to a pre-technological level of development.

B – Symbolian technology led to global warming.

C – Living on a hot planet, the Symbolians found it easy to develop an advanced technology.

D – Symbolian cities went up in flames during their dark ages.

E – As a result of global warming, the Symbolian civilisation collapsed to a pre-technological level of development.

Question 8: What is the best interpretation of the following coded message?

◀◀(❗⬛), ▶▶, (❗)(⬛)

A – Symbolian children are taller than Terran children.

B – Symbolian/Terran hybrid children are taller than either species.

C – Symbolian/Terran hybrid children are shorter than Symbolian children.

D – Symbolians and Terrans cannot interbreed to produce hybrid children.

E – Symbolian/Terran hybrid children are looked down on by both species.

Question 9: What is the best interpretation of the following coded message?

⬛🌲, ▶▶(⬛ⓘ☢/)

A – Symbolians have poured molten metal over their farmland.

B – Symbolian bridges span deep ravines in their countryside.

C – Symbolians don't like their harsh countryside.

D – Symbolia has many dangerous molten metal rivers outside of its cities.

E – Symbolians want to see new planets with exciting farming techniques.

Question 10: What is the best interpretation of the following coded message?

▶▶(⚡ ⤙⤙), ◀◀(🕷 ⤙⤙), ▼ ▶▶ 🔥, ⚡⬤

A – The Symbolian fleet fought the Terran Space Navy over Earth.

B – It took a battle in Earth orbit for the Terran Space Navy to defeat the Symbolians.

C – The Terran Space Navy engaged the Symbolian fleet over Symbolia.

D – Earth declared war on Symbolia by launching a Space Navy attack.

E – The Symbolian fleet could never defeat Earth because it's outnumbered by the Terran Space Navy.

enlarge terrainspace spce chrloh symbol spa
spa
Question 11: What is the best interpretation of the following coded message?
late
never

🕷 🚌 🚌, ▼ (▶ ▼)
angry
terran
plofu

A – Symbolians never built the roads to support their ground cars.

B – Symbolians never let their ground cars run late.

C – Symbolian ground cars always run late.

D – The Symbolians will catch the later ground car.

E – The ground car will come later on to pick up the Symbolians.

Question 12: What is the best interpretation of the following coded message?

⚡ 🕷 ❤, _ ", 🔥(⚡👤🕷👤)

A – Symbolians and Terrans are working together in an attempt to solve their mutual farming crisis.

B – Symbolians like Terrans because they solved their farming crisis.

C – Terrans used the Symbolian solution to countryside deforestation on Earth.

D – Both Earth and Symbolia suffered from a severe food production problem.

E – It is not possible for there to be a joint solution to the Terran/Symbolian farming crisis.

Question 13: What is the best interpretation of the following coded message?

(NB: **Two** options are correct)

A – 'The primitive Terran Space Navy will be no match for our space and ground forces', the Symbolian Admiral cried rally the planet.

B – The Terran Space Navy has been defeated by the Symbolian Admiral's forces.

C – The Terran Space Navy blockaded Symbolia, causing their leader to charge at them in his spaceship.

D – The Symbolian Prime Minister intends to attack primitive Earth with his fleet and army.

E – The Symbolian Admiral encouraged his people by telling them that the inferior Terran Fleet would fall to their fleet and army.

Question 14: What is the best interpretation of the following coded message?

(NB: **Two** options are correct.)

A – The Symbolian loved playing 'Forever and For Always' loudly.

B – The Symbolian currently likes 'It's Now or Never' a lot.

C – The Symbolian enjoys playing 'Never Forget' loudly.

D – The Symbolian loved listening to 'We Have All the Time in the World' many times.

E – The Symbolian listens to 'Time after Time'.

Question 15: What is the best interpretation of the following coded message?

A – The Terran was reluctant to loan the Symbolian his e-book reader.

B – The Terran secretly liked the Symbolian because of his large library.

C – The Symbolian had an advanced electronic library of Terran books.

D – The Terran felt that the Symbolian was hiding e-books from him.

E – The Symbolian liked the Terran enough to lend him the technical books he wanted.

Question 16: What is the best interpretation of the following coded message?

A – Terran ships convert desert planets into arable planets.

B – Terran colony ships contain technology to convert desert into farmland.

C – Terran colony ships were launched because Earth's farmland was turned into desert.

D – Large technologically advanced Terran ships seek out new hot arable planets.

E – The Terran Space Navy uses advanced technology to subjugate both desert and arable planets.

Question 17: What is the best interpretation of the following coded message?

(NB: **Two** options are correct.)

A – The Symbolian moved home because of changeable weather.

B – The Symbolian might move home because of the cold weather.

C – The Symbolian's home planet is often cold.

D – Symbolian homes are cold and draughty.

E – The Symbolian's home might be uprooted in a winter storm.

Question 18: What is the best interpretation of the following coded message?

! 🚌, _ 🕸, 🕷🛫/

A – Terran ground cars are prone to break down on Symbolian country roads.

B – Terran ground cars sometimes drive down Symbolian country roads.

C – Terran ground cars aren't often found on Symbolian roads.

D – Terran ground cars are sometimes found on Symbolian roads.

E – Terrans often avoid using their ground cars on Symbolian country roads.

Question 19: Which **two** of the following would be the most useful additions to our translated knowledge of the Symbolian language when attempting to convey the following message?

Terran bridges are much more likely to undergo metal fatigue than Symbolian ones because they are made from inferior metal that undergoes more deformation on extended use.

A – deformation

B – worse

C – fatigue

D – bridge

E – usage

Question 20: What is the best interpretation of the following coded message?

!🕸, ⊖(▸ 🕸 ▾ !■), 🕷🚌

A – The Terran couldn't drive his car because the instruments were all in Symbolian.

B – The Symbolian could drive his car on Terran roads because he understood Terran.

C – The Terran got frustrated with the lack of a Terran translation for the manual in his Symbolian hire car.

D – The Terran refused to get into the Symbolian's car.

E – The Terran laughed at the lack of a Terran translation for the construction manual for his Symbolian kit car.

Question 21: What is the best way to translate the following into Symbolian?

The wreckage of the ancient Symbolian spaceship was found orbiting one of their moons.

A. ⊛(▶▶▮ ▶ ▶▶▮ ▼)⤝, ⊛●, ✸◀◀

B. ✸◀◀, ⊛(▶ ▼)⤝, ⊛●◀◀

C. ✸◀◀, ⊛(_ ▶ _ ▼)⤝, ⊛●◀◀

D. ✸▶▶, ⊛(▶▶▮ ▶ ▶▶▮ ▼)⤝, ⊛●▶▶

E. ✸◀◀, ⊛(▶▶▮ ▶ ▶▶▮ ▼)⤝, ⊛●◀◀

Question 22: What is the best interpretation of the following coded message?

⸮(⟋▮), ✸▶▶, ●●●

(NB: **Two** options are correct.)

A – Terran television is the worst in the galaxy.

B – Terran telecommunications are the best in the galaxy.

C – Terrans use electronic communication systems to stay in touch across the galaxy.

D – Terran email is plagued by spammers on every colony.

E – The Terrans spent a fortune upgrading their inferior information database.

Question 23: What is the best interpretation of the following coded message?

♥, ⸮▶▶(🏘️), ♥◀◀, ⸮◀◀(🏰▶▶)

A – I would like to be wealthy enough to buy houses in the country and the city.

B – I would rather own two houses than a big city.

C – I would rather be first in a village than second in Rome.

D – The big Terran liked his two houses in the countryside and his small one in the city.

E – The Terran bought two big houses and one small city.

Question 24: What is the best way to translate the following into Symbolian?

This world is the best of all possible worlds.

A. ●, (●●●)
B. ●, _, (●●●)
C. ●, ♥ ♥(●●●)
D. ♥ ►►●, (●●●)
E. ✹ ►►●, ♥(●●●)

Question 25: What is the best interpretation of the following coded message?

❗❗, ⁓ ♥, (❗❗)♥

A – Men like spending time with other men.
B – Mankind will always like strong leaders.
C – Men are doomed to be ruled over by tyrants.
D – The husbands hated their wives.
E – Men freely believe that which they desire.

Question 26: What is the best interpretation of the following coded message?

♥ ⁓, ✹ ①, (❗❗)►►◄

A – The fire on the old galleon caused many deaths.
B – The sailing ship was brutally hot on deck.
C – Many people died when cosmic radiation penetrated the spaceship.
D – The spaceship passed through a solar storm with few fatalities.
E – The spaceship passed through the solar storm, but with many fatalities.

Answer 1

A – The large Terran metal Spaceship is hot.

$$\text{▶} \text{!} \text{♻} \text{➤, ①}$$

= Enlarge Terran Metal Spaceship, Hot

= The large Terran metal Spaceship is hot

The first symbol 'enlarge' eliminates choice D because D makes no mention of spaceship size. The other four choices all have 'Terran Spaceship' but C and E skip mentioning 'metal'. Between A and B, only B interprets the 'hot' symbol. Note that the comma separates the phrase describing the spaceship from the fact that it became hot.

Attention is therefore required to the literal translation of the symbols, the placement of commas to group ideas or clauses together, and the relationships between these clauses in the sentence being translated. In this first example, doing so is straightforward but when a large number of symbols and commas are used, the degree of ambiguity in translation rises, forcing you to sometimes decide which option is best, or even 'least-worst'. This inherent ambiguity is a deliberate part of the test.

Answer 2

E – The hostile Symbolian Spaceship fired lasers at the Terran Spaceship.

$$\text{●} \text{※} \text{➤, ⚡, !➤}$$

= Angry Symbolian Spaceship, Laser, Terran Spaceship

= The hostile Symbolian Spaceship fired lasers at the Terran Spaceship

Answer 3

$$\text{B. (✛ ••) !, ▣ ●, ※}$$

The Terran driving the ground car ruthlessly crashed into the Symbolian.

= Ruthless Terran, Ground Car Hostile, Symbolian

= (Cold Calm) Terran, Ground Car Angry, Symbolian

Answer 4

C – The Terran will give the book as a present to the Symbolian in his home.

= Terran Friendly Later, Book, Symbolian (Symbolian Home)

= The Terran will be Friendly, Book, Symbolian in his home

= The Terran will do something friendly with the book to the Symbolian in his home

= The Terran will give the book as a present to the Symbolian in his home

The first three symbols tell us 'Terran friendly later', which refers to the Terran being friendly in the future. Foil A says that the Terran is unfriendly in the future and Foil B makes no mention of the Terran being friendly later but instead says that the Terran is angry now. The last three symbols translate to Symbolian (Symbolian home). E incorrectly translates this phrase to the Terran home. D does not refer to the Symbolian playing a part in the transaction. This brings us to C.

Answer 5

A – Symbolian farmland is increasingly being converted into road use as their cities expand.

= Symbolian Farmland, Now Enlarge Road, City Enlarge

= Symbolian Farmland, now more roads, cities expand

= Symbolian Farmland is increasingly being converted into road use as their cities expand

B contains no information about the changes in size. C applies the wrong changes in size, as does E. D talks about profitability, which isn't included in the code and doesn't mention the roads.

Answer 6

D – The Terran Space Navy is threatening orbital bombardment should the Symbolian fugitives not immediately emerge from their hiding place.

= Terran Spaceship Spaceship, Later Angry Laser Planet, Symbolian Symbolian Shy, Now House Shrink

= Terran Space Navy, will fire lasers on planet, Symbolians Shy now Shrink from House

= The Terran Space Navy will fire lasers on planet if the Symbolian fugitives don't right now leave their house

= The Terran Space Navy is threatening orbital bombardment should the Symbolian fugitives not immediately emerge from their hiding place

Answer 7

E – As a result of global warming, the Symbolian civilisation collapsed to a pre-technological level of development.

= Planet Hot Increase, Later, Symbolian City City, Shrink, Wooden

This may be an appropriate place to discuss comma placement. Could it be that 'later' is by itself separated by commas to show that time passes? If it had been together in a phrase with 'Symbolian city city', it would instead refer to something happening to the cities in the future because that part of the translation would be 'later Symbolian city city'.

= Planet warming, caused Symbolian cities, shrink to wooden

= Global warming caused Symbolian civilisation to collapse to wooden

= As a result of global warming, the Symbolian civilisation collapsed to a pre-technological level of development

The question uses the word 'wooden' to describe a more primitive technology. To decipher this question, you need to accept that because wooden things generally precede metal things, then if the Symbolian city (civilisation) is now wooden, and it got here by shrinking, the earlier civilisation must have been more technologically advanced.

This need to apply lateral thinking illustrates a difference between this subtest and the verbal reasoning subtest. The verbal reasoning subtest requires you to use only simple logic, but decision analysis allows and requires you to manipulate and merge concepts together.

Answer 8

B – Symbolian/Terran hybrid children are taller than either species.

$$\blacktriangleleft\blacktriangleleft\,(\,\dot{\mathbf{i}}\,\text{\ding{92}}\,),\ \ \blacktriangleright\blacktriangleright,\ (\,\dot{\mathbf{i}}\,)(\,\text{\ding{92}}\,)$$

= Shrink (Terran Symbolian), Enlarge, (Terran)(Symbolian)

= small (product of Terran and Symbolian), bigger, (Terran) (Symbolian)

= Terran/Symbolian hybrid children are bigger than Terrans and Symbolians

= Terran/Symbolian hybrid children are taller than either species

Note that the question uses the same set of symbols (those for 'enlarge' and 'shrink') to conduct two different operations within the same code based on placement of parentheses. This is an example of why you need imagination and lateral thinking when you encode or decode using a restricted set of symbols. The translation is a little uncertain, but you can still find a 'best' interpretation. In question 9, 'shrink' is used as a description whereas here it's used as an operation. If used descriptively in this case, it can be translated as: Hybrid is small, Terran & Symbolian both large, which is the opposite of the desired meaning.

Answer 9

D – Symbolia has many dangerous molten metal rivers outside of its cities.

$$\text{\ding{92}}\,\blacktriangle,\ \blacktriangleright\blacktriangleright(\text{\ding{92}}\,\textcircled{1}\,\mathbf{\ddot{\delta}}\,\diagup\,)$$

= Symbolian Farmland, Enlarge(Angry Hot Metal Road)

= Symbolian Farmland has many angry molten metal roads

= Symbolian countryside has many dangerous molten metal rivers

= Symbolian has many dangerous molten metal rivers outside of its cities

Answer 10

E – The Symbolian fleet could never defeat Earth because it's outnumbered by the Terran Space Navy.

$$\blacktriangleright\blacktriangleright(\dot{!} \rightleftharpoons \rightleftharpoons), \blacktriangleleft\blacktriangleleft(\text{❋}\rightleftharpoons \rightleftharpoons), \blacktriangledown\blacktriangleright\blacktriangleright\text{❋}, \dot{!}\bullet$$

= Enlarge (Terran Spaceship Spaceship), Shrink (Symbolian Spaceship Spaceship), Later Never Angry, Terran Planet

= Large Terran fleet small Symbolian fleet could never angry Earth

= The Terran fleet outnumbers the Symbolian fleet could never defeat Earth

= The Symbolian fleet could never defeat Earth because it's outnumbered by the Terran Space Navy

Answer 11

C – Symbolian ground cars always run late.

$$\text{❋}\,🚌\,🚌, \blacktriangledown\ (\blacktriangleright\blacktriangledown)$$

= Symbolian Ground Car Ground Car, Later (Now Later)

= Symbolian ground cars, later (always)

= Symbolian ground cars are always later

= Symbolian ground cars always run late

Answer 12

A – Symbolians and Terrans are working together in an attempt to solve their mutual farming crisis.

$$\dot{!}\,\text{❋}\,\heartsuit, \_\,\text{··}, \text{❋}(\dot{!}⛏\text{❋}⛏)$$

= Terran Symbolian Friendly, Maybe Calm, Angry (Terran Farmland Symbolian Farmland)

= Terrans and Symbolians Friendly to Maybe Calm, Angry (mutual Farmland)

= Terrans and Symbolians are working together to possibly calm the mutual farmland crisis

= Symbolians and Terrans are working together in an attempt to solve the their mutual farming crisis

Answer 13

A – 'The primitive Terran Space Navy will be no match for our space and ground forces', the Symbolian Admiral cried rally the planet.

And

E – The Symbolian Admiral encouraged his people by telling them that the inferior Terran Fleet would fall to their fleet and army.

▸▸ ▓, ▸▸ ▓●, ▾, ▓(⤛⤜)(🚃🚃), ▓◂◂, ♥(🏙🏙), ▮(⤛⤜)

= Enlarge Symbolian, Enlarge Symbolian Planet, Later, Symbolian (Spaceship Spaceship) (Ground Car Ground Car), Angry Shrink, Wooden (City City), Terran (Spaceship Spaceship)

= Major Symbolian, make all Symbolian people bigger, later, Symbolian fleet and Symbolian ground troops, aggressively shrink, primitive civilisation, Terran fleet

= The Symbolian Admiral encouraged his people that later Symbolian fleet and army defeat primitive Terran fleet

= 'The primitive Terran Space Navy will be no match for our space and ground forces', the Symbolian Admiral cried rally the planet

And

= The Symbolian Admiral encouraged his people by telling them that the inferior Terran Fleet would fall to their fleet and army

English is a versatile language, and often you can use many phrases to give the same essential meaning. If you parse down the sentences in this question into their basic meanings, you can see that answers A and E say the same thing. The kind of conceptual code that the Symbolians use (and, indeed, that you find in the decision analysis subtest in general) is much stricter than English, because the code has fewer ways of expressing any given idea.

A quick way to solve questions where more than one answer is correct is to look for pairs of equivalent, but differently phrased answers. If you can see only one pair of answers in the set of options and the question asks you to choose two options, that pair of answers are probably correct.

Be careful not to get caught out using this shortcut in questions that contain two pairs of equivalent options.

Answer 14

A – The Symbolian loved playing 'Forever and For Always' loudly.

And

D – The Symbolian loved listening to 'We Have All the Time in the World' many times.

= Symbolian, Friendly, Now Later, Now Later, Enlarge

= The Symbolian loves Forever Always loudly/many

= The Symbolian loved playing 'Forever and For Always' loudly

And

= The Symbolian loved listening to 'We Have All the Time in the World' many times

This question creates the rather odd mental image of an alien getting down to Shania Twain and Louis Armstrong. The question is also a more subtle exploration of the ambiguity you may find in the decision analysis subtest. Some elements of the answers do not exist in the code, forcing you to fill in the gaps in small ways. For example, no code exists for 'playing' or 'listening'.

This makes excluding the other answer options harder. You can rule out B, because the middle two pairs of symbols are the same, not opposites. You can also exclude C: Adding in elements to account for 'Never', 'Forget' and 'playing' is more of a manipulation of the code's translation than the two correct answers, which involve the addition of a maximum of two elements. Finally, E doesn't fully express the 'Friendly' symbol so isn't the best interpretation.

A is the better of the two remaining interpretations, as forever is synonymous with 'for always'. D is a harder conceptual stretch, and if the question only asked for a single answer, could be excluded. However, the question asks for two answers, and D is the second best translation.

Answer 15

A – The Terran was reluctant to loan the Symbolian his e-book reader.

= Terran, Shy Friendly, Metal Laser Book, Symbolian

= The Terran, reluctant be nice, e-book reader, to Symbolian

= The Terran was reluctant to loan the Symbolian his e-book reader

C, D and E can all be excluded on the basis of the subject and object of the sentence not matching the order of the code. Neither A nor B are ideal translations so you must choose the 'least worst'. A is superior because it is less hard to translate 'shy friendly' into reluctant, than to translate 'metal laser book' into large library. Choosing between two frustratingly, but not equally, poor options sometimes happens in this subtest.

Being open to the potential alternative and metaphorical meanings of unusual collections of symbols, but still being alert to maintain the syntactical meaning of the code, is challenging. You need to be imaginative and to work within boundaries at the same time.

In any real-life decision-making situation, hard decisions are hard precisely because you can neither ignore the limits of reality nor use conventional solutions to solve the problem. Harnessing your imagination is the key to good decision-making.

Answer 16

B – Terran colony ships contain technology to convert desert into farmland.

= Terran Planet Spaceship Spaceship, Metal (City City), Hot Farmland, Later, Friendly Farmland

= Terran Planet ships, advanced civilisation, desert, later, farmland

= Terran colony ships have technology desert become farmland

= Terran colony ships contain technology to convert desert into farmland

In this question, the 'Friendly' symbol next to the second 'Farmland' symbol acts as a contextual contrast to the 'Hot' symbol next to the first 'Farmland' symbol. If you later convert 'hot farmland' to 'friendly farmland', you can deduce that the original hotness wasn't the friendly hotness associated with lots of sunshine over fertile land but was the unfriendly hotness of a desert.

Answer 17

B – The Symbolian might move home because of the cold weather.

And

E – The Symbolian's home might be uprooted in a winter storm.

= Symbolian House, Maybe, Angry Cold

= The Symbolian House may cold is bad

= The Symbolian might move home because of the cold weather

And

= The Symbolian's home might be uprooted in a winter storm

Although no code exists for 'moving' or 'uprooting', only these two options include all the other translations of the symbols used in the question, retain their relationships to each other, and introduce the fewest additional elements.

Answer 18

A – Terran ground cars are prone to break down on Symbolian country roads.

= Terran Ground Car, Maybe Angry, Symbolian Farmland Road

= Terran ground cars, can become angry, Symbolian country roads

= Terran grounds cars are prone to break down on Symbolian country roads

Neither the code for 'ground car' nor the code for 'road' is repeated to indicate plurality in the Symbolian message, unlike usage in previous questions. However, as all the potential answer options use plural forms, no extra ambiguity results. If the meaning is clear, sometimes Symbolians don't bothering pluralising.

English has its fair share of variable and sloppy usage but still retains contextual meaning. If you use abbreviations when you text your friends, you're probably guilty of significantly worse omissions.

Answer 19
A – deformation

And

D – bridge

This question is quite difficult. All the possible answers would help to convey the message. In addition, you can send the message by combining existing symbols in the Symbolian language. The question asks you to decide which extra terms would be most helpful – in other words, which new symbols give you the most bang for your buck in conveying the message.

Choosing 'bridge' as one answer is relatively straightforward. Conveying the full meaning of a bridge using the existing symbols is quite difficult. Combining 'metal' and 'road' gives you some sense of what a bridge is but lacks the concept of it being *above* something. As a last resort, you can try to use the 'enlarge' symbol to convey the bridge being above something, but this option is unsatisfactory, as the 'enlarge' symbol would more logically mean 'bigger' rather than 'above'.

Choosing 'deformation' as the other correct answer is a bit harder. You can depict the concept of deformation fairly accurately using the Symbolian equivalent of something along the lines of 'Now, Later, Now Maybe, Later Maybe'. But this expression is quite a mouthful – or should we say 'eyeful' in the case of the Symbolian language!

You can convey the options of 'worse', 'fatigue' and 'usage' more simply using the existing symbols. 'Worse' can be 'Enlarge Angry'. 'Fatigue' can be 'Angry', because you need to convey the stress associated with metal fatigue rather than a sense of sleepiness. You can omit 'usage' altogether from the message, as the other elements of the message imply this concept.

Adding a symbol for 'deformation' alongside one for 'bridge' is more efficient than any of the other options.

Answer 20

C – The Terran got frustrated with the lack of a Terran translation for the manual in his Symbolian hire car.

¡▓, ⊖(▸ ▒ ▾ ¡▓), ▒ ▩

= Terran Angry, Shy (Now Symbolian Later Terran Book), Symbolian Ground Car

= Terran Angry, Shy (Terran translation Book), Symbolian car

= Terran Angry, lack of (Terran translation Book), Symbolian car

= The Terran got frustrated with the lack of a Terran translation for the manual in his Symbolian hire car

Answer 21

E. ▓◂◂, ▒ (▸▸▮ ▸ ▸▸▮ ▾)⌣, ▒ ⬤◂◂

= Angry Shrink, Symbolian (Never Now Never Later) Spaceship, Symbolian Planet Shrink

= break into smaller bits, Symbolian (not present nor future) spaceship, Symbolian smaller than planet

= wrecked, Symbolian (past) spaceship, Symbolian moon

= The wreckage of the ancient Symbolian spaceship was found orbiting one of their moons

Answer 22
A – Terran television is the worst in the galaxy.

And

D – Terran email is plagued by spammers on every colony.

= Terran (Laser Book), Angry Enlarge, Planet Planet Planet

= Terran television very bad every planet

= Terran television is the worst in the galaxy

And

= Terran (Laser Book), Angry Enlarge, Planet Planet Planet

= Terran email, lots of bad, every planet

= Terran email is plagued by spammers on every colony

Answer 23
C – I would rather be first in a village than second in Rome.

= Friendly, Terran Enlarge (House House), Friendly Shrink, Terran Shrink (City Enlarge)

= Like, Terran big (village), like less, Terran small (big city)

= Like first in village, less like second in big city

= I would rather be first is a village than second in Rome

Satisfaction

The translation 'I would rather be first in a village than second in Rome' is a paraphrase of a quote by the ancient philosopher Epicurus, who espoused the value of being happy about being in control of your own life rather than constantly trying to chase greater things. The original quote invoked an Iberian village, but trying to encode Iberian in Symbolian seemed like too much of a big task, even for this question-setter.

Answer 24

D. ♥ ⇥● , (●●●)

= Friendly Enlarge Planet, (Planet Planet Planet)

= Like lot planet, all planets

= This world is the best of all possible worlds

A Panglossian outlook

The German philosopher Leibniz first coined the phrase 'This world is the best of all possible worlds' in an attempt to explain why a benevolent and omnipotent god would create a world with such suffering as ours. Leibniz argued that if this world was the one God chose for us, then this world must be the best of all possible worlds that can exist, meaning that all the other possible worlds are even worse. This position was satirised by the French writer Voltaire in *Candide*. Candide's tutor Dr Pangloss uses the phrase to raise his spirits when he faces awful personal hardship. This kind of unrelenting and unrealistic optimism is now often termed 'Panglossian'.

Answer 25

E – Men freely believe that which they desire.

‼, ⁝♥, (‼)♥

= Terran Terran, Calm Friendly, (Terran Terran) Friendly

= Men, calmly like, what Men like

= Men freely believe that which they desire

B, C and D can rapidly be excluded due to those translations including terms absent from the code. It can be argued that A is a valid translation:

Man man, calm friendly, (man man) friendly = Men, subdued happiness, Men, happy = Men like spending time with other men. However, this phrase can be translated from Symbolian without the need for the final 'happy' symbol. Its presence indicates an additional layer of meaning, making E the preferable answer as it makes use of all the components of the code.

Classical psychology

The phrase 'Men freely believe that which they desire' comes from Julius Caesar, Emperor of Rome. This shrewd psychological insight reveals Caesar's innate political talent. The idea is that people are more easily persuaded by a weak argument that focuses on what they want and believe, than by a stronger argument that focuses on what is true. Also, when they make decisions, people generally believe themselves to be motivated by what is right but other people to be motivated by selfish personal interest. The field of social psychology describes this phenomenon more formally as the 'fundamental attribution error'.

Answer 26

A – The fire on the old galleon caused many deaths.

● ⤙, ✹ⓘ, (❢❢)▸▸▮

= Wooden Spaceship, Angry Hot, (Terran Terran) Never

= Wooden ship, bad Hot, (many people) never

= old ship, fire, many died

= The fire on the old galleon caused many deaths

Part III
Practice Tests

'I did so well in the UKCAT exam,
i've called my new cat 'UK.'

In this part . . .

*B*et some of you skipped directly to this part! We're not offended; we know you want to practice lots of UKCAT questions before test day.

The previous parts contain lots of background to the UKCAT that you really should know, though. And the explanations to some of the sample questions in Part II will deepen your understanding to the answers to some of the questions in this part too. So if you have time, it's worth going back and at least skimming over the earlier parts.

This part contains two full practice tests, and their answers and explanations. Try doing them under timed conditions to replicate the feel of the UKCAT!

Chapter 8

Practice Test One

- -

In This Chapter

▶ Working through a complete timed UKCAT practice test

- -

The best way to prepare for the UKCAT test is to do lots of practice questions under timed conditions. In this chapter, we give you a complete practice test, just like the real thing. We recommend you do the practice test in one session. Make sure that you allow the right amount of time for each part of the test (we show the UKCAT subtest timings in Table 8-1).

Table 8-1	Timings for the UKCAT Subtests
Subtest	*Time Allowed*
Verbal reasoning	22 minutes
Quantitative reasoning	23 minutes
Abstract reasoning	16 minutes
Decision analysis	32 minutes

If you've special educational needs and plan to sit the UKCATSEN, give yourself an extra 25 per cent of time. (For the low-down on the UKCATSEN, see Chapter 2.)

In Chapter 9, we give the answers and full explanations for the questions in this practice test.

Verbal Reasoning

Passage 1

Rome in Chaos
(Adapted from *The Decline and Fall of the Roman Empire*, by Edward Gibbon)

Pestilence and famine contributed to fill up the measure of the calamities of Rome. The first could be only imputed to the just indignation of the gods; but a monopoly of corn, was considered as the immediate cause of the second. The popular discontent at these calamities, after it had long circulated in whispers, broke out in the assembled circus. The people quitted their favourite amusements for the more delicious pleasure of revenge, rushed in crowds towards a palace in the suburbs, one of the emperor's retirements, and demanded, with angry clamours, the head of the public enemy.

Cleander ordered a body of Praetorian cavalry to sally forth, and disperse the seditious multitude. The multitude fled with precipitation towards the city but when the cavalry entered the streets, their pursuit was checked by a shower of stones and darts from the roofs and windows of the houses. The foot guards, who had been long jealous of the Praetorians, embraced the party of the people. The tumult became a regular engagement. The Praetorians gave way, oppressed with numbers; and the tide of popular fury returned with redoubled violence against the gates of the palace, where the Emperor Commodus lay, dissolved in luxury and alone, unconscious of the civil war.

Commodus started from his dream of pleasure, and commanded that the head of Cleander should be thrown out to the people. The desired spectacle instantly appeased the tumult; and he might even yet have regained the affection and confidence of his subjects.

A – True	B – False	C – Can't tell

Statement 1: A corn monopoly was partially responsible for the violence.

Statement 2: Commodus was asleep while the riot was taking place.

Statement 3: The crowd initially routed by cavalry fought back only once they retreated outside the city.

Statement 4: By sacrificing Cleander, Commodus regained the confidence of his subjects.

Passage 2

Exporting the Format
(Adapted from *Business the Jamie Oliver Way*, by Trevor Clawson)

Jamie Oliver's television career has taken a new international direction through an agreement to produce a series of six programmes specifically for the US market.

The show follows Oliver on an odyssey to Huntingdon, West Virginia, a town recognised as one of the most obese and unhealthy in the entire US. During his stay there, Oliver attempts to persuade and encourage the population to adopt a healthier diet.

As in the UK, he has his work cut out. According to the Centers for Disease Control and Prevention, around half the population of the Huntingdon-Ashland Metropolitan district are obese, and the area has the highest incidence of heart disease and diabetes in the US. To emphasise the point, in one of Oliver's early encounters – as reported in the *New York Times* – he meets an eight year old child suffering from type 2 diabetes and carrying 80 lbs more than her recommended weight.The US shows follow a long tradition of UK and European reality shows successfully adapted for the US market. If the US show proves a success, it will undoubtedly be re-exported back to the UK, underlining his global bankability.

A – True   **B – False**   **C – Can't tell**

Statement 5: The first person Oliver met during his TV show was the 8-year-old child with type 2 diabetes mentioned in the passage.

Statement 6: Around half the population of the Huntingdon-Ashland Metropolitan district are obese, with heart disease or diabetes.

Statement 7: British viewers may get to see the programme if it does well in America.

Statement 8: British reality TV formats can work well in the States.

Passage 3

Getting to the Bottom Line
(Adapted from *Where's the Sausage*, by David J. Taylor)

The Simpton's Sausages numbers made for sorry reading. The profitability of the core sausage business had been in decline for five years, with the brand trapped in a vicious downward cycle of increasing price promotion, leading to less funds for marketing and innovation, leading to less differentiation, more price promotion, and so on. In a way, I felt partly responsible for the nightmare we were having, having been part of the sales department's push for more promotional support to protect listings with the key supermarket chains such as Tesco, Sainsbury's and Asda-Walmart. At the same time, the supermarkets had been busy developing their 'own label' sausage ranges, such as Tesco's Finest and Sainsbury's Taste the Difference. Our market share had fallen off a cliff, dropping from 35% in 1999 to 19% in 2006. We had been squashed between the competitively priced supermarket brands at one end, and premium priced gourmet products at the other, from brands like Duchy's Originals and Porkinsons.

A – True   **B – False**   **C – Can't tell**

Statement 9: Price is the <u>only</u> determinant of sales in the sausage business.

Statement 10: One way of trying to protect listings with major retailers is with aggressive price promotion.

Statement 11: Squeezed profit margins for Simpton's Sausages over the past five years have resulted in less cash available for marketing.

Statement 12: Over a seven-year period, Simpton's went from selling more than one in three sausages to fewer than one in five.

Passage 4

And the winner is . . .
(Adapted from *Business the Simon Cowell Way*, by Trevor Clawson)

X Factor is one of the most popular shows on British television and – for good or for ill – it is the only prime-time music show running regularly on any of the major networks. Once upon a time, the BBC's *Top of the Pops* provided the main route to the television audience for mainstream pop acts. With that show long gone, *X Factor* has come to define what British pop music is, and how it is presented. And while *Top of the Pops* reflected the whole gamut of popular music, from rap and rock to novelty songs, *X Factor* is about Simon Cowell's vision. He owns the show, owns the successful acts and, if and when he signs them to his label, dictates the course of their careers.

The same is true, to some extent, of Cowell's Syco TV's second big commission for the UK market – *Britain's Got Talent*. As a more generalised talent show it doesn't necessarily throw up singers or potential recording artists as winners, but has nonetheless proved successful in finding artists for his Syco Music label. These include opera singer Paul Potts, winner of the first show, and Susan Boyle.

The relationship between Syco Music and Syco TV is there on the screen for all to see, but the television production unit is also swelling the coffers of Cowell and joint-venture partner Sony by successfully marketing and selling programmes and their formats around the world.

A – True **B – False** **C – Can't tell**

Statement 13: *X Factor* attracts the same audience demographic as *Top of the Pops* used to.

Statement 14: Simon Cowell has a financial interest in both *X Factor* and *Britain's Got Talent*.

Statement 15: Simon Cowell makes more money from *X Factor* than his joint-venture partner Sony does.

Statement 16: Cowell has an interest in Syco TV but not Syco Music.

Passage 5

Paradise
(Adapted from *The Rabbi and The Priest*, by Milton Goldsmith)

On the high road from Tscherkask to Togarog, and not far from the latter village, there stood, in the year 1850, a large and inhospitable-looking inn. Its shingled walls, whose rough surface no paint-brush had touched for long generations, seemed decaying from sheer old age. Its tiled roof was in a most dilapidated state, displaying large gaps imperfectly stuffed with straw, and serving rather to collect the rain and snow for the more thorough inundation of the rooms below than to protect them from the elements. The grounds about the house were in keeping with it in point of picturesque neglect, and were as innocent of cultivation as the building was of paint. A roughly paved path led from the highway to the tavern door. Two old and sickly poplar trees cast a poor and half-hearted shade upon the parched ground, and mournfully shook their leaves over the scene of desolation. The herbage grew in isolated patches on a black and uncultivated soil. Nature might have originally been friendly to the place, but generations of poverty and neglect had reduced it to a condition of wretched misery.

As was this particular spot, so was the entire village. Slavery had wound its chains about the inhabitants, stifling whatever energy they possessed, entailing upon them constant toil to satisfy the exorbitant demands of their task-masters. Hence, even with a genial sun and a southern climate, the fields were barren, the crops poor and the people sunk in abject poverty.

The dilapidated inn, or *kretschma*, was known in the vicinity by the ideal and appropriate name of 'Paradise' – appropriate, because in it many a sinner had been tempted and had fallen from grace.

A – True   **B – False**   **C – Can't tell**

Statement 17: The inn was closer to Togarog than to Tscherkask.

Statement 18: Crops were poor in the local area due to too little sunshine.

Statement 19: Straw was used to effectively patch the dilapidated roof.

Statement 20: Many of the local inhabitants were serfs.

Passage 6

The Raid of John Brown at Harper's Ferry
(Adapted from the book of the same name, by Reverend Samuel Leech)

The town of Harper's Ferry is located in Jefferson County, West Virginia. Lucerne in Switzerland does not excel in romantic grandeur of situation. On its northern front the Potomac sweeps along to pass the national capital, and the tomb of Washington, in its silent flow towards the sea. On its eastern side the Shenandoah hurries to empty its waters into the Potomac, that in perpetual wedlock they may greet the stormy Atlantic. Across the Potomac the Maryland Heights stand out as the tall sentinels of Nature. Beyond the Shenandoah are the Blue Ridge Mountains, fringing the westward boundary of Loudon County, Virginia. Between these rivers, and nestling inside of their very confluence, reposes Harper's Ferry. Back of its hills lies the famous Shenandoah Valley, celebrated for its natural scenery, its historic battles and 'Sheridan's Ride'. At Harper's Ferry the United States authorities early located an Arsenal and an Armoury.

Captain John Brown believed that if he could secure the arms and ammunition in these buildings, carry them into the fastnesses of the adjacent mountains, and then unfurl the flag of freedom for all slaves who would flock to his standard, the result would be a general uprising of slaves throughout the border states.

A – True   **B – False**   **C – Can't tell**

Statement 21: The author finds Harper's Ferry to be more beautiful than Lucerne.

Statement 22: Harper's Ferry is bounded by the Shenandoah and the Potomac.

Statement 23: The local slave population was ready to rise up.

Statement 24: Captain Brown intended to make his stand in the town, after securing the Arsenal and Armoury.

Passage 7

Something Wonderful
(Adapted from *The Railway Children*, by Edith Nesbit)

'I wish something would happen,' said the eldest child Bobbie, dreamily, 'something wonderful.'Now, curiously enough, this was just what happened. The old gentleman, who was very well known and respected at his particular station, had got there early that morning, and he had waited at the door where the young man stands holding the interesting machine that clips the tickets, and he had said something to every single passenger who passed through that door. And after nodding to what the old gentleman had said – and the nods expressed every shade of surprise, interest, doubt, cheerful pleasure, and grumpy agreement – each passenger had gone on to the platform and read one certain part of his newspaper. And when the passengers got into the train, they had told the other passengers who were already there what the old gentleman had said, and then the other passengers had also looked at their newspapers and seemed very astonished and, mostly, pleased. Then, when the train passed the fence where the three children were, newspapers and hands and handkerchiefs were waved madly, till all that side of the train was fluttery with white like the pictures of the King's Coronation in the biograph at Maskelyne and Cook's. To the children it almost seemed as though the train itself was alive, and was at last responding to the love that they had given it so freely and so long.

A – True   **B – False**   **C – Can't tell**

Statement 25: Bobbie knew something wonderful was going to happen.

Statement 26: The old gentlemen ensured that many train passengers would wave at the children from their windows.

Statement 27: The children loved seeing the train, even before it waved back at them.

Statement 28: The children knew why everyone was waving at them.

Passage 8

Social Commerce
(Adapted from *Socialnomics*, by Erik Qualman)

Social Commerce is upon us. What is social commerce exactly? It is a term that encompasses the transactional, search, and marketing components of social media. Social commerce harnesses the simple idea that people value the opinion of other people. What this truly means is that in the future we will no longer seek products and services; rather, they will find us. Nielsen reports 78 per cent of people trust their peers' opinions. This is neither a new concept, nor new to the Web.

What is new is that social media makes it so much easier to disseminate information. As the success of social media proves, people enjoy spreading information. This explains the popularity of Twitter, Foursquare, Gowalla, and so forth. These tools and products enable users to inform their friends what they are doing every minute of the day (I'm having an ice cream cone; check out this great article; listening to keynote speaker; etc.). Twitter is interesting from the standpoint that its popularity began with older generations, and time will tell how much of Generation Y and Z embrace Twitter. This is the exact opposite trend of Facebook, which was originally popular with the younger generations and then Generation X and Baby Boomers started to get engaged.

The most popular feature of Facebook and LinkedIn is status updates. Status updates enable users to continuously brag, boast, inform and vent to everyone in their network.

A – True   **B – False**   **C – Can't tell**

Statement 29: Social commerce is a buzzword for how social media affects businesses.

Statement 30: Facebook was originally popular because younger people are less socially inhibited than older generations.

Statement 31: Most sharing on social media is, in fact, a form of bragging.

Statement 32: Research suggests that most people trust their peers.

Passage 9

Chinese Water Crisis
(Adapted from *An Introduction to the Chinese Economy*, by Rongxing Guo)

China now faces almost all of the problems related to water resources that are faced by countries across the globe. China's rapid economic growth, industrialisation, and urbanisation have outpaced infrastructural investment and management capacity, and have created widespread problems of water scarcity. In the areas of the North China Plain, where about half of China's wheat and corn is grown and there are extensive peach orchards, drought is an ever-looming threat. With one-fifth of the world's population, China has only 8 per cent of the fresh water. China's annual renewable water reserves were about 2.8 trillion cubic meters, which ranked it fifth in the world, behind Brazil, Russia, Canada, and Indonesia, but ahead of the US. However, in terms of per capita availability of water reserves, China is one of the lowest in the world – barely one-quarter of the world average.

In the coming decades, China will be under severe water stress as defined by the international standard and there is already growing competition for water between communities, sectors of the economy, and individual provinces.

A – True   **B – False**   **C – Can't tell**

Statement 33: China will be unable to adequately manage its limited water supply.

Statement 34: China has 8% of the water it needs, by international standards.

Statement 35: China has less water than it needs, by international standards.

Statement 36: The North China Plain is a major agricultural centre in China.

Passage 10

The Dead Rise
(Adapted from *The Proper Care and Feeding of Zombies*,
by Mac Montandon)

In 2009, a small group of highly motivated Canadian mathematicians and researchers took up the humanitarian cause of modelling an infectious zombie outbreak.

The basic equation for determining the rate of a zombie outbreak contained three variables: Susceptibles, Zombies and Removed. The first two categories should be clear enough, and Removed simply refers to dead humans. They introduced a special parameter to account for Removed humans who subsequently become Zombies, and another one to allow for Zombies to be Removed by means of 'removing the head or destroying the brain'.

The results are chilling. If no action is taken, the zombie outbreak will overtake a city of half a million people in roughly four days. However, if counter-strikes by humans are permitted, it is possible for humans to win and eradicate the zombies within just ten days. This assumes that the attacks are 'sufficiently frequent, with increasing force, and assuming that the available resources can be mustered in time'.

A – True   **B – False**   **C – Can't tell**

Statement 37: Canadian researchers are interested in zombie outbreaks.

Statement 38: Zombies cannot be killed as they are already undead.

Statement 39: Zombie outbreaks take just days to overwhelm population centres.

Statement 40: Zombies cannot be defeated through superior firepower.

Passage 11

(Adapted from *Wine for Dummies*, by Ed McCarthy and Mary Ewing-Mulligan)

Back in 1855, when an Exposition took place in Paris, the organisers asked the Bordeaux Chamber of Commerce to develop a classification of Bordeaux wines. The Chamber of Commerce delegated the task to the Bordeaux wine brokers, the people who buy and re-sell the wines of Bordeaux. These merchants named 61 top red wines – 60 from the Medoc and one from what was then Graves (and today is known as Pessac-Leognan). According to the prices fetched by wines at the time and the existing reputations of the wines, they divided these 61 wines into five categories, known as *crus* or growths. (In Bordeaux, a *cru* refers to wine estate). Their listing is known as the classification of 1855; to this day, these classified growths enjoy special prestige among wine lovers.

The 1855 classification has held up remarkably well over time. Sure, a few of the 61 properties are not performing up to their classification today, while other unclassified chateaux now probably deserve to be included. But because of the politics involved, no changes in classification ranking have been made, with one dramatic exception. That exception was the upgrading of Chateau Mouton-Rothschild from a second growth to a first growth. The family estate's motto subsequently changed from 'First, I cannot be; second, I do not deign to be; Mouton, I am' to 'First, I am; second I was; Mouton does not change'.

A – True   **B – False**   **C – Can't tell**

Statement 41: In 1855, the Bordeaux Chamber of Commerce classified Bordeaux wines.

Statement 42: There are five *Premier Crus* in the 1855 classification.

Statement 43: The change of the Mouton-Rothschild motto following the wine's upgrade to first growth reflects their pride in the upgrade.

Statement 44: The Mouton-Rothschild motto is a play on words of the motto of a famous French noble House.

Quantitative Reasoning

Numerical presentation 1

FTSE All-Share Index Market Capitalisations

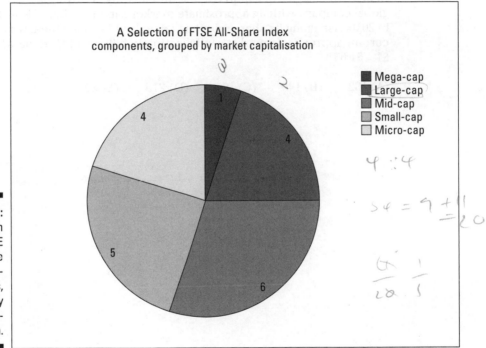

Figure 8-1: A selection of 20 FTSE All-Share Index components, grouped by market capitalisation.

Market capitalisation is a measure of how large a company is. It is calculated by multiplying the share price by the number of shares in circulation. Companies can be grouped into categories based on the size of their market capitalisation, or 'cap' for short. The largest companies are the mega-caps, followed by large-caps, mid-caps, small-caps and micro-caps. A selection of companies listed on the Stock Exchange were analysed and the chart in Figure 8-1 was created.

Item 1: What percentage of companies are at least large-caps in size?

(A) 5%   (B) 20%   (C) 25%   (D) 30%   (E) 45%

Item 2: What is the ratio of large-caps to micro-caps?

(A) 1:5   (B) 1:1   (C) 2:1   (D) 1:4   (E) 1:5

Item 3: Two large-caps merge, creating a new single mega-cap company. What is the approximate new percentage of mega-caps?

(A) 5.0%   (B) 5.3%   (C) 10.0%   (D) 10.5%   (E) 15.0%

Item 4: The mega-cap featured in the initial study is Royal Dutch Shell, a global company with an approximate market capitalisation of £165 billion in 2010. Assuming its share price has fallen by 15% since then, what is its current approximate market capitalisation in billions of US dollars? (Assume £1 = $1.63.)

(A) 132   (B) 140   (C) 165   (D) 215   (E) 229

Numerical presentation 2

Conflict in Afghanistan

Table 8-2	British Fatalities in Afghanistan in 2010
Month	*Number of Fatalities*
January	6
February	15
March	12
April	3
May	8
June	20
July	16
August	7
September	6
October	4
November	3
December	3

Item 5: Approximately what percentage of fatalities took place up to the end of June?

(A) 50%   (B) 62%   (C) 64%   (D) 78%   (E) 80%

Item 6: If you were a soldier in Afghanistan, approximately how many times greater were your chances of dying in the first half of the year compared with the second half, working solely from the statistics in the table?

(A) 1.64   (B) 1.78   (C) 2.00   (D) 3.49   (E) 3.50

Item 7: What was the mean number of British deaths per month in Afghanistan in 2010? Round your answer to one decimal place.

(A) 3.0   (B) 5.3   (C) 8.3   (D) 8.6   (E) 12.0

Item 8: In the deadliest month, by what percentage did deaths exceed the modal average, to the nearest whole per cent?

(A) 15%   (B) 380%   (C) 433%   (D) 567%   (E) 667%

Numerical presentation 3

Top Flight Material

Table 8-3 shows the 20 teams playing in the Premier League in the 2011–2012 season, together with the total number of years they've played in the top division of English football.

Table 8-3		Premiership Clubs Top Tier Years							
Arsenal	95	Everton	109	Newcastle United	81	Swansea City	3
Aston Villa	101	Fulham	23	Norwich City	22	Tottenham Hotspur	71
Blackburn Rovers	72	Liverpool	97	Queen's Park Rangers	22	West Bromwich Albion	73
Bolton Wanderers	73	Manchester City	83	Stoke City	56	Wigan Athletic	7
Chelsea	77	Man United	87	Sunderland	81	Wolves	63

John, a keen football statistician, decides to group the teams into categories, based on how many seasons they've been in the top flight and draws up the table shown in Table 8-4.

Table 8-4	John's Table of Premiership Clubs
Football Royalty (90+ seasons)	4
Aristocrats (70–89 seasons)	9
Bourgeoisie (20–69 seasons)	5
New Boys (19 or fewer seasons)	2

Item 9: Is there anything wrong with John's table?

    A – One too many in Football Royalty

    B – One too many in the Aristocrats

    C – One too few in the Bourgeoisie

    D – One too few in the New Boys

    E – No – his table is correct

Item 10: If all the current members of the top three categories remain in the Premiership for another 10 years, how many members of the Aristocrats will there be then?

    (A) 5   (B) 6   (C) 8   (D) 10   (E) 12

Item 11: Returning to the present day, what is the arithmetic mean number of seasons of top flight status held by the Football Royalty clubs? You may round your answer to the nearest whole number of seasons.

    (A) 98   (B) 100   (C) 101   (D) 105   (E) 122

Item 12: How many more years will it take Wigan Athletic to become Bourgeoisie, assuming that they get relegated out of the Premier League twice during that time and it takes them a season in the Championship each time to return to Premier League?

    (A) 9   (B) 13   (C) 14   (D) 15   (E) 17

Numerical presentation 4

Ryding High

Selection to the USA Ryder Cup Golf team is done through a points system. Players collect points based on how they do in tournaments throughout the year. The points of the top 20 players can be found in Table 8-5.

Table 8-5		Ryder Cup Points		
331	194	408	360	293
803	220	314	163	364
164	390	766	364	184
330	129	330	291	141

Item 13: The top eight players qualify automatically for inclusion in the team. What is the minimum current score that would qualify?

(A) 331   (B) 330   (C) 314   (D) 293   (E) 291

Item 14: What is the range of points?

(A) 625   (B) 637   (C) 662   (D) 673   (E) 674

Item 15: What percentage of the top 20 players would qualify with a cut-off score of 295?

(A) 45%   (B) 50%   (C) 55%   (D) 60%   (E) 65%

Item 16: To the nearest whole per cent, by what percentage would the average point score of the bottom five players have to increase to meet a 295 point cut-off?

(A) 12%   (B) 39%   (C) 56%   (D) 89%   (E) 100%

Numerical presentation 5

Speed Test

Items 17–20 refer to the Nurburgring Nordschliefe car test track located in Germany.

Nurburgring test times are based on a 20.6-km lap, and times are given in a minutes and seconds format such that 8:55 would be 8 minutes and 55 seconds, for example. Speeds are commonly reported in kilometres per hour (km/h) or miles per hour (mph).

If needed, you may assume that 1 mile = 1.6 km.

Item 17: The fastest car around the Nurburgring is the Radical SR8 LM, recording a lap time of 6:48. What was its average speed in miles per hour, to the nearest whole number?

(A) 12   (B) 114   (C) 162   (D) 181   (E) 182

Item 18: The Pagani Zonda F Clubsport took 33:04 to complete three laps. Assuming that 652 seconds was lost due to mechanical problems and time spent recovering from these problems, what would have been its average lap time without these issues?

(A) 0:74   (B) 7:24   (C) 7:40   (D) 11:01   (E) 22:12

Item 19: The Radical mentioned in Item 17 weighs just 680 kg. The Zonda mentioned in Item 18 weighs 1210 kg. If Zonda's maximum power is 650 horsepower (hp), what approximately would the Radical need to put out to maintain the same maximal power to weight ratio as the Zonda?

(A) 365 hp   (B) 366 hp   (C) 368 hp   (D) 382 hp   (E) 1157 hp

Item 20: The Zonda now does three fresh laps. The first lap manages an average speed of 120 mph, the second a lap time of 7:23 and the third is 5% quicker than the first. What is the approximate average speed of the Zonda across these three laps of the Nurburgring?

(A) 3 km/s   (B) 117 km/h   (C) 117 mph   (D) 185 mph   (E) 187 mph

Numerical presentation 6

Population Demographics

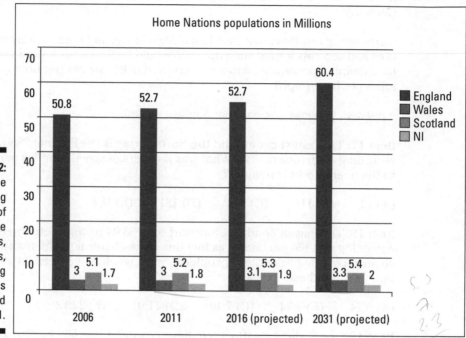

Figure 8-2:
The changing population of the UK Home Nations, in millions, including projections for 2016 and 2031.

Home Nations populations in Millions

England
Wales
Scotland
NI

50.8 / 3 / 5.1 / 1.7 — 2006
52.7 / 3 / 5.2 / 1.8 — 2011
52.7 / 3.1 / 5.3 / 1.9 — 2016 (projected)
60.4 / 3.3 / 5.4 / 2 — 2031 (projected)

Item 21: In 2011, what is the ratio of the English to the rest of the Home Nations?

(A) 1:1.19   (B) 1:1.20   (C) 1.24:1   (D) 5.18:1   (E) 5.27:1

Item 22: Which of the following statements is supported by the information in the chart?

A – The Northern Irish population is very gradually falling over the period charted.

B – On average, the Scottish population is increasing at a faster rate than the English population between 2006 and 2031.

C – The English make up a greater proportion of the total population in 2031 than in 2011.

D – The Welsh population is projected to increase by approximately 10% between 2016 and 2031.

E – By 2016, the English and Scottish populations will represent less than 90% of the overall population of the Home Nations.

Item 23: What is the approximate overall percentage population increase of the Home Nations in 2031 compared with 2011?

(A) 10.2%   (B) 13.4%   (C) 14.6%   (D) 17.3%   (E) 18.9%

Item 24: What is the range in millions between the English and the Welsh across the entire period charted?

(A) 9.6   (B) 55.3   (C) 57.1   (D) 57.4   (E) 58.7

Numerical presentation 7

Well-Heeled

James is just starting his career, and decides to buy three pairs of shoes to suit any basic professional need (black plain cap-toe oxfords, dark brown wingtip oxfords and burgundy penny loafers).

He is undecided whether to buy high-quality but expensive Northampton Classics or cheaper but limited-lifespan Mass Markets so draws up Tables 8-6 and 8-7 to compare the costs and help him decide.

Table 8-6	Northampton Classics
Pair of shoes	£650
Factory recrafting and resoling (required every five years; can be done a maximum of three times per shoe)	£120 per pair
High-quality polish (total annual cost)	£20
Lasted shoe trees (pair)	£50
Expected lifetime, with good upkeep	20 years per pair

Table 8-7	Mass Markets
Pair of shoes	£75
Cheap polish (total annual cost)	£5
Cheap shoe trees (pair)	£10
Expected lifetime, with good upkeep	2 years per pair

Item 25: How much would it cost James to wear Northampton Classics over a 40-year career, assuming that he can reuse the old shoe trees in any new pairs of shoes he needs to buy over that career?

(A) £5,060   (B) £6,210   (C) £7,010   (D) £7,160   (E) £7,730

Item 26: How much would it cost him to wear Mass Markets over the same career? (Assume that the cheaper shoe trees break and need to be re-bought once every 20 years.)

(A) £1,760   (B) £4,560   (C) £4,565   (D) £4,730   (E) £4,760

Item 27: Which of the following statements is false?

    A – Northampton Classics are more expensive over a career lifetime than Mass Markets.

    B – If cost is the only determinant of purchase, James should buy Mass Markets.

    C – If James finds the aesthetic value and craftsmanship of Northampton Classics to be superior to that of Mass Markets, then he may find them worth spending extra money on.

    D – The annual cost of wearing Northampton Classics is £175.25.

    E – The annual cost of wearing Mass Markets is £110.00.

Item 28: James decides to buy Northampton Classics, but decides to start off with four pairs of shoes instead of three, and for that fourth pair adds dark brown Chelsea boots to his collection. This addition reduces the frequency of wearing of each pair and so proportionally reduces the required frequency of resoling. If resoling is the limiting factor determining the overall lifespan of the shoe, how many years will each pair now last him?

    (A) 22.5   (B) 24.3   (C) 25.5   (D) 26.7   (E) 30.3

Numerical presentation 8

Hitting the Sales

A market research firm is hired by the British Chambers of Commerce to study how shopping habits of the public varied in response to a Bank of England interest rate cut of 50 basis points. They compared shoppers with variable mortgages and without mortgages (or with fixed rate mortgages), and measured how many of each group increased their weekly discretionary expenditure by at least 10% in the aftermath of the rate cut.

Table 8-8	Effect of Monetary Policy on Shopping Habits		
	Variable Mortgage Holders	Fixed/No Mortgage Holders	Total
Would not increase expenditure by 10+%	52	89	141
Would increase expenditure by 10+%	133	111	244

Item 29: Approximately, what are the odds of a variable mortgage holder increasing expenditure by at least 10% compared with those who do not hold variable mortgages?

(A) 1:1   (B) 3:2   (C) 2:1   (D) 3:1   (E) 5:1

Item 30: What percentage of variable mortgage holders increased their expenditure by at least 10%? Round your answer to the nearest whole per cent.

(A) 21%   (B) 39%   (C) 55%   (D) 72%   (E) 256%

Item 31: What is the difference between the proportion of people who increased expenditure by at least 10% and who were variable mortgage holders compared to the proportion of who increased expenditure by at least 10% but were fixed/no mortgage holders?

(A) 0.16   (B) 0.18   (C) 0.56   (D) 0.72   (E) 1.20

Item 32: What is the chance that a person selected at random from the study sample has neither a variable mortgage nor increased their expenditure by at least 10% in response to the Bank of England base rate cut?

(A) 13.5%   (B) 23.1%   (C) 28.8%   (D) 34.5%   (E) 37.4%

Numerical presentation 9

In at the Deep End

Preparation for the London 2012 Olympics included the design of a new swimming pool to meet FINA long-course standards. The dimensions of such a swimming pool are shown schematically in Figure 8-3.

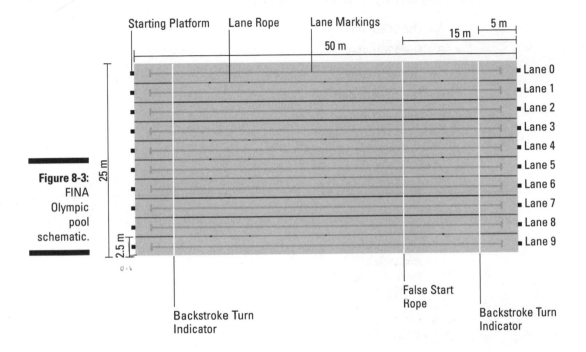

Figure 8-3: FINA Olympic pool schematic.

Item 33: Assuming an average depth of 2 m, what is the total internal surface area of the empty pool in m²?

(A) 1,250 m²   (B) 1,550 m²   (C) 2,500 m²   (D) 2,800 m²   (E) 5,300 m²

Item 34: The pool needs to be tiled. As well as the internal surface area, the pool also needs to be tiled to a border that extends a further 0.5 m in both length and width beyond the pool's edge. If each tile is 10 cm x 10 cm, how many tiles are required in total?

(A) 7,600   (B) 147,400   (C) 155,000   (D) 162,600   (E) 162,700

Item 35: Pale blue tiles cost 15p each and will be used on the bulk, but 2,500 tiles need to be dark blue, which costs 18p per tile. Another 7,500 tiles need to be non-slip, which cost 30p each. What is the total cost of the tiles?

(A) £24,390   (B) £24,690   (C) £25,590   (D) £27,090   (E) £48,780

Item 36: It takes a tiler 5 minutes to lay a tile. Assuming that 10 people work a simultaneous 8-hour tiling day and don't interfere in each other's work, on what day do they complete the entire job?

     A – The 169th day

     B – The 170th day

     C – The 504th day

     D – The 1,694th day

     E – The 2,033rd day

Abstract Reasoning

Display 1

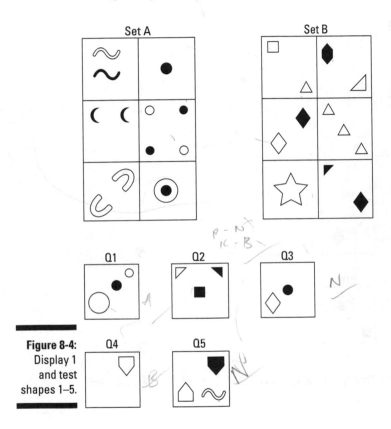

Figure 8-4:
Display 1
and test
shapes 1–5.

For each of the five questions, choose Set A, Set B, or Neither Set.

Display 2

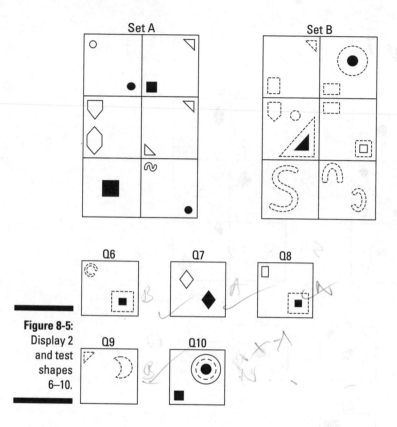

Figure 8-5:
Display 2
and test
shapes
6–10.

For each of the five questions, choose Set A, Set B, or Neither Set.

Display 3

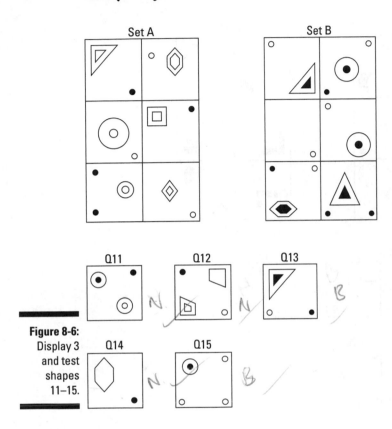

Figure 8-6:
Display 3
and test
shapes
11–15.

For each of the five questions, choose Set A, Set B, or Neither Set.

Display 4

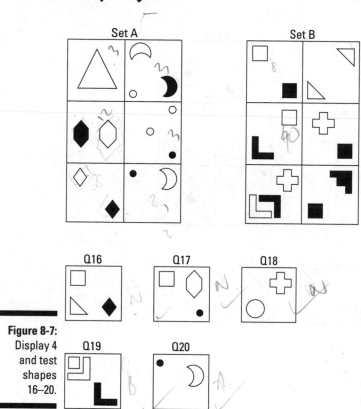

Figure 8-7:
Display 4
and test
shapes
16–20.

For each of the five questions, choose Set A, Set B, or Neither Set.

Display 5

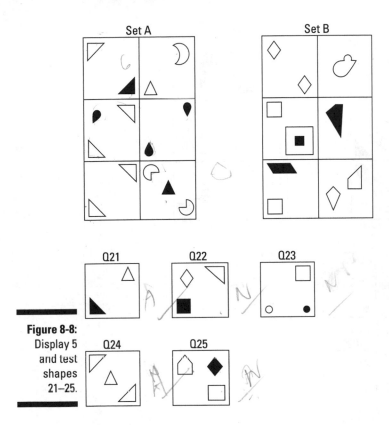

Figure 8-8:
Display 5
and test
shapes
21–25.

For each of the five questions, choose Set A, Set B, or Neither Set.

Display 6

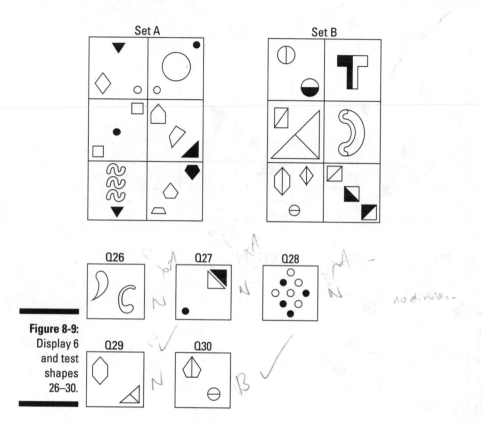

Figure 8-9:
Display 6
and test
shapes
26–30.

For each of the five questions, choose Set A, Set B, or Neither Set.

Display 7

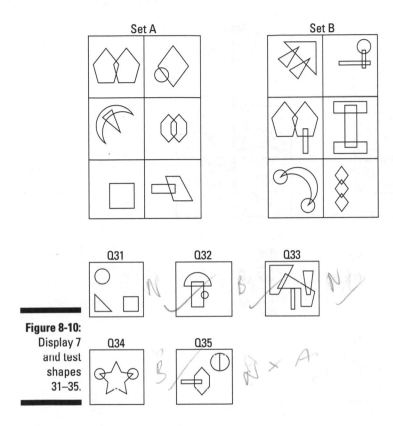

Figure 8-10:
Display 7
and test
shapes
31–35.

For each of the five questions, choose Set A, Set B, or Neither Set.

Display 8

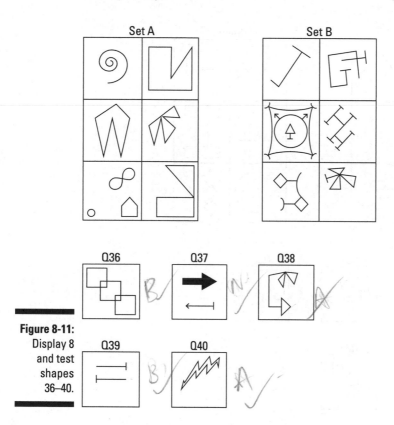

Figure 8-11:
Display 8
and test
shapes
36–40.

For each of the five questions, choose Set A, Set B, or Neither Set.

Display 9

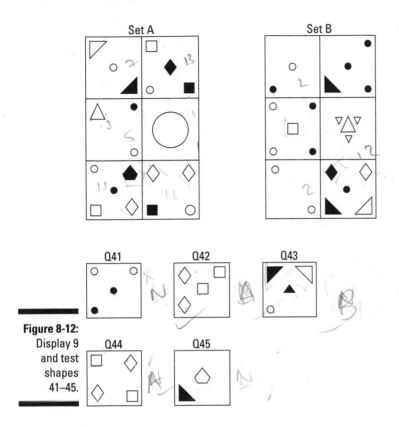

Figure 8-12:
Display 9
and test
shapes
41–45.

For each of the five questions, choose Set A, Set B, or Neither Set.

Display 10

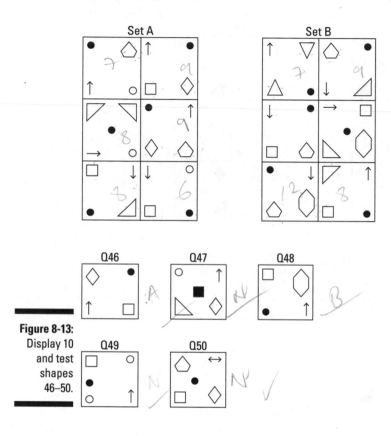

Figure 8-13:
Display 10
and test
shapes
46–50.

For each of the five questions, choose Set A, Set B, or Neither Set.

Display 11

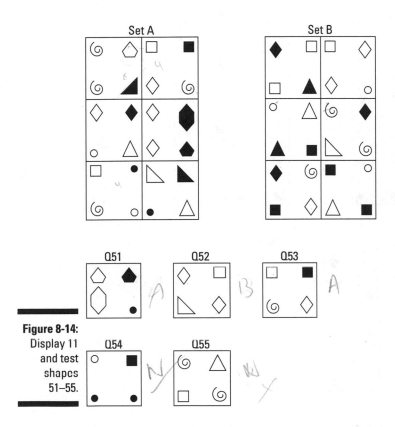

Figure 8-14:
Display 11
and test
shapes
51–55.

For each of the five questions, choose Set A, Set B, or Neither Set.

Display 12

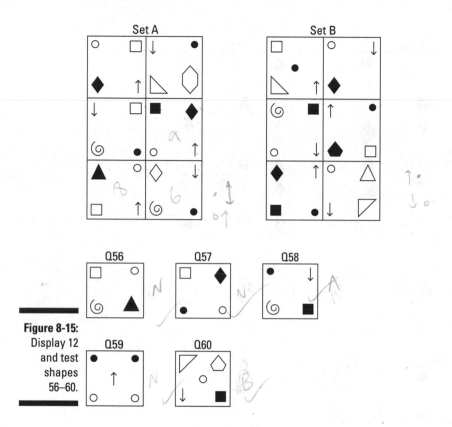

Figure 8-15:
Display 12
and test
shapes
56–60.

For each of the five questions, choose Set A, Set B, or Neither Set.

Display 13

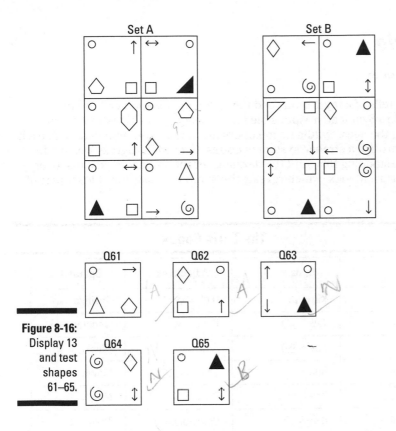

Figure 8-16:
Display 13
and test
shapes
61–65.

For each of the five questions, choose Set A, Set B, or Neither Set.

Decision Analysis

Scenario

The Turin Codex

Legend tells of a mysterious and powerful organisation called The Penumbra Syndicate responsible for influencing world history down through the ages. Syndicate members are said to communicate with each other through a strange system of codes, but little progress was made in understanding this until the dazzling recent archaeological discovery of The Turin Codex, which reveals the symbolic basis for at least part of the code.

Table 8-9		The Turin Codex	
Nouns	**Verbs**	**Adjectives**	**Operator**
I = O	Kill = 💣☀	Rich = ✡	Positive = ♩
You = ●	Talk = 📖	Poor = ❄	Negative = ℘
He = ■	Pay = ✉	Angry = ☹	Quickly = ☞
King = ᠌᠊	Run = ♉	Calm = ☺	Slowly = ☜
Pope = ✝	Sail = ♒	Brave = ♠	Now = ♌
Queen = ♍	Ride = ♐	Cowardly = ☙	Then = ⌛
Cardinal = ♎	Take = ❽		Conditional = ♎
Knight = ♄	Burn = ♋		
Peasant = ∕ ♦			
Home = ❖			

Armed with the Codex, your task is to decipher the following messages written in the Penumbra Syndicate's code, convert some others into Penumbra code, and so save the world from their malign and pervasive influence!

Question 1: What is the best interpretation of the following Penumbra message?

⌂, ⧗ ☄ , ᗡ

Ⓐ – The king will be killed by the cardinal.

B – The cardinal has killed the king.

C – The cardinal will be killed by the king.

D – The king has talked to the cardinal.

E – The king might kill the cardinal.

Question 2: What is the best interpretation of the following Penumbra message?

♍, ⧗ 📖, ᗡ, ⊠, (◐ ●)

A – The king will pay the queen.

Ⓑ – The king will persuade the queen to talk to us.

C – The queen will persuade the king to pay us.

D – The queen will talk to the king.

E – The queen will tell the king to fight.

Question 3: What is the best interpretation of the following Penumbra message?

✟, ⤢, ⌂ ⌂

A – The pope fights his cardinals.

Ⓑ – The pope rides to meet his cardinals.

C – The pope bribes his cardinals.

D – The cardinals plot against the pope.

E – The cardinals plot against each other to become pope.

Question 4: What is the best interpretation of the following Penumbra message?

♙♙,♌ ♟

A – The battle will be won by the knights.

B – No knights fought in the previous war.

C – Knights and bishops will fight together.

D – The knights will not fight us today.

E – No knight will dare challenge the king.

Question 5: What is the best interpretation of the following Penumbra message?

♍,☹,👓;☞♟,☹ (💣 💣)

A – The queen is furious at the king's rapid retreat from battle.

B – The king was routed in the battle.

C – The queen and king were forced to flee the battle.

D – No king would leave his queen to be lost in battle.

E – Defeating the queen is the fastest way to beat the king.

Question 6: What is the best way to translate the following into Penumbra code?

Bribe the Pope to defy the King.

A. ✉,✝,☹📖,👓

B. ✝,☹📖,✉ 👓

C. ♙,✝,☹📖,👓

D. 💣,☹📖,✉,👓

E. ☹📖,💣,✝,👓

Question 7: What is the best interpretation of the following Penumbra message?

$$\spadesuit \; \blacklozenge, \; \Omega \; (\textbf{8} \; \textit{P}) \; \bullet \; \boxtimes$$

A – The bribed peasants will lie to you.

B – The peasants will kill the knight if you bribe them.

C – The peasants will revolt if you bribe them.

D – The peasants may not choose to take your bribe.

E – The bribed peasants will commit regicide.

Question 8: What is the best interpretation of the following Penumbra message?

$$\maltese \; (\text{P} \; \text{P}), \; \textbf{8} \; \smiley, \; \omega \; \frown$$

A – The knights need a rich king.

B – The king will pay his knights handsomely.

C – The knights get rich by killing the king.

D – Wealthy knights will remain loyal to the pope.

E – Rich knights will remain loyal to the king.

Question 9: What is the best interpretation of the following Penumbra message?

$$\dagger, \smiley \; \text{\Large 📖}, \; \blacklozenge; \; \text{P} \; \triangle, \; \varodot$$

A – The pope calmly ordered the execution of the rebel cardinal by burning at the stake.

B – The cardinal ordered his pope to be executed.

C – The pope furiously ordered that his rebellious cardinal be burned to death.

D – The pope demanded the death of all renegade cardinals.

E – The pope fumed as he excommunicated the rebel cardinal.

Question 10: What is the best interpretation of the following Penumbra message?

$$♦♦,♠⊗,☺(❖❖),℘(⋿⋿)$$

    A – The peasants bravely fought the knights away from their village.

    B – The brave peasants took the evil knight's castle.

    C – The peasants fought bravely to defend their homes from the evil knights.

    D – The peasants were terrified but still fought off the evil knights.

    E – The evil knights charged the brave peasants.

Question 11: What is the best interpretation of the following Penumbra message?

$$O⊠,●〰,Ravenna,☒♦⸙⌂$$

    A – Sailing to Ravenna with the cardinal can be lethal.

    B – The Cardinal of Ravenna kills all who arrive at his port.

    C – The Cardinal of Ravenna hires sailors as assassins.

    D – I will pay you to sail to Ravenna and kill the cardinal there.

    E – Paying the Cardinal of Ravenna is the only way to avoid death.

Question 12: Penumbra messages are often signed with the following inscription:

$$(O●)☺(⚕↑✝)$$

What is the best interpretation of this phrase?

    A – From the shadows, we rule.

    B – We control kings, popes and peasants.

    C – We subdue both king and pope.

    D – Neither king nor pope can defeat us.

    E – The king will bow before us.

Question 13: What is the best interpretation of the following Penumbra message?

☝◆, ♂(☹ 🜚※)

A – The peasant fought the knight.

B – The knight and his squire fight bravely.

C – The knight and his entourage fought off the pope.

D – The knight carried his squire into battle.

E – The knight fought his serfs.

Question 14: What is the best interpretation of the following Penumbra message?

A – The king burned his city to the ground.

B – The king was burned to death in his city.

C – The city burned around the invading king.

D – The invaders ordered the king's city to be torched.

E – The king ordered a scorched earth policy to protect his city.

Question 15: What is the best interpretation of the following Penumbra message?

●✗⚑, 𝄢

A – Ride to the king as fast as you can!

B – The king flees from you.

C – Let the king ride to meet you.

D – The king's cavalry is swifter than you.

E – You can outrun the king's mounted troops.

Question 16: For this question, you may assume that the Pope lives in the Vatican City. Use the Turin Codes to encode the following into a message that the Penumbra Syndicate will think is from their own operative:

Burn the Vatican City immediately!

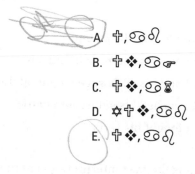

A. ✞,👁️♌

B. ✞❖,👁️☞

C. ✞❖,👁️⌛

D. ✿✞❖,👁️♌

E. ✞❖,👁️♌

Question 17: What is the best interpretation of the following Penumbra message?

(◐●)(♉),♌(◐,●,■)

A – I'm trapped – you have to get help now!

B – We're trapped – call for back-up immediately!

C – We're trapped; it's now every man for himself.

D – Don't move – I'll come to help you.

E – We must all remain perfectly still.

Question 18: What is the best interpretation of the following Penumbra message?

☙(●●),◐⌛(☹💧❇️)

A – You coward – I will not become angry with you.

B – I will not become a coward like you.

C – I will kill all cowards.

D – You're all cowards; I will fight again another day.

E – Cowardly behaviour does not save you from me.

Question 19: What is the best interpretation of the following Penumbra message?

$$\text{♎ (☇⌒⚇❋), (◐●)⊗♂}$$

A – The cowardly king will not stop me.

B – If we bankrupt the king, we may still win.

C – The king is poor but I am not.

D – The king will pay me enough to no longer be poor.

E – The king is generous while I am a thief.

Question 20: What is the best interpretation of the following Penumbra message?

$$\text{♦♦, ✉♂♂,☇⌒♱}$$

A – The peasants stole from the king and the pope.

B – The king stole from the peasants to give to the church.

C – The church taxed the peasants to pay the king.

D – The pope stole the people's money to bribe the king.

E – The peasants are taxed excessively by both church and state.

Question 21: What is the best interpretation of the following Penumbra message?

$$\text{♍⊞✉, ▥, △, ♙▥, ♍(☇⌒(♄♂))}$$

A – The queen paid the cardinal to keep her affair with the king's chief knight secret.

B – The cardinal's refusal to talk to the queen led to an uprising by the knights.

C – The queen paid the cardinal to promote the king's knight-in-chief.

D – The queen paid the cardinal to arrange for the king to kill his chief nobleman.

E – The king and queen arranged for the knights to bribe the cardinal.

Question 22: The Turin Codex is an incomplete portion of modern Penumbra Syndicate code. In particular, the code has been added to over the centuries to include symbols for things that simply weren't in existence at the time the Codex was laid down. Which two of the following would be the most useful additions to Syndicate code if attempting to convey the following message?

Modern politicians need to use the internet, television and road tours to communicate effectively with their people.

A – Politician

B – Internet

C – Television

D – Road tours

E – Communicate

Question 23: What is the best way to translate the following into Syndicate code?

To have and to hold,

from this day forward,

for better, for worse,

for richer, for poorer,

in sickness, and in health.

A. ✪,♗ (♫,♑,✿♫,❄ ♫, ♠⁂➠,☺♫)

B. ✪,♌ (♫,♑,✿♫,❄ ♫, ♠⁂➠,☺♫)

C. ♌♗ (♫,♑,✿♫,❄ ♫, ♠⁂➠,☺♫)

D. ✪,♌♗ (♫,♑,✿♫,❄ ♫, ♠⁂➠,☺♫)

E. ✪ (♫,♑,✿♫,❄ ♫, ♠⁂➠,☺♫)

Question 24: What is the best way to translate the following into Syndicate code?

Whoever wants to be happy, let him be so: of tomorrow there's no knowing.

A. ☺(☺♂), ⧗(♎♑)

B. ☺(☺♂), ♎(⧗♑)

C. ☺(☺♂), ⧗(♎,♎♑)

D. ☺♂, ⧗(♎,♎♑)

E. (☺☺)♂, ⧗♎♑

Question 25: What is the best way to translate the following into Syndicate code?

The gold is hidden in the cardinal's palace.

A. ⛩❖,♚✿

B. ⛩❖,♚❖(✿✿)

C. ♚⛩❖,✿✿

D. ♚(✿✿),⛩

E. ⛩❖,♚(✿✿)

Question 26: What is the best way to translate the following into Syndicate code?

The knight charged on horseback into the satanic cult's fire.

A. ♘,✗,♙🏛✝⛩⛩),☾☉

B. ♘,✗☞,✝⛩⛩,☾☉

C. ♘,✗☞,♙(✝⛩⛩),☾☉

D. ♘,♉☞,♙(✝⛩⛩),☾☉

E. ♘,✗☜,♙(✝⛩⛩),☾☉

Chapter 9

Practice Test One: Answers and Explanations

In This Chapter

▶ Answering the questions to Practice Test One
▶ Understanding the answers

Verbal Reasoning

Answer 1
A – True

To the population of Rome, the corn monopoly 'was considered the immediate cause' of the famine. The famine, alongside pestilence (disease), was one of the 'calamities of Rome' that led to the 'popular discontent' that culminated in the violent scenes of the passage. The passage therefore describes a logical sequence starting with corn monopoly and ending with the violence.

You don't need to know whether the corn monopoly was actually the cause of the famine in order to determine the statement's veracity – you simply need to know that the Romans considered it to be true. The Romans may or may not have been correct.

Answer 2
A – True

The passage describes Commodus as waking from a 'dream of pleasure' and being previously unconscious of the civil war. Therefore, Commodus was asleep when these events took place.

Answer 3

B – False

The passage says that missiles thrown from houses on the streets checked the pursuit of the Praetorian cavalry. Therefore the crowd didn't retreat outside the city but fought the Praetorians from within the city.

Answer 4

C – Can't tell

The passage only says that he 'might even have regained . . . the confidence of his subjects', not that he did so. You still don't know the actual eventual outcome by the end of the passage.

Answer 5

C – Can't tell

The passage only says that the unfortunate 8-year-old was one of Oliver's early encounters, not the first person he met. The child may have been the first person or not, but you can't be certain from the passage. The complicating presence of the clause regarding the *New York Times* between dashes in the relevant sentence of the passage encourages careless eyes to miss the crucial qualifier.

Answer 6

C – Can't tell

The passage confirms that around half the population are obese. It says that these people have one of the highest incidences of heart disease and diabetes, but it doesn't say what that incidence is, so you can't tell whether the incidence is around half, higher or lower. Therefore, you can't prove or disprove the statement's truth based on the information in the passage.

A fatal ending

In reality, Commodus became increasingly megalomaniacal in the years that followed, including renaming Rome in his own honour. Together with an economic and farming crisis, this problem led to his massive unpopularity and eventually to his assassination. Commodus was Emperor of Rome for 12 years, a lengthy duration that may surprise you if you know of him from the movie *Gladiator*. Commodus enjoyed competing in the gladiatorial arena, though doing so brought him more scorn from the Roman elite, who viewed this behaviour as scandalous.

Beware of statements that include one probably true fact and then tag on facts that you can't prove. Wrongly selecting 'True' as your answer here is easy.

If the statement began with the phrase 'The passage says that . . .', the answer would be 'False' rather than 'Can't tell', because the statement would then be a specific case rather than a general statement.

Answer 7

A – True

The passage says that if the show does well in the US, it will be re-exported to the UK. Therefore, British viewers would be able to see the show.

Answer 8

A – True

The passage says there is a long tradition of UK reality shows being success-fully adapted to the US. Therefore, these formats can work well in America.

Answer 9

B – False

Price is certainly a determinant of the sale of sausages but other factors play a part, such as the development of own brand by the supermarkets and the need for differentiation as mentioned in the first paragraph as well as the attraction of premium price products mentioned in the second paragraph.

Highly exclusionary ('only') or totally universal ('all') statements are often false. Read the passage carefully to determine whether the text really does support the statement.

Answer 10

A – True

The first paragraph states that promotional support was recommended by the sales department to protect listings with the major supermarkets.

Answer 11

A – True

The first paragraph states that 'profitability of the core sausage business had been in decline for five years, with the brand trapped in a vicious downward cycle of increasing price promotion, leading to less funds for marketing and innovation'. Thus, falling profits mean less money for marketing.

Polarising profits

The sausage firm featured in the excerpt is fictional, but the dilemma faced by the company is real. Operating as an undifferentiated mass-market retailer is increasingly hard. Sales are increasingly driven either to low-cost budget brands or to high-end, highly differentiated elite products. The middle-market needs to focus on getting across what makes it unique in order to maintain margins and avoid entering a price war that it can't win against low-cost brands.

Answer 12

A – True

Sales dropped from 35% to 19% between 1999 and 2006.

Answer 13

C – Can't tell

Although the passage confirms that both shows were prime-time music programmes, the two shows don't necessarily attract the same audience demographic.

Answer 14

A – True

The passage confirms that Syco TV makes both *X Factor* and *Britain's Got Talent*, and that Syco TV is Cowell's. Thus, Cowell has a financial interest in both shows.

Answer 15

C – Can't tell

Based on the information in the passage, you can't tell which partner makes more money.

Answer 16

B – False

The article confirms, in different places, that both Syco TV and Syco Music are at least partly Cowell's.

Answer 17

C – Can't tell

The passages states that the inn is 'not far' from Togarog, but you can't tell whether the inn is closer to Togarog or to Tscherkask. The implication of the text is that the inn is closer to Togarog, but you can't logically derive this information.

Answer 18

B – False

The passage describes the sun as genial, so the poor crop yield can't be the result of too little sunshine.

Answer 19

B – False

Straw was indeed used to patch the roof, but even in this state the passage describes the roof as being ineffective.

Answer 20

A – True

The passage says about the village: 'Slavery had wound its chain around the inhabitants'. Thus, most of the local inhabitants must have been unfree, or, to use the feudal terminology of the statement, serfs.

An autocratic regime

Russia in the year 1850 was a highly authoritarian society, built upon feudal lines, with power concentrated in the hands of the tsar and the higher ranks of the nobility. Much of the citizenry of imperial Russia was peasantry, many within the unfree serf class. Russia clung to centralised feudal structures long after most other European nations had made at least some efforts to disseminate power more widely. This concentration of political and economic power led to significant abuses. When the central power of the tsars finally weakened following the expenditures associated with the First World War, the door opened for the Bolshevik Revolution of 1917, and the subsequent creation of the Soviet Union, which proved just as dictatorial as the imperial regime it replaced. Even following the collapse of Communism, the Russian electorate has shown a consistent preference for autocratic candidates for the presidency.

Answer 21
A – True

The author compares the town of Harper's Ferry favourably with Lucerne. You can logically say that the author finds the town more beautiful.

Answer 22
A – True

The passage is quite flowery but it does state that the town is faced on at least two sides by the Shenandoah River and the Potomac River, and that you can find it 'nestling inside' the confluence (joining point) of these two rivers.

Answer 23
C – Can't tell

Captain Brown believed this statement to be true, but the passage doesn't provide the information required for you to say whether it was true. In reality, the slave population remained surprisingly loyal even during the Civil War itself, but how much of this loyalty was down to habit or fear – rather than satisfaction with current arrangements – is uncertain.

Answer 24
B – False

The passage says that after securing the Arsenal and Armoury, Brown planned to return to the mountainous regions of the area to rally slave support. Therefore, he didn't intend to make a stand in the town.

Answer 25
B – False

She only 'wished' something wonderful would happen. Although she doesn't know if something wonderful will or won't happen, the answer to the statement is not 'Can't tell', because her uncertainty is definitively different from the statement. The answer is therefore 'False'.

Answer 26
C – Can't tell

The passage goes to great lengths to tell us that the old gentlemen spoke to every passenger in turn – but to preserve story surprise the passage doesn't tell you what the gentlemen actually said to the passengers. Even with the benefit of the hindsight granted by the rest of the passage, you still don't know whether his request was limited to the passengers all reading the requested article in the newspaper (which was then followed by a spontaneous and contagious waving by the passengers on passing the children), or whether the waving was included in his request. After you read the article, assuming that the waving is prearranged is easy – but you can't conclude that it was prearranged definitively from the passage.

Answer 27

A – True

The passage states that the children had given their love to the train freely for a long time before the events of the passage.

Answer 28

C – Can't tell

You can't be certain of what the three children knew was going to happen. You can say that Bobbie didn't expect it to happen, because in the first sentence she wished for something unexpectedly wonderful to happen. But you can't tell what the other two children knew, or didn't know, about the events of that day and their cause. Without spoiling the ending of *The Railway Children*, we can safely reveal that in the novel none of the children expected or understood the happy reason for the waving – but they soon would.

Answer 29

A – True

The passage describes social media as 'a term that encompasses the transactional, search, and marketing components of social media'. This description is logically equivalent to being a descriptive term for how social media affects businesses.

Answer 30

C – Can't tell

Although the passage says that younger generations of people were the first to adopt Facebook, the text doesn't provide any reasons for this early adoption. The reason may be that younger people are less socially inhibited, but equally the reason may be that younger people have less experience in understanding how maintaining definite boundaries of social interaction can be helpful. Or maybe the effect is random and no reason exists. More prosaically, the reason may be that Facebook was originally restricted to college students, and so most older people were unable to sign up, giving Facebook cachet status among younger groups.

Answer 31

C – Can't tell

The passage describes status updates as being at least partially an outlet for bragging. The passage also describes functions other than updating your status. The passage doesn't indicate how common bragging is relative to other updates – and of course, status updates aren't the entirety of sharing on social media.

Answer 32

A – True

The passage quotes a Nielsen study suggesting that 78 per cent of people trust their peers. Whether they're wise to do so is another matter entirely, but the question merely asks whether most do or don't.

Answer 33

C – Can't tell

The passage essentially says that water scarcity will be an increasingly difficult problem for China to manage, but it doesn't say that China will be unable to manage the issue.

Answer 34

C – Can't tell

The passage tells you that China has 8 per cent of the world's fresh water, and that China has less water than it needs by international standards, but the passage doesn't mention what percentage of its water needs China actually has.

Answer 35

A – True

The article unequivocally states that China has less than a quarter of the world average in terms of per capita availability of water reserves. It also states that 'China will be under severe water stress as defined by the international standard'. By combining this information with the earlier sentence that states China has widespread problems of water scarcity, you can deduce that China already has less water than it needs by international standards.

Answer 36
A – True

The article states that the North China Plain grows half of China's wheat and corn and also has extensive peach orchards. This information is enough to classify the area as a major agricultural centre – you don't need to know *how* major (and indeed you can't work out how major from the text).

Answer 37
C – Can't tell

You know only that a small group of Canadian researchers were interested enough in zombies to model an outbreak. You've no information on what the rest of the Canadian research community thought about it. Though we can guess that they may have chuckled . . .

Answer 38
B – False

You can remove – kill – zombies by pursuing the rather graphic procedure described in the passage.

Answer 39
A – True

The study demonstrated that a city of half a million people can be overwhelmed within four days.

Answer 40
B – False

The study called for frequent and increasingly forceful attacks to eradicate the zombie threat. Thus, superior firepower can defeat zombies.

Answer 41
B – False

The 1855 Exposition organisers asked the Bordeaux Chamber of Commerce to classify the wines, but the Chamber delegated the task to the Bordeaux wine merchants. Therefore, the wine merchants actually classified the wines.

Answer 42

C – Can't tell

Five *Premier Crus* (Chateaux Latour, Lafite Rothschild, Margaux, Haut-Brion and Mouton-Rothschild) do indeed exist, but you can't obtain this information from the passage.

Answer 43

C – Can't tell

Although you may assume that the Baron de Rothschild would be proud of his wine finally being regarded as a *Premier Cru* (especially given the outside knowledge that he lobbied the French government intensively for the change), the wording of the change itself is the only information in the passage. You may think that the passage suggests pride, but you may also take the ending clause that 'Mouton does not change' to be scorn for the entire classification system.

Answer 44

C – Can't tell

Without outside information, you can't tell.

Rohan I am

The Mouton-Rothschild motto is a play on words of the family motto of Henri II, Duke of Rohan (1579–1683), who was a prominent leader of the French Huguenots. Huguenots were French Protestants, and tensions between Protestantism and Catholicism in France erupted into civil war during the latter half of the 16th century.

Although the Catholics were most fervently supported by the House of Guise, the ruling House of Valois also generally supported the Catholics. The Bourbons and the Rohans sided with the Huguenots. Thus, the wars gradually took on a dynastic quality – a contest between these noble houses for the right to the French crown. The Bourbons eventually won, and Henry IV became the first Bourbon King of France.

The proud Rohan motto was 'King I cannot be; Duke I do not deign to be; Rohan I am'.

Quantitative Reasoning

Answer 1
C – 25%

Four large-caps and one mega-cap are present, making five companies at least large-cap in size. As the selection under consideration includes 20 companies, the percentage is $(5 \div 20) \times 100 = 25\%$.

Answer 2
B – 1:1

Four large-caps and four micro-caps are present, so the ratio is 4:4 = 1:1.

Answer 3
D – 10.5%

The merger of two large-caps to form a mega-cap means that there are now two mega-caps. However, the total number of companies falls to 19 from 20, as a result of the merger. The new percentage of mega-caps is therefore $(2 \div 19) \times 100 = 10.5\%$ (approximately).

Answer 4
E – 229

The current market cap in sterling is 165 billion × 0.85 = 140.25 billion. Converting to US dollars gives 140.25 × 1.63 = 228.6075 billion = \$229 billion (approximately).

Answer 5
B – 62%

103 total fatalities have occurred, and 64 up to the end of June, so the percentage is $(64 \div 103) \times 100 = 62\%$ to the nearest whole number.

Answer 6
A – 1.64

You already know that of 103 total fatalities, 64 took place in the first half of the year, which means that 103 – 64 = 39 fatalities occurred in the second half of the year. To find out how many times greater were your chances of dying in the first half compared with the second half, you divide one by the other:

64 ÷ 39 = 1.64 to two decimal places.

Answer 7
D – 8.6

You calculate the mean by dividing the total by the number of categories. In this case, you divide 103 ÷ 12 = 8.6 to one decimal place.

Answer 8
D – 567%

The modal average is the number that occurs most frequently, in this case three fatalities, which occurred in April, November and December. The deadliest month was June, with 20 fatalities – 17 more deaths than the mode. Expressed as a percentage:

$$(17 \div 3) \times 100 = 567\% \text{ to the nearest whole number.}$$

Answer 9
E – No – his table is correct

For this question, you need to replicate the work that John put into drawing up his table. If you do so, you find that his table is correct.

Answer 10
B – 6

Four clubs would move up to the Football Royalty group (Man U, Man City, Newcastle, Sunderland) and one club would move up into the Aristocrats (Wolves). Given the current starting point of nine clubs in the Aristocrats, the net change of –3 would leave the Aristocrats with six clubs (Chelsea, Bolton, West Brom, Blackburn, Spurs, Wolves).

An alternate solution would be to note that the Aristocrats grouping in Table 8-4 requires teams to have between 70 and 89 seasons in the top flight. If ten seasons were added to each value, the future Aristocrats would have current rankings of 60–79. According to Table 8-3, six teams are within these margins.

Answer 11
C – 101

This question demands a fairly straightforward calculation. The four Football Royalty clubs of Everton, Aston Villa, Liverpool and Arsenal have 109, 101, 97, and 95 seasons respectively, making a total of 402 seasons between them.

402 ÷ 4 = 100.5, which you round up to 101 to the nearest whole season.

Answer 12

D – 15

Wigan Athletic currently has 7 years in the top flight and needs a total of 20 years to become Bourgeoisie, which is an extra 13 years. However, if Wigan is relegated twice and takes a year each time to return to the Premiership, the total number of years required is 15.

Answer 13

A – 331

You simply need to find the eighth highest score in the table, which is 331.

Answer 14

E – 674

The range is the difference between the highest and lowest figures in the sample. In this case, the range is 803 – 129 = 674.

Answer 15

C – 55%

A cut-off score of 295 allows 11 players to qualify. As a percentage, this is $(11 \div 20) \times 100 = 55\%$.

Answer 16

D – 89%

The current average score of the bottom five players is (129 + 141 + 163 + 164 + 184) ÷ 5 = 156.2.

To reach a score of 295, the average score would have to increase by (295 ÷ 156.2) = 138.8 points. Expressed as a percentage of the current average, this is 138.8 ÷ 156.2 × 100 = 89% to the nearest whole percentage point.

Note that this represents an increase *of* 189% on the current average, but an increase *by* 89%.

This type of data display can be quickly analysed by ranking the data values relative to one another vertically on your portable white board. A quick glance tells us we'll be going from 100–800. The first entry, 331, should go about one third of the way down the page. The next entry of 803 should go toward the bottom. 164 should be placed near the top. 330 should go immediately above 331 with no extra space for new entries . . . and so on. After all data are placed in order, the first three questions are simple to answer.

Answer 17

B – 114

The Radical SR LM takes 6 minutes 48 seconds (= 408 seconds) to do 20.6 km. You calculate speed by dividing the distance travelled by the time taken, but you also need to convert the units into miles and hours:

$(20.6 \div 1.6) \div (408 \div 3,600) = (20.6 \times 3,600) \div (1.6 \times 408) = 113.6$ (approximately) = 114 mph to the nearest whole number.

Answer 18

B – 7:24

The Zonda takes 33:04 to complete three laps, but 652 seconds of this time is wasted time. Without this wasted time, the Zonda would have taken $[(33 \times 60) + 4] – 652 = 1,332$ seconds to complete three laps. This is $1,332 \div 3 = 444$ seconds per lap.

Converting to minutes, you get $444 \div 60 = 7.4$ minutes or 7:24.

Answer 19

A – 365 hp

This answer is a simple ratio:

$680 \div 1210 \times 650 = 365$ hp (approximately).

Answer 20

C – 117 mph

This question isn't difficult, but the large number of calculations with many different units involved increases your chances of making a careless error. A survey of the units in the answer choices tells us that we need to choose km/h or mph for our calculation and convert to the other system if our answer does not match.

Lap 1: 120 mph = $120 \times 1.6 = 192$ km/h

Lap 2: 7:23 for 20.6 km = 443 seconds for 20.6 km = $20.6 \div (443 \div 3,600) = 167.40$ km/h to the nearest hundreth

Lap 3: $192 \times 105 \div 100 = 201.6$ km/h

Average speed = $(192 + 167.40 + 201.6) \div 3 = 187$ km/h

This figure does not match any of the km/h answer choices, which means that we need to convert to mph and hope for the best!

Converting to mph gives you 187 ÷ 1.6 = 116.88 (approximately), which rounds to 117 mph.

Answer 21
E – 5.27:1

The ratio is 52.7:(3 + 5.2 + 1.8) = 52.7:10 = 5.27:1

Answer 22
C – The English make up a greater proportion of the total population in 2031 than in 2011.

You can derive this answer by working through each proposition in turn. The English make up about 84% of the population in 2011 and about 85% in 2031, which is a greater proportion.

Answer 23
B – 13.4%

> Population in 2011 = (52.7 + 3 + 5.2 + 1.8) = 62.7 million
>
> Population in 2031 = (60.4 + 3.3 + 5.4 + 2) = 71.1 million
>
> Population increase = 71.1 – 62.7 = 8.4 million

The percentage increase is 8.4 ÷ 62.7 × 100 = 13.4% (approximately).

Answer 24
D – 57.4

The range is the difference between the maximum and minimum values of the data – in this case, the maximum is the English population (60.4 million in 2031) and the minimum is the Welsh population (3 million in 2006). The difference is (60.4 – 3) = 57.4 million.

Answer 25
C – £7,010

Each pair of Northampton Classics lasts 20 years. James has a 40-year career, so he needs two pairs of each of the three types of shoe he wants to buy, making a total requirement of six pairs. The shoe cost is therefore £650 × 6 = £3,900.

He needs to resole each pair three times during its 20-year lifespan, giving a total of (6 × 3) = 18 resoles. The resoling cost is £120 × 18 = £2,160.

The polish costs are £20 × 40 years = £800.

James needs only three pairs of shoe trees, because he can reuse them. Tree costs are £50 × 3 = £150.

The total cost for wearing Northampton Classics over 40 years is therefore (£3,900 + £2,160 + £800 + £150) = £7,010.

Answer 26

E – £4,760

James needs 20 pairs of each type of shoe, making a total of (20 × 3) = 60 pairs. The total shoe cost is therefore 60 × £75 = £4,500.

The shoe polish costs are £5 × 40 = £200. James needs six pairs of shoe trees, because they last only 20 years, making a total tree cost of 6 × £10 = £60.

The total cost of wearing Mass Markets is therefore (£4,500 + £200 + £60) = £4,760.

Answer 27

E – The annual cost of wearing Mass Markets is £110

This figure is false. The actual cost is £4,760 ÷ 40 = £119. All the other statements are true.

Answer 28

D – 26.7

The new resoling interval is proportionally increased to 4 ÷ 3 × 5 years = 6.67 years.

Worth it or not?

You can see from the calculations in Answers 25–28 that James needs to decide whether he wants to spend an extra £56.25 per year to wear Northampton Classics in terms of any extra pleasure he derives from the purchase of a more beautiful artisanal product. This annual difference is relatively small compared with the vast difference in upfront shoe purchase price. Although the manufacturers' names are fictional, the figures and assumptions in this question are realistic.

James can still resole each pair of shoes three times, meaning the shoes now last 6.67 + (6.67 × 3) = 26.7 years (approximately).

Alternatively, you can simply multiply the initial 20-year lifespan figure by 4 ÷ 3.

Answer 29
C – 2:1

The odds of a variable mortgage holder increasing expenditure are 133 ÷ 52 (the number of variable mortgage holders who increased expenditure divided by the number of variable mortgage holders who didn't increase expenditure).

The odds of a non-mortgage holder increasing expenditure are 111 ÷ 89 (the number of non-mortgage holders who increased expenditure divided by the number of non-mortgage holders who didn't increase expenditure).

To calculate how much more likely the holder will increase expenditure compared with the non-holder, you compare 133 ÷ 52 with 111 ÷ 89:

(133 ÷ 52) ÷ (111 ÷ 89) = 2.56 ÷ 1.25 = 2.05 = 2:1 (approximately).

You can't simply compare the raw figures of 133:111, because the total number of people in each group differs – so you're not comparing like with like. You need to figure out the odds within each group and then compare the two odds with each other to find the overall odds.

Answer 30
D – 72%

133 increased out of a total of (52 + 133) = 185. The percentage is therefore 133 ÷ 185 × 100 = 72% to the nearest whole per cent.

Medical statistics I

Statisticians call the calculation in Answer 29 the odds ratio. Odds ratios occur frequently in medical and scientific papers when the authors want to judge whether a treatment (for example a new antibiotic) has a benefit compared with either an old treatment or no treatment at all (for example a placebo).

Answer 31
A – 0.16

The proportion of people who increased expenditure by at least 10% and who were variable mortgage holders is 133 ÷ (53+133) = 0.72 (approximately). (This calculation is the same as in Answer 30, but without converting the answer into a percentage.)

The proportion of people increasing expenditure in the non-mortgage group is 111 ÷ (111+89) = 0.56 (approximately). The difference is (0.72 – 0.56) = 0.16.

Answer 32
B – 23.1%

The study has a total of 385, of whom 89 meet the criteria. The percentage likelihood ('chance') of randomly picking one of these people is therefore 89 ÷ 385 × 100 = 23.1% (approximately).

Answer 33
B – 1550 m^2

This calculation is a relatively simple one:

Wall surface area = $2(50 \times 2) + 2(25 \times 2)$ = 300 m^2

Bottom surface area = 50×25 = 1,250 m^2

Total internal surface area = 300 + 1,250 = 1,550 m^2

Medical statistics II

Statisticians describe the calculation in Answer 31 as the (absolute) risk difference. If, instead of comparing expenditure levels in groups with and without variable rate mortgages, you compare health outcomes in groups of sick people taking and not taking a new drug, you can invert the risk difference to calculate the number needed to treat (NNT) – that is, the number of people you need to give the new drug to in order to successfully treat one person.

In the mortgage example, the NNT doesn't mean much – but if you describe it in words you can say 'the number of people without variable mortgages who need to switch to variable mortgages in order to be statistically sure that at least one extra person would be influenced enough by the interest rate cut to increase their expenditure by at least 10 per cent'.

Answer 34
D – 162,600

This question requires careful thought and calculation. The internal surface area is 1,550 square metres. Each tile measures 10 cm × 10 cm, or 0.1 m × 0.1 m. The internal surface area therefore requires 1,550 ÷ (0.1 × 0.1) = 155,000 tiles.

You also need to calculate the border. You can break down the border into two rectangles that measure [(50 + 0.5 + 0.5) × 0.5] and two rectangles that measure (25 × 0.5).

Alternatively you can break down the border into two rectangles that measure (50 × 0.5), two rectangles that measure (25 × 0.5) and four corner squares that measure (0.5 × 0.5).

The total area of the border is 76 square metres.

As each tile measures 0.1 m × 0.1 m, the border needs [76 ÷ (0.1 × 0.1] = 7,600 tiles. Adding that to the internal surface area tiles gives 155,000 + 7,600 = 162,600.

Answer 35
C – £25,590

The total number of tiles is 162,600, of which 2,500 are dark blue and 7,500 are non-slip, leaving 152,600 pale blue. The cost is therefore:

(152,600 × 0.15) + (2,500 × 0.18) + (7,500 × 0.3) = 22,890 + 450 + 2,250 = £25,590

Answer 36
B – The 170th day

You've 162,600 tiles at 5 minutes per tile = 813, 000 minutes = 13,550 hours of work. Ten tilers working simultaneously means that each needs to do 13,550 ÷ 10 = 1,355 hours of work.

Each tiler works eight hours a day, so the team takes 1,355 ÷ 8 = 169.37 days.

However, the tilers complete the job not on the 169th day but on the 170th day, because any fraction above a whole number of days pushes the job into the following day. The normal practice of rounding down when the figure after the decimal point is less than 5 doesn't apply here.

Abstract Reasoning

Display 1

1. Set A; **2.** Set B; **3.** Neither set; **4.** Set B; **5.** Neither set

Explanation

All the shapes in Set A have curved edges. All the shapes in Set B have straight edges. The size, colour and orientation of the shapes demonstrate no commonality within the sets.

Test shape 1 contains only shapes with curved edges and therefore falls into Set A. Test shapes 2 and 4 contain only shapes with straight edges and so fall into Set B. Test shapes 3 and 5 contain shapes with both curved and straight edges and therefore don't fall into either set.

Display 2

6. Set B; **7.** Set A; **8.** Neither set; **9.** Set B; **10.** Set A

Explanation

All the objects in Set A have solid outer edges . . . and no interruptions in any edges. All the objects in Set B have outer edges with interruptions regardless of the inner edges. The exact nature of the overall shape, the colour and the orientation show no consistent features of commonality.

Test shapes 7 and 10 have only objects with solid uninterrupted outer edges and so fall within Set A. Test shapes 6 and 9 have interrupted outlines and so fall in Set B. Test shape 8 contains objects with both solid and interrupted outlines and so falls into neither set.

Display 3

11. Neither set; **12.** Neither set; **13.** Set B; **14.** Neither set; **15.** Set B

Explanation

All members of both sets contain exactly one large shape and one or two smaller shapes.

All the examples in Set A contain a large shape that is internally replicated with a shape of the same colour. For instance, the top-left item contains a large white triangle with a smaller white inner triangle, and the top-right item contains a large white hexagon with a smaller white inner hexagon.

All the examples in Set B contain a large shape that is internally replicated with a shape of the opposite colour. For instance, the top-left item contains a large triangle with a smaller black inner triangle, and the top-right item contains a large white circle with a smaller black inner circle within it.

The placement and orientation of the large object within the box are irrelevant, and any small shapes featured in each item show no consistent features of commonality.

Test shape 12 contains a large object that is replicated internally by a smaller white item but as it has a second large shape it goes into neither set. Test shapes 13 and 15 have large objects that are internally replicated with smaller black objects and so fit in Set B. Test shape 11 has both types of internal replication and so falls into neither set. Test shape 14 has no internal replication whatsoever and so falls into neither set.

Display 4

16. Neither set; **17.** Neither set; **18.** Neither set; **19.** Set B; **20.** Set A

Explanation

All the examples in Set A contain items with no right-angles. All the examples in Set B contain items with at least one right-angle. The exact nature of the overall shape, the colour and the orientation show no consistent features of commonality.

Test shape 20 contains objects with no right-angles and so belongs to Set A. Test shape 19 has only right-angled figures and so belongs to Set B. Test shapes 16, 17 and 18 have objects both with and without right-angles and so aren't either Set A or Set B.

Display 5

21. Set A; **22.** Neither set; **23.** Neither set; **24.** Set A; **25.** Neither set

Explanation

All of Set A's objects have three borders and all of Set B's objects have four borders.

Test shapes 21 and 24 contain only three-sided objects and so are Set A. Test shapes 22, 23 and 25 contain objects with varying numbers of sides and so fall into neither set.

Display 6

26. Set A; **27.** Set A; **28.** Set A; **29.** Neither set; **30.** Set B

Explanation

Set A's objects are undivided. Set B's objects are subdivided.

Test shapes 26, 27 and 28 contain objects without subdivision and so belong in Set A. Test shape 30 has subdivided objects and so is part of Set B. Test shape 29 has a mixture of whole and divided objects and so isn't in Set A or Set B.

Display 7

31. Neither set; **32.** Set B; **33.** Neither set; **34.** Set B; **35.** Set A

Explanation

The shapes in Set A overlap only once, whereas the shapes in Set B overlap twice.

Test shape 35 has only one area of overlap and so is in Set A. Test shapes 32 and 34 have two overlapping areas and so belong to Set B. Test shape 31 has no overlaps and test shape 33 has three overlaps, and so both fall into neither set.

Display 8

36. Set B; **37.** Neither set; **38.** Set A; **39.** Set B; **40.** Set A

Explanation

You can draw every shape in Set A continuously without lifting your pen from the paper or backtracking. To draw Set B's shapes, you need to lift the pen at least once or backtrack.

Test shapes 38 and 40 fit in Set A. Test shapes 36 and 39 are part of Set B. Test shape 37 contains one element that you can draw without lifting your pen; however, test shape 37 also contains one element that you can't draw without lifting your pen and so fits in neither set.

Because drawing the shapes in Set B require you to lift your pen at least once, some may try to argue that test shape 37 belongs to Set B. This line of argument says that even though one of its elements can be drawn without lifting your pen, as the other requires lifting, the test shape as an overall picture requires at least one lift and therefore falls within Set B.

The reason this line of argument is incorrect is that the bottom-left shape in Set A also contains multiple elements. All its component elements can be drawn without lifting. This fact allows us to postulate a rule that in cases where a shape has multiple elements, all those component elements must follow the overall rule of the shape. Test shape 37 has one element that follows the rule of Set A, and another element that follows Set B's rule, and this confirms it in neither set.

Display 9

41. Neither set; **42.** Set A; **43.** Set B; **44.** Set A; **45.** Neither set

Explanation

The pictures in Set A all contain the same number of objects as the object with the most edges. The pictures in Set B have one more object than the object with the most edges.

Test shapes 42 and 44 fall into Set A. Test shape 43 is part of Set B. Test shapes 41 and 45 obey neither set's rule.

Display 10

46. Set A; **47.** Neither set; **48.** Set B; **49.** Neither set; **50.** Neither set

Explanation

The black circle is the key to these sets. In Set A, if the black circle is at the top of the shape, the arrow points up. If the black circle is in the middle, the arrow is horizontal. If the black circle is at the bottom, the arrow points down. In Set B, the top/bottom rule is reversed but the middle rule remains the same.

Test shape 46 obeys Set A's rules. Test shape 48 obeys Set B's rules. Test shape 47 has no black circle and so belongs to neither set. Test shapes 49 and 50 fall into neither set because the arrows do not obey the rules of either set.

Display 11

51. Set A; **52.** Set B; **53.** Set A; **54.** Neither set; **55.** Set B

Explanation

In Set A, the identical objects are in vertical or horizontal alignment. In Set B, the identical objects are in diagonal alignment. Colour is irrelevant.

Test shapes 51 and 53 are in Set A. Test shapes 52 and 55 are in Set B. Test shape 54 has both horizontal/vertical and diagonal alignment and so belongs to neither set.

Display 12

56. Neither set; **57.** Neither set; **58.** Set A; **59.** Neither set; **60.** Set B

Explanation

If you see a white circle and an upward-pointing arrow, or a black circle and a downward-pointing arrow, the shape belongs to Set A. The rules are reversed for Set B.

Test shape 58 is in Set A. Test shape 60 is in Set B. Test shapes 56 and 57 have no arrow and so fall into neither set. Test shape 59's arrow points in the correct direction for the presence of white circles in Set A but points in the wrong direction for the presence of black circles in Set A; therefore it isn't in Set A. Similar logic rules Test shape 59 out of Set B, and so it belongs to neither set.

Display 13

61. Set A; **62.** Set A; **63.** Neither set; **64.** Neither set; **65.** Set B

Explanation

These set rules are quite complex. In Set A, if you see a white circle, the arrow points to the right. However, an additional white square makes the arrow point up. If you also see a black shape, the arrow is double-headed and is horizontal.

In Set B, a white circle causes the arrow to point to the left. However, an additional white square makes the arrow point down. If you also see a black object, the arrow is double-headed and vertical.

Test shapes 61 and 62 are in Set A. Test shape 65 is in Set B. Test shape 63 has conflicting arrows and no square, and so it belongs to neither set. Test shape 64 has no circle and so is part of neither set.

Decision Analysis

Answer 1
A – The king will be killed by the cardinal.

$$\text{🔔}, \text{⌛💣}, \text{♋}$$

= Cardinal, Then Kill, King

= Cardinal, kill at some point in the future, king

= The king will be killed by the cardinal

You can't express the future perfect tense using the Turin Codex, but this answer is as close as you can get. No other option fits the code anyway.

Answer 2
C – The queen will persuade the king to pay us.

$$\text{♍}, \text{⌛📖}, \text{♋}, \text{✉}, (\text{◖●})$$

= Queen, Then Talk, King, Pay (I you)

= The queen will talk to the king to pay us

= The queen will persuade the king to pay us

Answer 3
B – The pope rides to meet his cardinals.

$$\text{✝}, \text{↗}, \text{🔔🔔}$$

= Pope, Ride, Cardinal Cardinal

= The pope rides cardinals

= The pope rides to meet his cardinals

Without reading the options, you may leave the translation as 'The pope rides cardinals', although this phrase doesn't sound terribly dignified . . .

Answer 4

D – The knights will not fight us today.

$$\text{⚑⚑, ♌♟}$$

= Knight Knight, Now Cowardly

= Knights, are now cowardly

= The knights will not fight us today

You can encode this message in other ways, but only this choice from the list of options is a plausible decoding.

Answer 5

A – The queen is furious at the king's rapid retreat from battle.

$$\text{♍, ☹, ⚔, ☞♟, ☹(💣💣)}$$

= Queen, Angry, King, Quickly Cowardly, Angry(Kill Kill)

= Queen is angry with king, rapid retreat from site of violent killings

= The queen is furious at the king's rapid retreat from battle

Answer 6

$$\text{A. ✉, ✝, ☹📖, ⚔}$$

= Pay, Pope, Angry Talk, King

= Bribe the pope to talk angrily to the king

= Bribe the pope to defy the king

The other options do not translate correctly to the English phrase in the question. Option B is Pope, Angry Talk, Pay King. This option potentially may mean that the pope is defying the king, but the pairing of the symbols of pay and king together most plausibly translate to the king being paid something (maybe taxes?).

Option C mentions a knight, which is not in the English phrase. Option D invokes killing as well as defiant talk, and doesn't mention the pope, so is a worse translation. Option E includes the pope, but also includes killing and the late placement of the symbol for pope suggests that both the pope and the king are being killed and angrily spoken to.

Answer 7

D – The peasants may not choose to take your bribe.

$$◆ ◆, \; ⏛ (⑧), \; ● ⊠$$

= Peasant Peasant, Conditional (Take Negative), You Pay

= Peasants, may not take, your payment

= The peasants may not choose to take your bribe

You can quickly eliminate some of the other answers by comparing what symbols are present in the options. The English phrase talks about choosing, but several options include the symbols for 'angry' or 'kill'. These can be rapidly excluded as possible answers.

Answer 8

E – Rich knights will remain loyal to the king.

$$✡ (⤙ ⤙), \; ⧖ ☺, \; ⟿$$

= Rich (Knight Knight), Then Calm, King

= Rich knights will stay calm, king

= Rich knights will remain loyal to the king

Answer 9

A – The pope calmly ordered the execution of the rebel cardinal by burning at the stake.

$$✝, \; ☺ 📖, \; ◆, \; ⌑, \; ♋$$

= Pope, Calm Talk, Kill, Negative Cardinal, Burn

= The pope calmly ordered the execution of the bad cardinal by burning

= The pope calmly ordered the execution of the rebel cardinal by burning at the stake

Despite the absence of any code for 'stake', this answer is the best-fit (or least-worst) option from the choices available.

The roles of the pope and the cardinal are reversed in Option B. Option C is wrong as the code has the symbol for calm, but the pope in option C is furious, implying a greater degree of agitation. Option D has the cardinals (plural), but no indication exists in the code of more than one cardinal. Option E is wrong because, like option C, it has a more animated pope than implied by the use of the symbol for calm.

Answer 10

C – The peasants fought bravely to defend their homes from the evil knights.

$$\blacklozenge\blacklozenge, \ \bullet\odot, \ \odot(\diamond\diamond), \ \wp(\looparrowright\looparrowright)$$

= Peasant, Peasant, Brave Angry, Calm (Home Home), Negative (Knight Knight)

= The peasants, bravely angry to keep calm homes from bad knights

= The peasants fought bravely to defend their homes from the evil knights

Answer 11

D – I will pay you to sail to Ravenna and kill the cardinal there.

$$\bullet\boxtimes, \ \bullet\approx, \ \text{Ravenna}, \ \otimes\blacklozenge, \ \triangle$$

= I Pay, You Sail, Ravenna, Then Kill, Cardinal

= I pay you to sail to Ravenna and then kill the cardinal

= I will pay you to sail to Ravenna and kill the cardinal there

Answer 12

C – We subdue both king and pope.

$$(\textbf{O} \bullet) \ominus (\mathit{6} \dagger)$$

= (I You) Calm (King Pope)

= We subdue both king and pope

Answer 13

B – The knight and his squire fight bravely.

$$\mathrel{\rule[0.3ex]{0.8em}{0.1ex}} \blacklozenge , \; \psi (\otimes \blacklozenge \ast)$$

= Knight Peasant, Positive (Angry Kill)

= The knight and peasant fight well

= The knight and his squire fight bravely

Answer 16

E – The King ordered a scorched earth policy to protect his city.

$$\mathit{6} , \; \square , \; \mathfrak{I} , \; \ominus (\mathit{6} \diamond)$$

= King, Talk, Burn, Calm (King City)

= The king ordered burning to calm his city

= The king ordered a scorched earth policy to protect his city

This answer is only a loose translation, but is the only option of those listed that comes close to translating the code.

Scorched earth

The term 'scorched earth policy' originates from the policy of a retreating army burning all the crops within its own territory to deprive an invading army of that food source. The policy was ruthless because it guaranteed widespread starvation in one's own land, even if the invader was subsequently successfully repelled. Nowadays, the term is a metaphor to describe an equally ruthless policy designed to spite others at considerable personal cost.

Answer 15
A – Ride to the king as fast as you can!

= You Ride Quickly, King

= Ride to the king as fast as you can!

Answer 16

E. ✝ ❖ , ☾ ♌

Burn the Vatican City immediately!

= Pope Home, Burn Now

= Burn the pope's home now

= Burn the Vatican City immediately!

Answer 17
C – We're trapped; it's now every man for himself!

(◉ ●)(♉ ♑), ♌(◉ ,   ● , ■)

= (I You)(Run Negative), Now(I, You, He)

= We (cannot run), it's now all of us separate

= We're trapped; it's now every man for himself!

Answer 18

D – You're all cowards; I will fight again another day.

$$☞(● ●), ⬤⌛(☹💧💦)$$

= Cowardly (You You), I Then (Angry Kill)

= You all are cowardly; I will later fight

= You're all cowards; I will fight again another day

Answer 19

B – If we bankrupt the king, we may still win.

$$♎(🐌⌛❄), (⬤ ●)✡👆$$

= Conditional (King Then Poor), (I You) Take Positive

= If the king is then poor, we will be able to take successfully

= If we bankrupt the king, wc may still win

Answer 20

E – The peasants are taxed excessively by both church and state.

$$💧💧, ✉👆👆, 🐌✝$$

= Peasant Peasant, Pay Positive Positive, King Pope

= Peasants, pay a lot, state church

= The peasants are taxed excessively by both church and state

Answer 21

A – The queen paid the cardinal to keep her affair with the king's chief knight secret.

$$♍, ✉, 📖, 🔔, ☞📖, ♍(🐌(☞👆))$$

= Queen, Pay, Cardinal, Negative Talk, Queen (King(Knight Positive))

= The queen paid the cardinal to not talk about queen (king's chief knight)

= The queen paid the cardinal to not talk about the queen with king's chief knight

= The queen paid the cardinal to keep her affair with the king's chief knight secret

Answer 22

B – Internet

And

C – Television

You can encode the word 'Politician' with 'Talk Knight' or 'Talk Peasant', depending on your level of respect for politicians. The term 'Road Tours' may be 'Ride Quickly' – or even 'Ride Quickly, Peasant Peasant Home' if you want to convey a sense of visiting the electorate. You can paraphrase the word 'Communicate' by using 'Talk'.

Conveying the words 'Internet' or 'Television' effectively without some new code is much harder.

Answer 23

D. ⑧, ♌⌛(☝, ☝, ✡☝, ❄☝, 💣☝, ☺☝)

= Take, Now Then (Positive, Negative, Rich Positive, Poor Positive, Kill Slowly, Calm Positive)

= Have by taking, from this day forward (good, bad, richer, poorer, ill, well)

= To have and to hold, from this day forward, for better, for worse, for richer, for poorer, in sickness, and in health

This phrase is an excerpt from the traditional marriage vows.

Answer 24

C. ☺(☺◑), ⌛(♎, ♎𝒫)

= Calm (Calm Positive), Then (Conditional, Conditional Negative)

= Calm (Happy), Then (may be, may be not)

= Let be happy, future may be or may not be

= Whoever wants to be happy, let him be so: of tomorrow there's no knowing

This phrase is a partial quote from Lorenzo de' Medici, also known as Lorenzo the Magnificent, de facto ruler of Renaissance Florence. His death marked the end of the Golden Age of Florence, making the quote even more poignant.

Answer 25

B. 🔔❖, 𝒫❖(✡✡)

= Cardinal Home, Cowardly Home (Rich Rich)

= Cardinal's home is cowardly home of riches

= The cardinal's palace is the cowardly home of gold

= The gold is hidden in the cardinal's palace

Answer 26

C. ⚑, ↗☞. 𝒫(✝🔔🔔), 👁

= Knight, Ride Quickly, Negative (Pope Cardinal Cardinal), Burn

= The knight charged on horseback, Negative (god's church), Burn

= The knight charged on horseback, satanic cult's, burning

= The knight charged on horseback into the satanic cult's fire

Chapter 10

Practice Test Two

In This Chapter

▶ Doing a complete timed UKCAT practice test

*T*his test is the second of two complete UKCAT practice tests that we include in this book (the other complete test is in Chapter 8). You can do the two tests in any order. They both stand up on their own as a way of doing lots of practice questions under timed conditions.

We recommend you work through this test in one session, allocating the right amount of time to each part of the test (we show the UKCAT subtest timings in Table 10-1).

Table 10-1	Timings for the UKCAT Subtests
Subtest	**Time Allowed**
Verbal reasoning	22 minutes
Quantitative reasoning	23 minutes
Abstract reasoning	16 minutes
Decision analysis	32 minutes

If you've special educational needs and plan to sit the UKCATSEN, you can give yourself an extra 25 per cent of time. (For more about the UKCATSEN, see Chapter 2.)

In Chapter 11, we give the answers and full explanations for the questions in this practice test.

Verbal Reasoning

Passage 1

High Noon
(Adapted from *Celestial Navigation*, by Tom Cunliffe)

Local noon occurs at the moment when the Sun, on its journey from east to west, crosses the observer's meridian. At any one time, you are on a particular terrestrial meridian of longitude. When the Sun bears exactly due south or due north of you, or once in a lifetime is right over your head (at your zenith), its celestial meridian (its Greenwich Hour Angle) will correspond to your longitude.

As we are about to see, if you can observe the altitude of any celestial body when it is exactly on your meridian, a surprisingly simple calculation leads to the latitude. Since finding this is half the battle, and because the Sun is very much in evidence at noon, the noon sight has always been the cornerstone of the navigator's day.

Obviously, the Greenwich time of noon is going to vary from location to location as the Sun appears to travel around the Earth. When you are sitting on deck with your sextant, you can tell when the Sun has reached its noon altitude because it doesn't get any higher. Nevertheless, you don't want to be hanging around all day waiting for it, so it helps to work out the approximate time of local noon.

A – True **B – False** **C – Can't tell**

A **Statement 1:** Your longitude equals the celestial meridian at noon.

 Statement 2: The noon sighting of the Sun is important to navigators because it allows them to calculate their position.

C **Statement 3:** The Sun is at your zenith when it is directly beneath you.

 Statement 4: The Earth revolves around the Sun.

Passage 2

This Isn't Just Food . . .
(Adapted from *Where's the Sausage*, by David J. Taylor)

I got some welcome inspiration from a Marks & Spencer's chocolate pudding advert Claire and I saw on Saturday night. In contrast to our pizza ad, the second this one started I knew which brand it was for. I recognised the music, although it was almost drowned out by the moans and groans that Claire was making next to me on the sofa. Her reaction was understandable, as the chocolate pudding in question did look amazing. The film did a great job of celebrating the product, taking time to show a fork appearing and then piercing the pud with a river of steaming sauce pouring out. The languorous voice-over then told us that 'This isn't just food; this is M&S food.' It was more than that even; it was food porn.

The effectiveness of the commercial was confirmed in two ways. First, when we sat down to dinner after the kids had finally gone to bed, we had M&S chocolate pud for dessert. Second, and more importantly, a quick bit of Googling led me to the news that M&S and their agency had won the Grand Prix for their work, which had played a major role in the brand's turnaround and increased pudding sales by a whopping 288%.

A – True   **B – False**   **C – Can't tell**

A

Statement 5: Brand awareness can be reinforced by an easily recognisable soundtrack.

C

Statement 6: An advertising campaign needs to target women like Claire.

B

Statement 7: Marks & Spencer's advertising campaign led to a 288% increase in food sales.

A

Statement 8: The author is impressed by M&S's advertising.

Passage 3

Independence
(Adapted from *Business the Simon Cowell Way*, by Trevor Clawson)

As he continues to grow his global television and music interests, Simon Cowell is in an enviable position. He's rich. He has a close and mutually beneficial commercial relationship with Sony. And, above all, he's in control of his own destiny to a degree that most people in and outside of the music and entertainment industries can only dream of.

But Cowell's autonomy has been hard won. His early attempts to work independently of the big guns of the record industry ended in failure. Since then Cowell has adopted a different strategy. Rather than working independently of the music industry, he built his businesses in partnership with a corporate. First with BMG and now with Sony, while remaining a high-profile leader rather than a cog in the bigger machine. It's a neat trick.

His 50–50 joint venture with Sony, Syco, is an example of enlightened self-interest in action. From Sony's perspective, Cowell is one of a rare breed of golden geese laying golden eggs. Meanwhile, Cowell continues to work with a company that has the resources to help him put his ideas into practice, and his name remains firmly above the door of Syco for the foreseeable future.

The upshot of all this is that Cowell is a living embodiment of the old maxim: You don't get rich on a salary.

A – True   **B – False**   **C – Can't tell**

Statement 9: Simon Cowell has more autonomy than most music professionals.

Statement 10: Simon Cowell is profitable for Sony.

Statement 11: Simon Cowell has always been successful.

Statement 12: According to the author, enlightened self-interest underpins Simon Cowell's relatively large degree of personal autonomy in his relationship with Sony.

Passage 4

You Will Be Assimilated!
(Adapted from *Sociology For Dummies*, by Nasar Meer and Jay Gabler)

Not all ethnic groups are immigrant groups – most societies have a number of indigenous ethnic groups as well as ethnic groups that have come from elsewhere, plus there are ethnic groups not associated with a place of origin. Still, almost all sociologists interested in race and ethnicity find themselves looking closely at the experiences of immigrants.

The members of the Chicago School were among the first sociologists to really look closely at immigration. The turn of the 20th century saw a wave of immigration to the United States that transformed America's social landscape, and that transformation was most visible in big cities like Chicago, where the new arrivals went looking for work.

Initially, sociologists thought immigration could be understood in terms of 'assimilation'. The word assimilation means to be absorbed into, to become one of. America was seen as a great 'melting pot' where people from all different places arrived to be incorporated into one big whole.

The theory of assimilation has it that people arrive speaking their native languages, wearing their native styles of dress, and otherwise practising the traditions of their home countries. Over time, they are assimilated into their new community, adopting that country's language and traditions. If that's the way in works, the study of immigration is just the study of why some groups assimilate more quickly and peacefully than others.

A – True   **B – False**   **C – Can't tell**

A **Statement 13:** Immigration can result in the arrival of new ethnic groups into a society.

C **Statement 14:** Immigration is largely driven by economic factors.

A **Statement 15:** Assimilation assumes that the eventual outcome of immigration is integration into the existing community's traditions.

C **Statement 16:** Immigration is the study of why some groups assimilate more quickly and peacefully than others.

Passage 5

Get Me the Best You Have
(**Adapted from** *Business the Jamie Oliver Way*, **by Trevor Clawson**)

Oliver has not been slow to recruit big hitters into all parts of his organisation and to work with strong personalities.

As the commissioning editor at Channel 4 and series producer on *Jamie's School Dinners* says, Oliver knows when to delegate to other people, 'The thing about Jamie is he spots talent, recognises what everyone else's strengths are and then lets you do what you're good at. He understood we needed great TV moments, as programme makers.'

Away from the camera, Oliver has appointed expert managers to his businesses. They have included David Page, formerly managing director of Indian food company Patak, who joined Oliver's Fresh Retail Ventures in 2007. He wasted no time in signalling his plans to take the company on a fast growth curve.

Oliver's TV production company also has an experienced hand at the helm. Recruited from Diverse Productions – a key supplier of programmes to Channel 4 – Roy Ackerman joined Fresh One with a brief to diversify from a portfolio of shows that were largely centred around Oliver.

Employing high flyers as managers is about more than putting the day-to-day management of a growing business in safe hands. They bring in expertise in their chosen industries, coupled with their own managerial skills. They also make a business more sustainable and in some cases saleable.

A – True   **B – False**   **C – Can't tell**

 Statement 17: Channel 4's commissioning editor believes that great TV moments are essential to programme-making.

 Statement 18: Roy Ackerman plans to make more shows centred around Jamie Oliver.

 Statement 19: High-flying managers have the potential to increase an owner's wealth.

 Statement 20: Fresh Retail Ventures has been on a fast growth curve since 2007.

Passage 6

Digital Pennies
(Adapted from *Socialnomics*, by Erik Qualman)

It's inevitable that all of our broadcasts will eventually be pushed through the internet and a majority will be viewed on tablets and iPads. Brand budgets that historically went to television, magazine ads, and outdoor boards are moving to digital channels for three main reasons: 1) the audience has moved there, 2) it's more cost-effective, and 3) it's easier to track. What will happen?

In the short-term there will be companies that are able to take advantage of this transition. Just as online travel agents were able to take advantage for suppliers and make a slow progression to web bookings, aggressive conduit companies will be able to deliver what the audience wants. The same holds true for online distributors of music jumping on the opportunity made available by the ineptness of the music industry to embrace digital music.

At the beginning of 2008, Jeff Zucker, the boss of NBC Universal, told an audience of TV executives that their biggest challenge was to ensure 'that we do not end up trading analogue dollars for digital pennies.' Zucker understood that the audience was moving online faster than advertisers were, thus leaving media companies in a position of possibly losing advertising revenue and having their inventory devalued if and when they moved online with their TV content.

A – True   **B – False**   **C – Can't tell**

Statement 21: It's inevitable that a majority of broadcasts will be watched on iPads.

Statement 22: The ability to track digital channels is a key reason behind a shift in advertising budgets to the digital sphere.

Statement 23: Viewer numbers and advertising budgets do not necessarily move synchronously to fresh platforms.

Statement 24: Eventually, online broadcasters should be able to attract roughly comparable revenue to normal TV broadcasters.

Passage 7

Taking Advantage
(Adapted from *The Art of War*, by Sun Tzu)

If the enemy be at rest in comfortable quarters, harass him; if he be living in plenty, cut off his supplies; if sitting composedly awaiting attack, cause him to move. This may be done by appearing where the enemy is not, and assaulting unexpected points.

If we go where the enemy is not, we may go a thousand leagues without exhaustion. If we attack those positions which the enemy has not defended, we invariably take them; but on defence we must be strong, even where we are not likely to be attacked.

Against those skilful in attack, the enemy does not know where to defend; against those skilful in defence, the enemy does not know where to attack.

Now the secrets of the art of offence are not to be easily apprehended, as a certain shape or noise can be understood, of the senses; but when these secrets are learnt, the enemy is mastered.

We attack, and the enemy cannot resist, because we attack his insufficiency; we retire and the enemy cannot pursue, because we retire too quickly.

The leader who changes his tactics in accordance with his adversary, and thereby controls the issue, may be called the God of War.

A – True   **B – False**   **C – Can't tell**

 Statement 25: Sun Tzu recommends that you should defeat an opponent in an entrenched position by aggressively attacking him there.

Statement 26: Mobility is an essential component of successful warfare.

Statement 27: The lessons of *The Art of War* may be interpreted metaphorically for modern civilian life.

Statement 28: To be successful in warfare requires a general to be flexible enough to respond to changing situations.

Passage 8

Princely Acts
(Adapted from *The Prince* by Niccolo Machiavelli)

Nothing makes a Prince so well thought of as to undertake great enterprises and give striking proofs of his capacity.

Among the Princes of our time, Ferdinand of Aragon, present King of Spain, may almost be accounted a new Prince since from one of the weakest he has become, for fame and glory, the foremost King in Christendom. And if you consider his achievements you will find them all great and some extraordinary.

In the beginning of his reign he made war on Granada, which enterprise was the foundation of his power. At first he carried the war leisurely, without fear of interruption, and kept the attention and thoughts of the Barons of Castile so completely occupied with it that they had no time to think of home. Meanwhile, he insensibly acquired reputation among them and authority over them. With the money of the Church and of his subjects, he was able to maintain his armies, and during the prolonged contest, to lay the foundations of that military discipline which afterwards made him so famous. Moreover, to enable him to engage in still greater undertakings, always covering himself with the cloak of religion, he had recourse to what may be called pious cruelty, in driving out and clearing his kingdom of the Moors; than which exploit none could be more wonderful or uncommon.

A – True   **B – False**   **C – Can't tell**

Statement 29: Ferdinand of Aragon's achievements are not that surprising given his background.

Statement 30: Ferdinand used his position of power to build loyalty among his nobles.

Statement 31: Religion can be used as a justification of the exercise of temporal power.

Statement 32: Spain had previously been partly occupied by the Moors.

Passage 9

Indestructible
(Adapted from *Wine For Dummies*, by Ed McCarthy and
Mary Ewing-Mulligan)

The legendary wine called Madeira comes from the island of the same name, which sits in the Atlantic Ocean nearer to Africa than Europe. Madeira is a subtropical island whose precarious hillside vineyards rise straight up from the ocean. The island is a province of Portugal, but the British have always run its wine trade. Historically, Madeira could even be considered something of an American wine, for this is the wine that American Colonists drank.

Madeira can lay claim to being the world's longest-lived wine. A few years ago, we were fortunate enough to try a 1799 Vintage Madeira that was still perfectly fine. Only Hungary's Tokaji Azsu can rival Madeira in longevity, and that's true only of its rarest examples, such as its Essencia.

Although Madeira's fortified wines were quite the rage 200 years ago, the island's vineyards were devastated at the end of the 19th century, first by mildew and then by the phylloxera louse. Most vineyards were replanted with lesser grapes. The very best Madeira wines are still those from the old days, vintage-dated wines from 1920 back to 1795. The prices aren't outrageous either (£200–£300 a bottle), considering what other wines that old, such as Bordeaux, cost.

A – True   **B – False**   **C – Can't tell**

Statement 33: Madeira is a British-American wine.

Statement 34: Madeira lasts centuries because it has already undergone oxidisation.

Statement 35: Phylloxera devastated the wine industry towards the end of the 19th century.

Statement 36: A vintage Madeira is good value for money compared to Bordeaux.

Passage 10

Capitalist Communists
(Adapted from *An Introduction to the Chinese Economy*, by Rongxing Guo)

While China's reform has been a strong driver of its economic growth, it has also derived a series of socioeconomic problems. Prior to the reform, China was an egalitarian society in terms of income distribution. In the initial stage of the reform, the policy of 'letting some people get rich first' (*rang yi bufen ren xian fui qilai*) was adopted in order to overcome egalitarianism in income distribution, to promote efficiency with strong incentives, and ultimately realise common prosperity based on an enlarged pie. But this policy has quickly enlarged income gaps between different groups of people.

According to the Gini coefficient, China has very high levels of inequality, only lower than a few nations in Latin America and Africa. However, there is a different view with respect to this issue: that China's current income inequality has been overestimated and, if measured in terms of purchasing power parity (PPP) rates, China's apparent income inequality should be reduced considerably, as in most cases the price levels in poor areas are much lower than those in rich areas.

A – True   **B – False**   **C – Can't tell**

Statement 37: China has moved at least some of the way towards a capitalist economic structure.

Statement 38: Income inequality is an inevitable function of a liberalising economy.

Statement 39: PPP is a better measure of income inequality than the Gini coefficient.

Statement 40: If inflation increases in China, it negatively impacts the poorest in China.

Passage 11

As Constant as the North Star
(Adapted from *Celestial Navigation*, by Tom Cunliffe)

As every schoolboy knows, the Pole Star is located directly over the North Pole, for which it is named. Alone amongst the heavenly bodies it sits apparently still while the whole 'bowl of night' revolves in splendour around it. Because of its unique situation almost exactly on the Earth's axis, a corrected altitude of Polaris delivers, without further ado, the observer's latitude. Long before the Sun's declination was tabulated, Polaris was giving early navigators a yardstick for north-south distance. They didn't know the Earth was round, so they had no idea why it worked. We do, and it goes like this.

Since the terrestrial horizon is a tangent to the Earth's surface (and hence forms a right angle with the radius which designates the observer's latitude), the altitude of Polaris above this tangent is the same as the angle subtended by the observer's azimuth at the centre of the Earth. This is, of course, his latitude.

This works out because the distance of Polaris being for all practical purposes infinite, the line joining Polaris to the observer is parallel to the axis of the Earth.

A – True   **B – False**   **C – Can't tell**

Statement 41: Polaris permits an approximate calculation of longitude by measuring its altitude relative to the observer.

Statement 42: Polaris' relative constancy above the North Pole is what gives it its unique navigational utility.

Statement 43: Other stars appear to revolve around Polaris in the night sky.

Statement 44: If Polaris were closer to Earth, its navigational utility would be greatly enhanced as more accurate measurements of its altitude would be possible.

Quantitative Reasoning

Numerical presentation 1

MPs' Expenses

MPs Expenses Claims 2007 - 2008

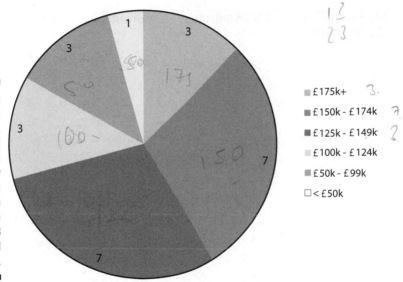

Figure 10-1: A selection of 24 MPs, categorised by the amount they claimed in expenses in the 2007–2008 financial year.

■ £175k+

■ £150k - £174k

■ £125k - £149k

□ £100k - £124k

■ £50k - £99k

□ < £50k

MPs' expenses claims were leaked to the press. Figure 10-1 shows the amounts claimed by a representative sample of 24 MPs (k = £1,000).

Item 1: Approximately what percentage of MPs claimed at least £125k?

(A) 12.5%   (B) 29.2%   (C) 41.7%   (D) 70.8%   (E) 82.3%

Item 2: What is the ratio of MPs claiming £150k or more to those claiming less than £150k?

(A) 1:7   (B) 5:7   (C) 17:7   (D) 5:12   (E) 1:8

Item 3: The MPs in the £100k–£124k category claimed a total of £340k between them. If the MP with the largest claim in this category claimed £121k, what is the maximum that one of the other MPs in this category may have claimed?

(A) £100.0k   (B) £105.5k   (C) £109.5k   (D) £119.0k   (E) £124.0k

Item 4: MPs have reduced their expenses claims by 19% since a new system for making claims was introduced. If the previous total bill for all 650 MPs was £98 million per year, what is the new annual total? Round your answer to the nearest million pounds.

(A) £19 million   (B) £28 million   (C) £62 million   (D) £79 million
(E) £81 million

Numerical presentation 2

US Jobs Data

Table 10-2	US Monthly Employment Gains
Month	**Jobs Added (Thousands)**
January	68
February	235
March	194
April	217
May	53
June	46
July	117

Item 5: What is the average number of jobs added per month, in thousands, to the nearest thousand?

(A) 78　　(B) 93　　(C) 115　　(D) 133　　(E) 235

Item 6: In what month was the 600,000th new job added in the year?

(A) February　　(B) March　　(C) April　　(D) May　　(E) June

Item 7: What was the approximate ratio of new jobs added in June and July versus those added in January and February?

(A) 1:1　　(B) 1:1.9　　(C) 1:2.2　　(D) 1:3　　(E) 1:7

Item 8: August jobs data showed a 23% increase over the average of the second quarter of the year. Approximately how many jobs were added in August, in thousands?

(A) 89　　(B) 105　　(C) 130　　(D) 144　　(E) 204

Numerical presentation 3

Inflation in the East

Table 10-3		Inflation Rates in Asian Economies (%)					
Japan	0.2	Singapore	5.2	Malaysia	3.1	Bangladesh	10.2
Philippines	4.0	India	8.6	Kazakhstan	8.5	Thailand	4.1
Sri Lanka	7.5	Taiwan	1.3	Hong Kong	5.6	China	6.5
Vietnam	22.2	South Korea	4.7	Pakistan	13.8	Indonesia	4.6

A first-year analyst at an investment bank is asked to categorise the data into the bands based on the inflation rate. He draws up Table 10-4.

Table 10-4	Asian Inflation, by Band
Band	*Number of Countries*
0–4.9%	7
5.0–9.9%	6
10.0–14.9%	1
>15%	2

Item 9: Is there anything wrong with Table 10-4?

    A – One too few in the 0–4.9% band

    B – One too many in the 0–4.9% band

    C – One too many in the >15% band

    D – One too few in the >15% band

    E – No – there is nothing wrong with the table

Item 10: What is the approximate average inflation rate of those countries in the 5.0–9.9% band?

(A) 5.4%   (B) 6.0%   (C) 7.0%   (D) 7.3%   (E) 7.5%

Item 11: By what percentage would Japan's inflation rate have to increase to match South Korea's?

(A) 2%   (B) 4.5%   (C) 91%   (D) 2,150%   (E) 2,250%

Item 12: India's GDP is $1.4 trillion. China's GDP is $5 trillion. What is the average rate of inflation across these two countries, assuming that the impact of each country's rate of inflation on the combined countries' rate of inflation is proportional to the GDP size of their economy?

(A) 7.0%   (B) 7.2%   (C) 7.4%   (D) 7.6%   (E) 25.6%

Numerical presentation 4

Under Par

Table 10-5 is a sample of the total number strokes taken by 20 players at the US PGA golf major tournament.

Table 10-5		US PGA Total Scores		
276	283	290	273	285
285	290	272	286	295
291	272	294	284	275
281	285	288	277	280

Item 13: What score was the modal average?

(A) 272   (B) 276   (C) 280   (D) 285   (E) 290

Item 14: What was the mean score? Round your answer to the nearest whole stroke.

(A) 277   (B) 279   (C) 281   (D) 282   (E) 283

Item 15: What percentage of scores were less than 286?

(A) 55%   (B) 60%   (C) 65%   (D) 70%   (E) 75%

Item 16: The top two players, KB and JD, were tied at 272 strokes, and went on to play a play-off over a further three holes. The odds of player KB winning the play-off were 5:11. Express these odds as a percentage chance of winning, rounding your answer to the nearest whole percentage.

(A) 19%   (B) 31%   (C) 45%   (D) 69%   (E) 81%

Numerical presentation 5

The Winner's Circle

Questions 17–20 refer to horse racing.

Horse races use imperial units of measurement. 1 mile = 8 furlongs = 1,760 yards.

Item 17: The Epsom Derby is held over 12 furlongs. In 2011, Pour Moi completed the course to win in 2 minutes and 35 seconds. How fast is this speed in miles per hour (mph)? Round your answer to the nearest whole mph.

(A) 15   (B) 23   (C) 35   (D) 184   (E) 279

Item 18: The third-placed horse, the Queen's Carlton House, finished 5 yards back from the winner mentioned in Item 17. What time did it complete the course in, assuming that Carlton House maintains a steady speed throughout the race? Round your answer to the first decimal place.

   A – 155.1 seconds

   B – 155.3 seconds

   C – 155.5 seconds

   D – 156.1 seconds

   E – 156.7 seconds

Item 19: The fastest ever Derby-winning time was the 2 minutes and 31 seconds recorded by Workforce in 2010. Assuming uniform speeds, by what approximate distance would Workforce have beaten Pour Moi?

(A) 62 yards   (B) 64 yards   (C) 66 yards   (D) 68 yards   (E) 70 yards

Item 20: The St Leger Stakes are held later in the year than the Derby, on a course measuring 1 mile, 6 furlongs and 132 yards. If a horse wins the St Leger by travelling at the same average speed as Pour Moi did when winning the Derby, what is its approximate winning time?

   A – 2 minutes 50 seconds

   B – 2 minutes 51 seconds

   C – 2 minutes 55 seconds

   D – 3 minutes

   E – 3 minutes 9 seconds

Numerical presentation 6

Eating into the Market

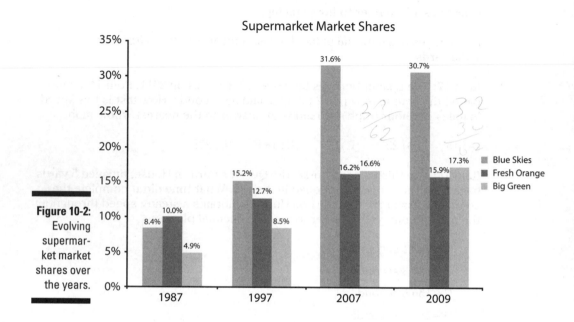

Figure 10-2: Evolving supermarket market shares over the years.

Figure 10-2 shows the changing market shares of three major UK supermarkets.

Item 21: In 1997, what is the approximate ratio of Blue Skies' market share to that of Big Green?

(A) 3:2   (B) 9:5   (C) 17:10   (D) 19:10   (E) 2:1

Item 22: Which of the following statements is supported by the information in the chart?

A – Blue Skies' market share is steadily increasing.

B – Big Green's market share is steadily falling.

C – The three supermarkets in the chart have taken an ever-increasing share of the overall market.

D – The combined market share of the three supermarkets suffered a fall in 2009.

E – Discount grocers are responsible for Blue Skies' market share fall in 2009 relative to 2007.

Item 23: Total grocery sales in the UK are approximately £125 billion per year. Roughly how much of that did Big Green take in 2009?

(A) £6.1 billion   (B) £10.6 billion   (C) £20.8 billion   (D) £21.6 billion
(E) £38.4 billon

Item 24: What is the range in market share between the three supermarkets in 1997?

(A) 6.7%   (B) 14.8%   (C) 15.0%   (D) 15.4%   (E) 26.7%

Numerical presentation 7

Keeping the Lights on

Catherine is looking to find a new electricity provider and has narrowed down her choice to Midlands Energy and Isis Energy. Their tariffs are shown in the tables below. Electricity usage is measured pence per kilo-watt hour (kWh) of usage and monthly refers to a 30-day period, whereas a quarter means 90 days.

Table 10-6	Midlands Energy Electricity Costs	
Energy Package	Cost per kWh	Daily Standing Charge
Quarterly billing	3.81p	29.97p
Monthly direct debit	3.59p	29.92p

Table 10-7	Isis Energy Electricity Costs		
Isis Energy Cheapest Package	Peak Cost per kWh	Off-Peak Cost per kWh	Daily Standing Charge
Domestic economy	15.01p	7.12p	25.56p

Item 25: Assuming that Catherine uses 12 kWh per day, how much more would it cost her per month using Midlands Energy quarterly billing than their monthly direct debit option?

(A) £0.80   (B) £0.81   (C) £21.90   (D) £22.71   (E) £44.61

Item 26: Of her daily usage of 12 kWh, one-third of Catherine's use is off-peak. How much does it cost her per month with Isis Energy?

(A) £7.67   (B) £8.54   (C) £36.02   (D) £44.56   (E) £52.24

Item 27: If Catherine reduced her electricity usage by 20%, and at the same time switched her consumption pattern to 60% off-peak, what would it now cost her with Isis Energy's package?

(A) £12.30   (B) £17.29   (C) £37.26   (D) £44.66   (E) £55.23

Item 28: Which of the following statements is false?

A – For Midlands Energy, quarterly billing is more expensive than monthly billing under all circumstances.

B – Isis Energy is cheaper than Midlands Energy Quarterly if Catherine's entire monthly energy consumption is less than 18 kWh off-peak.

C – If Catherine uses 200 kWh per month, Isis Energy can undercut Midlands Energy's price.

D – Even if Catherine increases her usage to 14 kWh, she will still find it cheaper to use Midlands Energy rather than Isis Energy.

E – Isis Energy's Domestic Economy package is most cost-effective for high-peak users.

Numerical presentation 8

Three Score and Ten

The UK government collects statistics on the life expectancy at birth of people across the different parts of the country. Table 10-8 contains the data for the various English regions, segregated by gender.

Table 10-8	Life Expectancy at Birth in Years	
Region	**Males**	**Females**
North East	75.8	80.1
North West	75.7	80.3
Yorkshire and the Humber	76.6	81.0
East Midlands	77.3	81.3
West Midlands	76.6	81.1
East of England	78.3	82.3
London	77.4	82.0
South East	78.5	82.4
South West	78.5	82.7

Item 29: What is the range of life expectancy in years between men and women, across England?

(A) 4.2   (B) 4.3   (C) 4.6   (D) 7.0   (E) 8.4

Item 30: What is the approximate average life expectancy in years for women across the English regions? You may assume that each region contributes in equal weight to the average.

(A) 77.2   (B) 77.3   (C) 81.1   (D) 81.4   (E) 81.5

Item 31: Expressed as a percentage, how much longer do women live than men in London?

(A) 5.1%   (B) 5.6%   (C) 5.9%   (D) 6.2%   (E) 6.5%

Item 32: Which of the following statements is true?

A – On average, men live longer than women.

B – A man born in the South West will, on average, live a longer life than a man born in the North East.

C – The regional variation in life expectancy is greater for women than for men.

D – A woman born in the North East will, on average, die before a man born in the South West on the same day.

E – The gender difference in life expectancy is least in the West Midlands.

Numerical presentation 9

Bottle Bank

George wants to convert his basement into a wine cellar. In order to do this, he needs to add in various racks and shelves. The basic dimensions of the room are depicted in Figure 10-3.

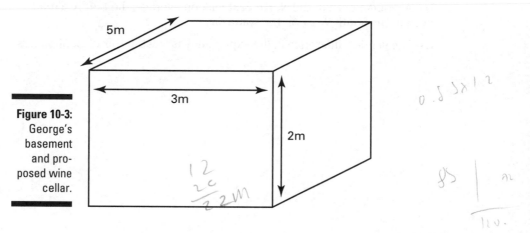

Figure 10-3:
George's basement and proposed wine cellar.

Item 33: George wants to line one long wall with wine racks. The rack is made from a modular system, with each module being 85 cm in height and 120 cm in length and containing up to 72 bottles. How many bottles can he store in the racks if he lines as much of the wall as he can with racks?

(A) 72   (B) 144   (C) 288   (D) 576   (E) 706

Item 34: Each module costs £120 excluding VAT. How much does it cost George to line the long wall with as many racks as possible? The rate of VAT is 20%.

(A) £576   (B) £960   (C) £1,152   (D) £1,177   (E) £1,412

Item 35: As well as the racks, George installs a climate control system for the wine cellar. This system costs him a total of £550 to buy and install. Electricity costs are a further 6,600 kWh per year, at a cost of 5p per kWh. Assuming that the capital purchase installation costs are amortised over a ten-year period, how much does it cost George to run the climate control system for a year?

(A) £330   (B) £385   (C) £715   (D) £3,300   (E) £3,850

Item 36: George buys six cases of wine to celebrate the completion of his new cellar. Cases contain a dozen bottles each. He buys three cases of Alsatian Gewurztraminer at £26 per bottle, two cases of Hermitage at £720 per case and a case of fine Bordeaux at £99 per bottle. How much would it cost him to fill his new cellar, at the same average cost per bottle and inclusive of these bottles?

(A) £2,254   (B) £3,564   (C) £12,936   (D) £28,512   (E) £155,232

Abstract Reasoning

Display 1

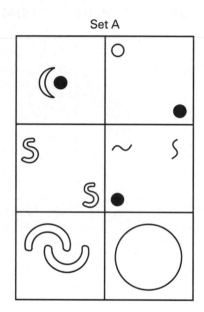
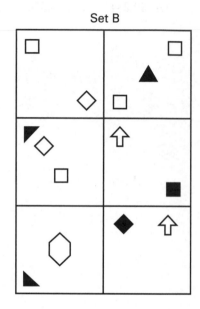

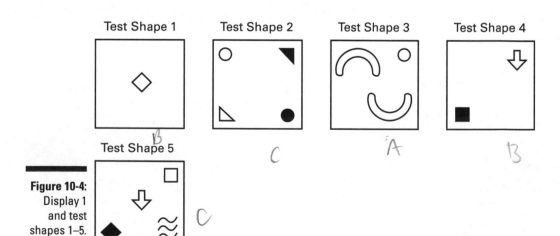

Figure 10-4: Display 1 and test shapes 1–5.

For each of the five test shapes, choose Set A, Set B, or Neither Set.

Display 2

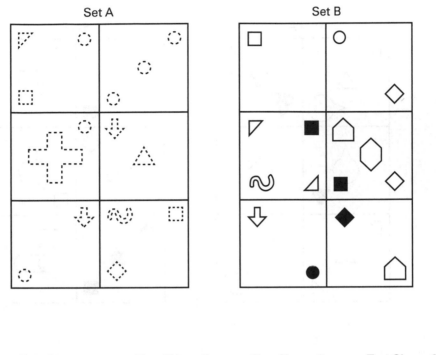

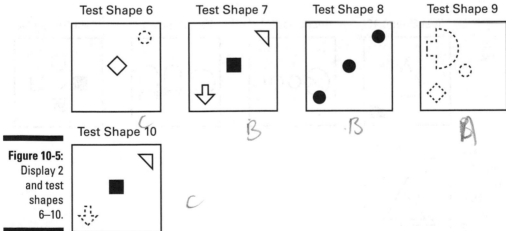

Figure 10-5: Display 2 and test shapes 6–10.

For each of the five test shapes, choose Set A, Set B, or Neither Set.

Display 3

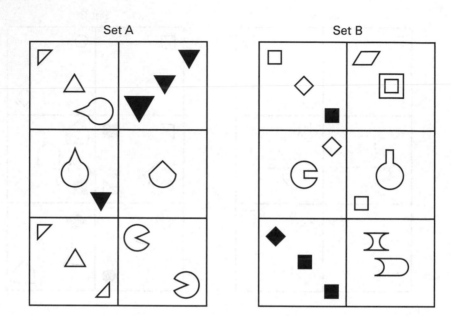

Set A   Set B

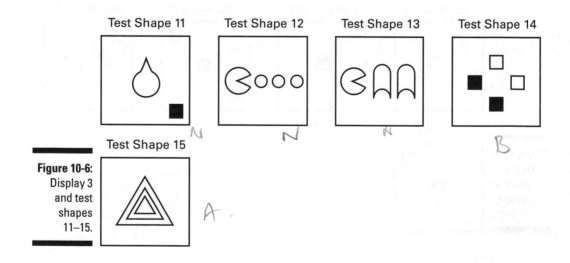

Test Shape 11   Test Shape 12   Test Shape 13   Test Shape 14

Test Shape 15

For each of the five test shapes, choose Set A, Set B, or Neither Set.

Display 4

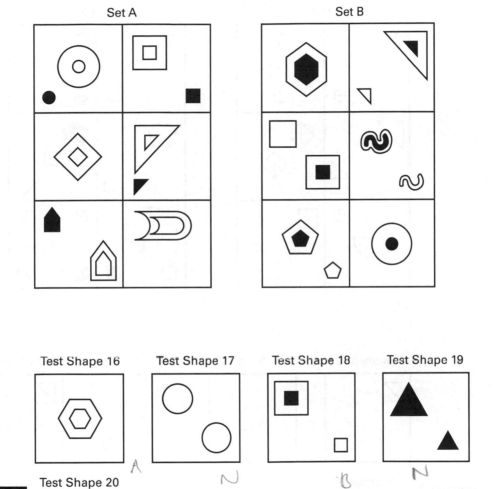

Figure 10-7: Display 4 and test shapes 16–20.

For each of the five test shapes, choose Set A, Set B, or Neither Set.

Display 5

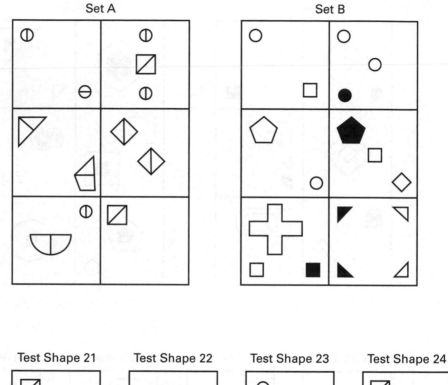

Set A   Set B

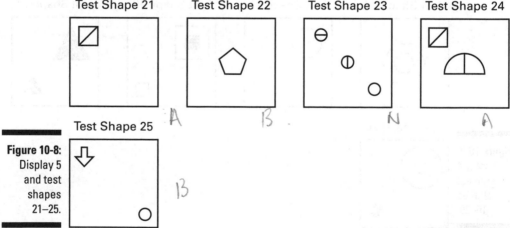

Test Shape 21   Test Shape 22   Test Shape 23   Test Shape 24

A   B   N   A

Test Shape 25

Figure 10-8:
Display 5
and test
shapes
21–25.

B

For each of the five test shapes, choose Set A, Set B, or Neither Set.

Display 6

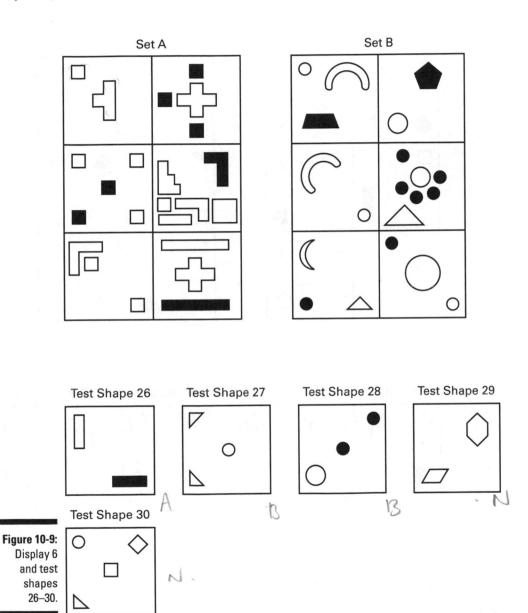

Figure 10-9: Display 6 and test shapes 26–30.

For each of the five test shapes, choose Set A, Set B, or Neither Set.

Display 7

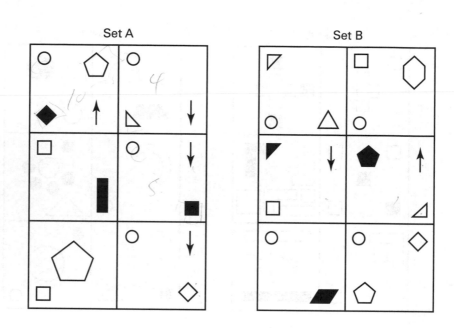

Set A   Set B

Test Shape 31   Test Shape 32   Test Shape 33   Test Shape 34

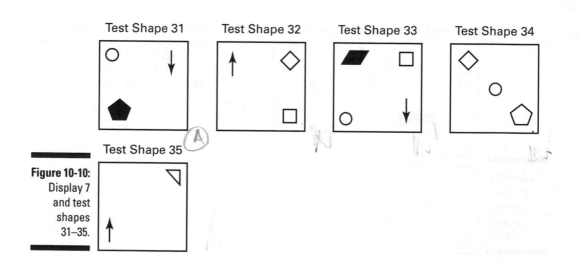

Test Shape 35

For each of the five test shapes, choose Set A, Set B, or Neither Set.

Display 8

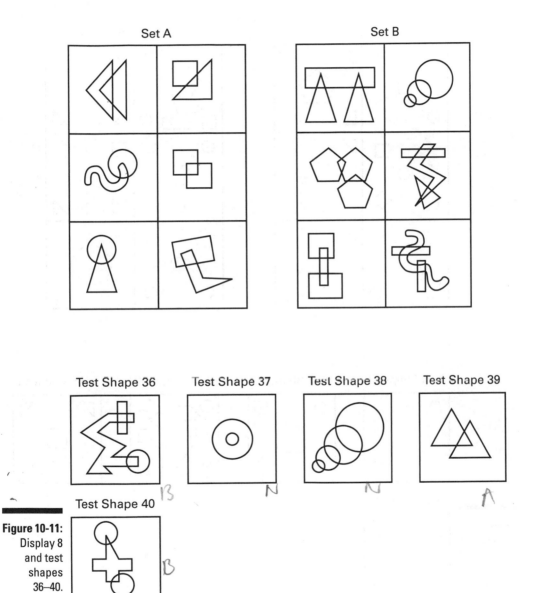

Figure 10-11: Display 8 and test shapes 36–40.

For each of the five test shapes, choose Set A, Set B, or Neither Set.

Display 9

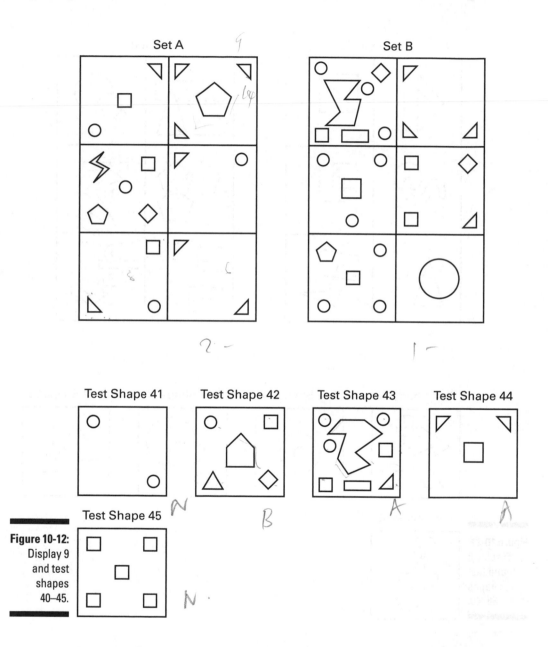

Figure 10-12: Display 9 and test shapes 40–45.

For each of the five test shapes, choose Set A, Set B, or Neither Set.

Display 10

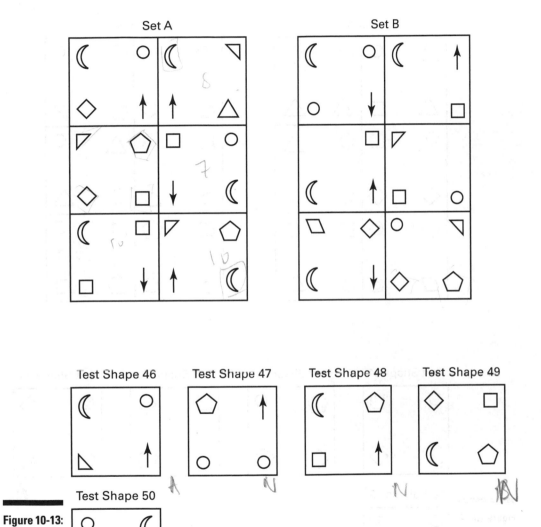

Figure 10-13: Display 10 and test shapes 46–50.

For each of the five test shapes, choose Set A, Set B, or Neither Set.

Display 11

Set A   Set B

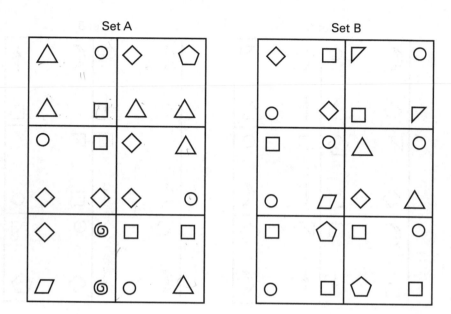

Test Shape 51   Test Shape 52   Test Shape 53   Test Shape 54

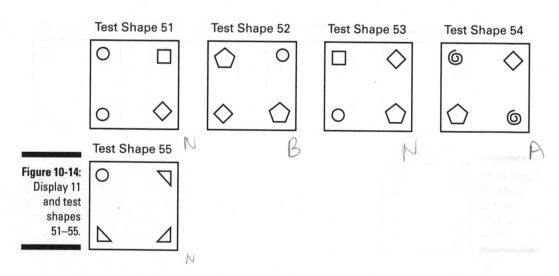

Test Shape 55

Figure 10-14:
Display 11
and test
shapes
51–55.

For each of the five test shapes, choose Set A, Set B, or Neither Set.

Display 12

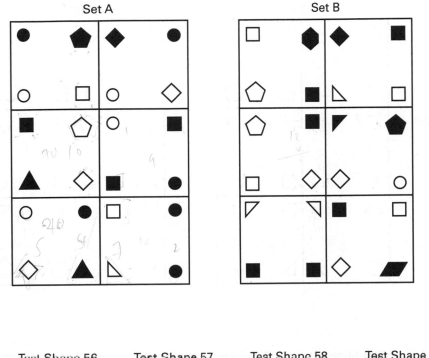

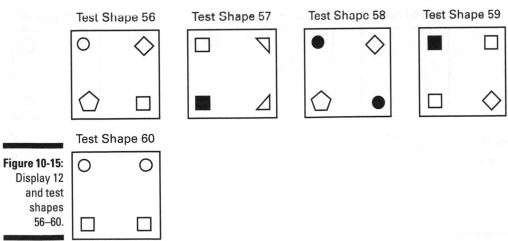

Figure 10-15: Display 12 and test shapes 56–60.

For each of the five test shapes, choose Set A, Set B, or Neither Set.

Display 13

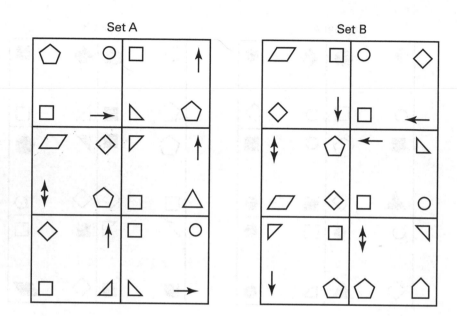

Set A   Set B

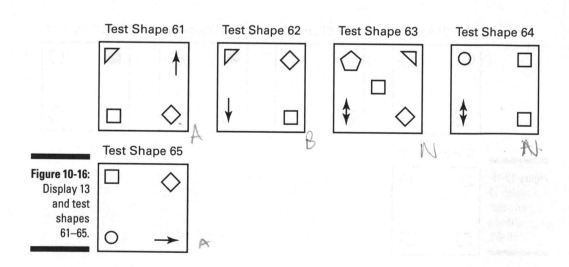

Test Shape 61   Test Shape 62   Test Shape 63   Test Shape 64

Test Shape 65

Figure 10-16:
Display 13
and test
shapes
61–65.

For each of the five test shapes, choose Set A, Set B, or Neither Set.

Decision Analysis

Scenario

Football Games

The intemperate manager of Cannons United has been banished from the dugout for swearing repeatedly at match officials. Prohibited from talking to his players, he is forced to communicate surreptitiously by passing written messages to his assistant manager down at the sidelines. In order to prevent the Football Association from proving that he's communicating to his team from the stands, the manager uses a complex code.

Table 10-9	The Manager's Code		
The Players	**The Pitch**	**Movements**	**Types**
Defender = ◄	Net = ⌃	Fast = ↺	Increase = ⇉
Midfielder = △	Goalposts = ⅃	Slow = ↻	Decrease = ⇇
Striker = ►	Penalty Spot = ⁝	Attack = →	Talk = ⇆
Keeper = ▽	Halfway Line = ‡	Defend = ←	Walk = ↔
Cannons = ▲	Corner = ↖	Score = ☝	Approve = ↘
Opponent = ▼	Whistle = ⌣	Shoot = ⚡	Disapprove = ⌢
Referee = ↺	Hand = ⊢	Pass = ↳	
Ball = ◢	Head = →ı		

You're the assistant manager, communicating via code with your unhappy boss sitting in the stands. Your boss depends on your help to change the course of the game.

Question 1: What is the best interpretation of the following coded message?

A – Pass the ball to the defender.

B – Pass the ball to the striker.

C – Pass the ball to the midfielder.

D – Pass the ball to the keeper.

E – The striker should shoot.

Question 2: What is the best interpretation of the following coded message?

↳, △, ↳, ▶, ⚡

A – Pass from midfield to striker, then shoot.

B – Pass from defence to the striker, then shoot.

C – Pass to midfield, then to the striker, then shoot.

D – Shoot frequently from midfield and from the striker.

E – Move midfield into attack and shoot.

Question 3: What is the best interpretation of the following coded message?

⇉(▲, ↳, ▼, ▲)

A – Move the ball around near their goal.

B – Attack a lot.

C – Stay in defence.

D – Don't attack.

E – Keep possession.

Question 4: What is the best interpretation of the following coded message?

$$\rightrightarrows ⌢, ↻$$

A – The referee will blow his whistle soon.

B – The referee should book the opposition.

C – The referee is going to book our player.

D – The referee is an idiot.

E – The referee can be bribed.

Question 5: What is the best interpretation of the following coded message?

$$↻, ⌣, \rightrightarrows(⌢ ⇆), ▼$$

A – Send off that opposition player, referee!

B – Substitute our player.

C – Tell the referee we're going to make a substitution.

D – The opposition is telling the referee they're substituting a player.

E – The opposition is trying to get our players sent off.

Question 6: What is the best interpretation of the following coded message?

$$◀◀(⌥), ←↖$$

A – Tell the defence to press forwards after this corner.

B – Two defenders should run from the goalposts in order to defend this corner.

C – I want one the defenders to take this corner.

D – I don't like the way the defence keeps hanging back near the goalposts on corners.

E – I want two defenders to stay near the goalposts to defend this corner.

Question 7: What is the best interpretation of the following coded message?

$$(\triangle \triangle), \rightarrow \circlearrowright$$

A – The midfield is running too fast.

B – The midfielders are going to get exhausted.

C – Midfield needs to attack faster.

D – I'm going to tell off the midfield for running too much.

E – Tell the midfield to run back and support the defence.

Question 8: What is the best interpretation of the following coded message?

$$(\blacktriangle \Updownarrow) \rightrightarrows, \blacktriangledown \Updownarrow$$

A – We need to score one more than them.

B – The opposition scored more than we did.

C – Score now, quick, while the opposition are attacking.

D – Don't pass, shoot and score!

E – We're getting better now that the opposition have scored.

Question 9: What is the best interpretation of the following coded message?

$$\circlearrowright, \blacktriangledown \blacktriangleleft, \leftmapsto \blacktriangleright$$

A – Referee, that was a clear handball by the opposition.

B – Referee, the opposing defender handballed!

C – Tell the referee to get his hand out of his pocket and book the opposition for handball.

D – I don't want the referee to see us handball while defending.

E – Tell the defence to handball, but distract the referee first.

Question 10: What is the best interpretation of the following coded message?

$$\text{≴▼}, \wedge, (\text{⋏⇶})\blacktriangleright$$

A – I hate the way you shoot.

B – Just score!

C – Tell that idiot striker to just hit the ball into the net!

D – Don't keep passing it around so much.

E – That was a bad shot.

Question 11: What is the best interpretation of the following coded message?

$$\blacktriangleright\text{≴}, \triangledown\leftarrow, \triangle\text{⇧}$$

A – The keeper let the striker and midfielder score.

B – The keeper tried to defend the midfielder's shot, letting the striker score.

C – The striker took a shot at the defending goalkeeper, after the midfielder scored.

D – The striker didn't score but the midfielder did.

E – The keeper saves from the striker, but the midfielder scores on the rebound.

Question 12: Translate the following into the manager's code:

Tell me if you want me to substitute a striker for a defender.

A. ⇆, (⇆↔)▶, ◀

B. ⇆, ▶, ◀

C. (⇆↔)▶, ◀

D. ⇆, (⇆↔)◀, ▶

E. ⇆, ⇆(▶), ◀

Question 13: What is the best interpretation of the following coded message?

↻ ↔, ▼ ‡

A – I want you all to attack now.

B – Shoot from where you are, quickly!

C – Pull everyone back into our own half to defend.

D – Run into their half.

E – Press forward into their half, slowly.

Question 14: What is the best interpretation of the following coded message?

(⇧ ⇧)(‿ ‡)

A – Score twice in each half.

B – Score a goal either half.

C – Score two goals in this half.

D – Scoring twice will win this match.

E – This match is a rematch.

Question 15: Translate the following into the manager's code:

Place the ball on the corner spot and score when the referee blows his whistle.

A. ◤↖, ↻‿, ⇧

B. ◤↖, ⇧, ↻‿

C. ↻‿, ⇧, ◤↖

D. ↻, ◤↖, ⇧

E. ⇧◤, ‿

Question 16: What is the best interpretation of the following coded message?

$$(\triangle \triangle) \mapsto \downarrow \; \blacktriangleright , \; \rightarrow \hspace{-0.5em}| \; \hat{\boxdot}$$

A – Tell the striker to head the ball in the net.

B – Midfield needs to pass up to the striker so he can head a goal.

C – The midfield are passing among themselves too much; give it to the striker so he can head the ball and score.

D – Pass quickly to the striker so he can head it into the goal.

E – Don't pass the ball to the striker, midfield; head it to him so he can score.

Question 17: What is the best interpretation of the following coded message?

$$\blacktriangle (\, \exists (\leftrightarrow \cup) \mapsto), \; \blacktriangleright \blacktriangleright$$

A – We need to pass the ball faster through the team up to the strikers.

B – More passing, more speed.

C – I need us pushing further up the pitch and getting the ball to the strikers.

D – I need everyone to run faster, pass more, and get the ball to the strikers.

E – Tell the strikers to hold the ball up and move more quickly.

Question 18: What is the best interpretation of the following coded message?

$$\searrow \blacktriangle , \; \exists \rightarrow$$

A – Congratulations, you won!

B – Don't wait for my approval, just attack!

C – Stop attacking, you've done what you needed to.

D – The attack's going well.

E – Well done, lads; now attack, attack, attack!

Question 19: What is the best interpretation of the following coded message?

$$\circlearrowleft \rightrightarrows (\circlearrowleft \smile),\ \rightrightarrows \leftarrow$$

A – Tell the referee to blow his whistle; we can't defend any longer.

B – The referee will blow his whistle any minute now; hang on!

C – Our defence is begging the referee to blow his whistle.

D – The referee is helping our defence with his interruptions of the game.

E – The referee has lost his whistle while running into defence.

Question 20: What is the best interpretation of the following coded message?

$$\blacktriangle (\blacktriangleleft \blacktriangleleft),\ \circlearrowleft \rightrightarrows$$

A – We need our defence to slow the game down.

B – Our defence have to speed the game up.

C – Their defenders are playing too slowly.

D – Their defenders are wasting time by talking to each other.

E – Break their defence quickly to end the game.

Question 21: What is the best interpretation of the following coded message?

$$\leftrightarrows,\ \blacktriangle (\triangle \triangle),\ \rightarrow (\hookleftarrow \hookrightarrow),\ \blacktriangle (\blacktriangleright \blacktriangleright)$$

A – We need our strikers to drop back and pass from midfield.

B – Our midfield aren't making enough attacking crosses to attack.

C – Get our midfield to send more penetrating crosses to the strikers.

D – If our midfield can attack more, we'll get more corners.

E – The midfield are passing to themselves too much, and not attacking.

Question 22: What is the best interpretation of the following coded message?

$$▼▼, ⇆, \circlearrowleft, (‿^)↔, ◀$$

A – The opposition players won't stop talking to the referee about our defender.

B – The referee is trying to decide whether to send off our defender.

C – Our defender managed to get the referee to send off their striker.

D – The opponents managed to get our defender sent off.

E – The opponents managed to get the referee to send our defender off the pitch.

Question 23: Which two of the following terms would be of most benefit if added to the code if you had to translate the following message into code?

If you don't start playing better, our owners are going to sell the lot of you.

A – Play

B – Match

C – Owner

D – Sell

E – Lot

Question 24: Which two of the following terms would be of most benefit if added to the code if you had to translate the following message into code?

I'm over the moon, but we'll still take each match as it comes and give 110%.

A – Match

B – Moon

C – Over

D – Calm

E – 110%

Question 25: What is the best interpretation of the following coded message?

$$▲◀(↖ ⌣), (▲◀▽)←^$$

A – Get one of our defenders to cover the goalpost nearest the corner, and another to stand next to the keeper and block the net.

B – Get our defenders near the goalposts and the keeper in front of the net.

C – Get one of our defenders on that corner spot and the other with the keeper in front of the net.

D – Get the defenders around the corner taker, and place the keeper in front of the net.

E – I want one defender on the nearside goalpost and the other out by the penalty spot.

Question 26: What is the best interpretation of the following coded message?

$$∪⇉(↻⌣), ▲↖, ⇧$$

A – Take the corner and score.

B – Force the corner by kicking the ball into touch in the last minute.

C – It's the last minute of the match, we have a corner . . . and score!

D – Score from this corner and we take the lead.

E – We need to get a last-minute corner.

Chapter 11
Practice Test Two: Answers and Explanations

• •

In This Chapter
▶ Answering the questions to Practice Test Two
▶ Understanding the answers

• •

Verbal Reasoning

Answer 1
A – True

This answer follows logically from the information in the first paragraph. You know that the Sun crosses the observer's meridian at noon – the Sun is no longer east or west of you. If the Sun is neither east nor west, it must be south or north (or, rarely, directly overhead). You also know that when the Sun is at this point, the celestial meridian corresponds to your longitude. Therefore, your longitude equals the celestial meridian at noon.

Answer 2
A – True

The first two paragraphs together tell you that you can calculate both longitude and latitude at noon. You also know that finding longitude and latitude is a cornerstone of the navigator's day. Therefore, you know that the noon sight allows you to calculate your position, which is important to navigators.

Answer 3
B – False

You know that the Sun is at your zenith when it is directly above you. When the Sun is directly beneath you (on the opposite side of the Earth), the Sun is at your nadir – but you don't need to know this fact to answer the question.

Answer 4
C – Can't tell

You know only that the Sun appears to travel around the Earth. The passage doesn't say whether the Earth revolves around the Sun.

Don't bring in your outside knowledge to help you answer the questions in the verbal reasoning subtest.

Answer 5
A – True

On hearing the music, the author immediately recognised the advert as being for Marks & Spencer. Thus, brand awareness is reinforced.

M&S isn't the only company to recognise the usefulness of having a catchy soundtrack, although we think that their choice of tune is a lot more melodious than the offerings from certain other companies.

Answer 6
C – Can't tell

Just because the chocolate pudding campaign worked on Claire doesn't necessarily mean that Claire is the target demographic or that Claire's demographic is important in all advertising campaigns.

Beware when reasoning from the specific to the general in the verbal reasoning subtest. Such logic can lead to you draw conclusions that the text doesn't necessarily support.

Answer 7
C – Can't tell

You know that pudding sales rose by 288%, but you don't know about the overall increase in food sales.

Answer 8
A – True

The overall tone of the passage is that of someone impressed by the advertising, from the enthusiastic description of the commercial itself to the specific sentence that he found it inspirational, and the exclamation mark at the end of the passage.

Answer 9
B – False

The passage is quite clear in its statement that Cowell has more autonomy than most people in the music industry.

Answer 10
A – True

Cowell is metaphorically described as laying golden eggs for Sony.

Answer 11
B – False

The passage documented failures in Cowell's early career.

Answer 12
A – True

The author explains Cowell's relationship with Sony as being a case of enlightened self-interest. He also says that Cowell has more autonomy within that relationship than most people in the music industry. Therefore, in the author's opinion, enlightened self-interest underpins that relative autonomy.

Answer 13
A – True

Although not all ethnic groups are immigrant groups, the passage says that sociologists interested in ethnicity study immigration and talks about immigrant groups as being from different cultures, countries and traditions to those of the host country.

Answer 14
C – Can't tell

The passage cites the search for work as one reason why immigration into the US in the early 20th century was concentrated in the major cities, but the text doesn't exclude other causes of immigration.

Answer 15
A – True

The passage defines assimilation alternatively as a great melting pot and as immigrants adopting the language and traditions of their new community.

Answer 16
C – Can't tell

The passage says that this is the case if the theory of assimilation is correct – but the text doesn't commit to saying whether the theory is actually correct.

Answer 17
A – True

The passage states this answer clearly.

Answer 18
B – False

Ackerman plans to diversify the portfolio of shows that Fresh One makes, which means that Ackerman plans to have fewer shows centred around Oliver and more shows centred on other things.

Answer 19
A – True

The passage says that they can make businesses more sustainable and saleable. Doing so would then have the potential to increase a business owner's wealth.

Answer 20
C – Can't tell

This was David Page's plan, but the passage doesn't tell you whether the plan was effective.

Answer 21
C – Can't tell

The passage tells you that a majority will be viewed on 'tablets and iPads', but the text doesn't give the relative popularity of each. Therefore, you can't tell whether the iPad subset alone would represent a majority of viewers.

At the time of writing, iPads are currently the most popular tablet device, but you can't use outside knowledge to determine an answer's veracity.

Answer 22
A – True

The passage cites this answer as one of the three reasons behind the shift.

Answer 23
A – True

The passage notes that online viewership is increasing at a faster rate than online advertising revenue.

Answer 24
C – Can't tell

This statement may well be correct, but the passage doesn't commit to this outcome. In fact, other factors may intervene to prevent digital eyeballs being worth as much as TV eyeballs to advertisers. For example, the demographic or people's attention to advertising may differ.

Answer 25
B – False

Sun Tzu suggests the opposite, using his strength in one position against him and attacking elsewhere instead. A less martial analogy would be to think about how to negotiate with someone: if the other person is particularly fixated by one issue, then attempting to compromise elsewhere and returning to the issue after the other situation has taken precedence in his mind may be a good idea.

Answer 26
A – True

Sun Tzu repeatedly returns to this theme of speed being crucial to successful warfare, in particular when he says 'the enemy cannot pursue, because we retire too quickly'. Similarly, speed of action is often crucial in making the most of your opportunities, otherwise someone else gets there first and exploits those opportunities.

Answer 27
C – Can't tell

The passage doesn't make this assertion. However, the explanations to Answers 25 and 26 show that, as with any philosophical text, the truths therein can be made more universal and relevant.

Answer 28
A – True

This statement is the overriding message of the passage. The text spells out this answer in the last paragraph.

Answer 29
B – False

You know that Ferdinand's throne was previously one of the weakest in Europe and that his achievements are extraordinary.

Answer 30
A – True

Ferdinand used his campaign against the Moors to 'insensibly' acquire reputation and authority over his senior noblemen.

Ferdinand was clearly aware that power is a custom or habit. If you become used to being commanded or dominated by others, breaking away from being controlled is increasingly hard. By conducting an extensive campaign against the Moors, Ferdinand's noblemen were used to taking orders from him. The fact that he was successful doubtless acted as positive reinforcement to cement this subconscious loyalty.

Answer 31
A – True

You know that Ferdinand 'covered himself in the cloak of religion' to continue driving the Moors out of Spain.

Answer 32
A – True

As the passage tells you that Ferdinand cleared his kingdom of the Moors, and that Ferdinand is King of Spain, logically you can deduce that Ferdinand cleared the Moors out of Spain. Therefore, the Moors must have previously occupied at least part of Spain.

In fact, the Moors (largely composed of Muslim North Africans) occupied much of the Iberian Peninsula during mediaeval times.

Answer 33
B – False

You know that Madeira is a province of Portugal, and so Madeira is a Portuguese wine.

Answer 34
C – Can't tell

This answer happens to be true – the wine is maderised (oxidised through heating) during the estufagem process that follows fermentation – but you can't deduce that the answer is true from the passage.

Answer 35
C – Can't tell

The passage discusses the impact of phylloxera only on Madeira, not on the wine industry in general.

In fact, phylloxera did have a devastating effect across the entire Old World wine industry and only grafting on to resistant rootstocks allowed the trade to survive to the present day.

Answer 36
A – True

You know that the prices aren't outrageous, and therefore you can deduce that vintage Madeira represents good value compared to Bordeaux.

Answer 37

A – True

You know that China has adopted a policy of letting some people get rich before others.

This concept is a primitive form of capitalism – although in reality China's central government continues to exert major control over the economic experiment.

Answer 38

C – Can't tell

The passage suggests that this statement is the case in China, but you can't generalise from this specific case. The precise effects of how capital and income distribute across different groups under different economic scenarios remain a complex area of debate among economists.

Answer 39

C – Can't tell

The passage specifically describes PPP as being only one view, and so you can't make absolute statements about the utility of PPP. However, intuitively this answer would make sense.

Answer 40

A – True

You know that despite significant income inequality, price levels in the poor areas are much lower than in the rich areas, which mitigates the effect in terms of PPP. Inflation would cause these prices to rise, which, given the lower level of income in the poor areas, would impact on poor people the most.

In fact, China's government is highly aware of this risk (partly because it fears loss of government authority in poor areas) and tries to manipulate the market to dampen the effect of inflation in these areas.

Answer 41

B – False

This measurement yields an approximate calculation of latitude.

Answer 42
A – True

The passage links the constancy of Polaris to a navigator's ability to use the star to approximate a latitude measurement.

Answer 43
A – True

This answer comes from the use of the poetic phrase 'bowl of night', though the meaning is transparent from the passage. The phrase 'bowl of night' comes from the English translation of a poem written by the Persian mathematician and astronomer Omar Khayyam.

Answer 44
B – False

You know that using the altitude of Polaris as a proxy measurement for the observer's latitude works only because the line joining Polaris to the observer is parallel to the axis of the Earth. You also know that this is the case only because for all practical purposes the distance of Polaris from the observer is effectively infinite. If the North Star were much closer to the observer, the star would be less useful to navigators.

Quantitative Reasoning

Answer 1

D – 70.8%

Seven MPs claimed between £125k and £149k. A further seven MPs claimed between £150k and £174k. A final three MPs claimed above £175k. Therefore, (7 + 7 + 3) = 17 out of a total of 24 MPs claimed at least £125k. As a percentage, 17 ÷ 24 x 100 = 70.8% to one decimal place.

Answer 2

B – 5:7

A total of 7 + 3 = 10 MPs claimed £150k or more, which means that (24 – 10) = 14 MPs claimed less than £150k. The ratio is 10:14, which you can simplify to 5:7.

Answer 3

D – £119.0k

This category contains only three MPs. If the total of their three claims is £340k and the largest claim is £121k, the sum of the other two is (340k – 121k) = 219k.

The question asks what is the maximum that one of these two MPs could have claimed. You need to assume that the other MP claims the minimum to remain in the category – 100k. The maximum remaining is therefore (219k – 100k) = £119.0k.

Answer 4

D – £79 million

The old total was £98 million and has reduced by 19%. The new total is therefore [98 million x (100 – 19)] ÷ 100 = £79 million.

Answer 5

D – 133

This question is a test of your ability to calculate an arithmetic mean:

(68 + 235 + 194 + 217 + 53 + 46 + 117) ÷ 7 = 133 in thousands and to the nearest whole thousand

Answer 6

C – April

You can calculate this answer by adding together the monthly data until you go beyond the 600,000th job. You pass the total in April.

Answer 7

B – 1:1.9

Jobs added in June and July = 46 + 117 = 163

Jobs added in January and February = 68 + 235 = 303

The ratio is 163:303, which you can simplify to 1:1.9 approximately.

Answer 8

C – 130

The second quarter is April, May and June. The average gain in these months is (217 + 53 + 46) ÷ 3 = 105.3 thousand to one decimal place. A 23% increase on this average is 105.3 x 123 ÷ 100 = 130 thousand (approximately).

Answer 9

C – One too many in the >15% band

You can derive this answer by doing the work the hypothetical analyst should have done and drawing up the table correctly.

Answer 10

C – 7.0%

The average is (5.2 + 8.6 + 8.5 + 7.5 + 5.6 + 6.5) ÷ 6 = 7.0% (approximately).

Answer 11

E – 2,250%

This question is more difficult than it appears. The question contains lots of different percentage figures, which can be confusing. Japan's figure is 0.2% and South Korea's figure is 4.7%. Japan's inflation rate has to be (4.7 – 0.2) = 4.5 percentage points higher to match South Korea – but the question doesn't ask you to calculate this. The question asks you by what percentage Japan's inflation rate has to increase to in order to match South Korea's 4.5 ÷ 0.2 x 100 = 2,250%.

Answer 12
A – 7.0%

India's inflation is 8.6% but contributes only a relative weighting of 1.4 ÷ (1.4+5). China's inflation is 6.5% but contributes 5 ÷ (1.4 + 5). The total combined rate of inflation is therefore:

(8.6 x 1.4 ÷ 6.4) + (6.5 x 5 ÷ 6.4) = 7.0% (approximately)

Answer 13
D – 285

The mode is the score that appears most frequently, which is 285.

Answer 14
E – 283

You calculate this answer by summing all the scores and dividing by the sample size: 5,662 ÷ 20 = 283, to the nearest whole stroke.

Answer 15
C – 65%

13 scores were less than 286, so the percentage is 13 ÷ 20 x 100 = 65%.

Answer 16
B – 31%

Odds of 5:11 mean that for every 5 times KB wins, JD wins 11 times. Therefore, out of a total of 16 games, KB wins 5 games. As a percentage, this chance of winning is 5 ÷ 16 x 100 = 31% to the nearest whole per cent.

Answer 17
C – 35

12 furlongs = 12 ÷ 8 = 1.5 miles

2 minutes and 35 seconds = 155 seconds = (155 ÷ 3,600) hours

The calculation for speed is distance ÷ time = 1.5 ÷ (155 ÷ 3,600) = 35 mph (approximately).

Answer 18
B – 155.3 seconds

This question is quite challenging. Pour Moi completes the course of 12 furlongs in 2 minutes and 35 seconds.

12 furlongs = 12 ÷ 8 x 1,760 = 2,640 yards

Therefore, Carlton House covers (2,640 – 5) = 2,635 yards in those same 155 seconds. You can then calculate the average speed of Carlton House and use the total race distance to calculate the third-placed horse's time to complete the course.

You can also take a mathematical shortcut. As the horse's speed is constant throughout the race, you can scale up the time that the winning horse took, based on the relative distances of the winner and the third-placed horse:

2,640 ÷ 2,635 x 155 = 155.3 seconds

Answer 19
D – 68 yards

If Workforce wins in 2 minutes 31 seconds (= 151 seconds), you need to know how far Pour Moi travels in that time to find out the distance Workforce beats Pour Moi by.

You know that each horse's speed is uniform, so you need to do a simple calculation based on the ratio of the two horses' individual winning times and the total course distance:

151 ÷ 155 x 2,640 (course length) = 2,572 yards

The difference between this and the course length gives you the hypothetical winning margin:

2,640 – 2,572 = 68 yards

Answer 20
E – 3 minutes 9 seconds

The St Leger course distance is 1 mile 6 furlongs 132 yards, or:

1,760 + (6 ÷ 8 x 1,760) + 132 = 1,760 + 1,320 + 132 = 3,212 yards

Pour Moi covered 2,640 yards in 155 seconds to win the Derby. The time the horse takes to cover 3,212 yards at the same speed is:

3,212 ÷ (2,640 ÷ 155) = 3,212 ÷ 2,640 x 155 = 189 seconds = 3 minutes 9 seconds

Answer 21
B – 9.5

In 1997, Blue Skies took 15.7% of the market and Big Green took 8.5%. The ratio between the two is 15.7:8.5, or approximately 1.8:1, which is equivalent to 9:5.

Answer 22
D – The combined market share of the three supermarkets suffered a fall in 2009.

All the other options are demonstrably false, or, in the case of option E, you can't prove them from the information in the chart.

Answer 23
D – £21.6 billion

125 billion x 17.3% = £21.6 billion

Answer 24
A – 6.7%

In 1997, the greatest market share was Blue Skies with 15.2% and the least market share was Big Green with 8.5%. The range is therefore (15.2 – 8.5) = 6.7%.

Answer 25
B – £0.81

12 kWh per day is 12 x 30 = 360 kWh usage per month.

With quarterly billing, Catherine pays (360 x 3.81p) + (30 x 29.97p) = 2,270.7p = £22.71 to the nearest penny. With monthly direct debit, Catherine pays (360 x 3.59p) + (30 x 29.92p) = 2,190p = £21.90 to the nearest penny.

The difference is (22.71 – 21.90) = £0.81.

Answer 26
E – £52.24

Off-peak daily use is $(12 \times 1 \div 3) = 4$ kWh. Peak daily use is $(12 - 4) - 8$ kWh.

> Monthly cost of off-peak use = 30 x 4 x 7.12p = 854.4p
>
> Monthly cost of peak use = 30 x 8 x 15.01p = 3,602.4p
>
> Monthly standing charge cost = 30 x 25.56p = 766.8p

The total cost is 854.4 + 3,602.4 + 766.8 = 5,223.6p = £52.24 to the nearest penny.

Answer 27
D – £44.66

New daily consumption is $(12 \times 80) \div 100 = 9.6$. Off-peak daily use is $(9.6 \times 60\%)$ = 5.76 kWh. Peak daily use is $(9.6 - 5.76) = 3.84$ kWh.

> Monthly cost of off-peak use = 30 x 5.76 x 7.12p = 1,230.3p
>
> Monthly cost of peak use = 30 x 3.84 x 15.01p = 1,729.1p to one decimal place
>
> Monthly standing charge cost = 30 x 25.56p = 766.8p

The total cost is 1,230.3 + 1,729.1 + 766.8 = 3,726.2p = £37.26 to the nearest penny.

Answer 28
C – If Catherine uses 200 kWh per month, Isis Energy can undercut Midlands Energy's price.

You can prove all the other options are true. More straightforwardly, from the calculations you do in the previous questions, you can see that Isis can't possibly be cheaper than Midlands at that level of consumption.

Answer 29
D – 7.0

The range is the difference between the maximum and minimum values: 82.7 – 75.7 = 7.0 years.

Answer 30
E – 81.5

The assumption regarding equal regional weighting lets you simply calculate the arithmetic mean to find the answer. In real life, the different regions contribute different numbers of people to the overall total, so you would have to weight their contribution to the overall English average by those populations. Your task in this question is much simpler:

$(80.1 + 80.3 + 81.0 + 81.3 + 81.1 + 82.3 + 82.0 + 82.4 + 82.7) \div 9 = 81.5$ to one decimal place

Answer 31
C – 5.9%

$(82.0 - 77.4) \div 77.4 \times 100 = 5.9\%$ to one decimal place

Answer 32
B – A man born in the South West will, on average, live a longer life than one born in the North East.

Be grateful when the correct option is early on in the list so you can stop testing the other propositions! However, if you do work through all the options to double-check, you can see that all the other statements are false.

Answer 33
D – 576

The long wall measures 5 m x 2 m. As each module measures 1.2 m x 0.85, you can fit a total of eight modules against the wall.

Trying to calculate this answer by working out the area of the wall and dividing by the area of the module is a mistake, because the modules by definition are the smallest component of the rack and so you can't break them up. Instead, you need to calculate how many modules fit lengthwise ($5 \div 1.2 = 4.17 = 4$ rounded down) and how many modules fit height-wise ($2 \div 0.85 = 2.35 = 2$ rounded down) and multiply the two figures = $(4 \times 2) = 8$.

Each module contains 72 bottles, so the total storage space is $72 \times 8 = 576$.

Answer 34
C – £1,152

You already know that you need eight racks, so the total cost excluding VAT is 8 x 120 = £960. Adding in the VAT at 20% gives 960 x 120 ÷ 100 = £1,152.

Answer 35
B – £385

The cost to purchase and install is £550. Amortised over ten years, this is 550 ÷ 10 = £55 per year. The cost of electricity per year is 6,600 x 5p = 3,3000p = £330.

Adding the two costs together gives (330 + 55) = £385.

Answer 36
D – £28,512

Three cases of Alsatian Gewurztraminer at £26 per bottle costs (3 x 12) x 26 = £936. Two cases of Hermitage at £720 per case costs 2 x 720 = £1,440. One case of fine Bordeaux at £99 per bottle costs (1 x 12) x 99 = £1,188.

The total cost is 936 + 1,440 + 1,188 = £3,564.

The average cost per bottle is 3,564 ÷ (6 x 12) = £49.50.

You know that George's cellar contains 576 bottles, so the total cost to fill the cellar, based on the average cost, is (£49.50 x 576) = £28,512.

Abstract Reasoning

Display 1

1. Set B; **2.** Neither set; **3.** Set A; **4.** Set B; **5.** Neither set

Explanation

All the shapes in Set A have curved edges. All the shapes in Set B have straight edges. The size, colour and orientation of the shapes demonstrate no commonality within sets.

Test shape 3 contains only shapes with curved edges and therefore falls into Set A. Test shapes 1 and 4 contain only shapes with straight edges and so fall into Set B. Test shapes 2 and 5 contain shapes with both curved and straight edges and therefore don't fit within either set.

Display 2

6. Neither set; **7.** Set B; **8.** Set B; **9.** Set A; **10.** Neither set

Explanation

All the objects in Set A have outer edges with interruptions. All the objects in Set B have solid outer edges. The exact nature of the overall shape, the colour and the orientation show no consistent features of commonality.

Test shapes 7 and 8 have only objects with solid uninterrupted outer edges and so fall within Set B. Test shape 9 has only interrupted outlines and so falls into Set A. Test shapes 6 and 10 contain objects with both solid and interrupted outlines and so fall into neither set.

Display 3

11. Neither set; **12.** Neither set; **13.** Neither set; **14.** Set B; **15.** Set A

Explanation

All the objects in Set A have three edges. All the objects in Set B have four edges. Test shape 15 contains only three-edged objects and so is in Set A. Test shape 14 has only four-edged objects and so is in Set B. Test shapes 11, 12 and 13 contain objects with varying numbers of edges and so fall into neither set.

Display 4

16. Neither set; **17.** Neither set; **18.** Set B; **19.** Neither set; **20.** Set A

Explanation

All the examples in Set A contain a shape that is internally replicated with a shape of the same colour. Any extra shapes on the outside have the opposite colour from the main shape. For instance, the top-left item contains a large white circle with a smaller white inner circle and a black outer shape (in this case, also a circle).

All the examples in Set B contain a shape that is internally replicated with a shape of the opposite colour. The extra shape on the outside has the same colour as the main shape. For instance, the top-left item contains a large white hexagon with a smaller black inner hexagon and no second outer object. The top-right item contains a large white triangle with a smaller black inner triangle within it and a white outer shape (in this case, a triangle).

The placement and orientation of the large object within the box are irrelevant. Any other shapes in each item show no consistent features of commonality.

Test shape 20 contains a large white object that is replicated internally by a smaller white item and a second outer object in the opposite colour from the big shape and so is in Set A. Test shape 18 has a large object that is internally replicated with a smaller black object and a second outer object in the same colour as the big shape, and so it fits in Set B.

Test shape 16 has a smaller object that is not an exact internal replication and so belongs to neither set. Test shapes 17 and 19 have no internal replication at all and so belong to neither set.

Display 5

21. Set A; **22.** Set B; **23.** Neither set; **24.** Set A; **25.** Set B

Explanation

Set A's objects are subdivided. Set B's objects are undivided.

Test shapes 21 and 24 and subdivided and so belong to Set A. Test shapes 22 and 25 are whole and so are part of Set B. Test shape 23 has a mixture of whole and divided objects so doesn't fit in either set.

Display 6

26. Set A; **27.** Neither set; **28.** Set B; **29.** Set B; **30.** Neither set

Explanation

All the examples in Set A contain only items with right-angles. All the examples in Set B contain only items with no right-angles. The exact nature of the overall shape, the colour and the orientation show no consistent features of commonality.

Test shape 26 contains only objects with right-angles and so belongs to Set A. Test shapes 28 and 29 have no right-angled figures and so belong to Set B. Test shapes 27 and 30 include objects with and without right-angles and so don't fit into either set.

Display 7

31. Set A; **32.** Set B; **33.** Set A; **34.** Set B; **35.** Set B

Explanation

In Set A, if you can see a circle, you also see an arrow. Conversely, if you see no circle, you don't see an arrow. Set B's rules are the opposite: If you can see a circle, you don't see an arrow; but if you see no circle, you can see an arrow. The colour and the direction of the arrow are irrelevant.

Test shapes 31 and 33 contain both circles and arrows and so are in Set A. Test shapes 32 and 35 contain no circle, but do have arrows, and so are in Set B. Test shape 34 has a circle but has no arrow and so is in Set B.

Display 8

36. Set B; **37.** Neither set; **38.** Neither set; **39.** Set A; **40.** Set B

Explanation

The shapes in Set A intersect only once. The shapes in Set B intersect twice.

Test shape 39 has only one intersection and so is in Set A. Test shapes 36 and 40 have two intersections and so belong to Set B. Test shape 37 has no overlaps and so is in neither set. Test shape 38 has three intersections and so isn't in either of the sets.

Display 9

41. Neither set; **42.** Set B; **43.** Set A; **44.** Set A; **45.** Neither set

Explanation

The pictures in Set A all contain one less object than the object with the most edges. The pictures in Set B all have the same number of sides as the object with most edges.

Test shapes 43 and 44 fall into Set A. Test shape 42 is in Set B. Test shapes 41 and 45 obey neither set's rules.

Display 10

46. Set A; **47.** Neither set; **48.** Set B; **49.** Neither set; **50.** Set A

Explanation

The sets in this question obey interacting conditional rules. In Set A, if you see a crescent moon, you also see an upward pointing arrow; if no moon is present, you see no arrow. If in addition to the crescent moon you also see a square, the arrow points downwards. A square on its own, without a crescent moon, has no impact at all.

In Set B, if you see a crescent moon, the arrow points down; if no moon is present, you see no arrow. If in addition to the moon you see a square, the arrow points upwards. A square on its own has no effect.

Test shapes 46 and 50 obey Set A's rules. Test shape 48 obeys Set B's rules. Test shape 47 has an arrow but no moon and so is in neither set. Test shape 49 has a moon but no arrow and so is in neither set.

Display 11

51. Set A; **52.** Set B; **53.** Neither set; **54.** Set B.; **55.** Neither set

Explanation

If the identical objects are in vertical or horizontal alignment, the shape falls into Set A. If the identical objects are in diagonal alignment, the shape is in Set B.

Test shape 51 is in Set A. Test shapes 52 and 54 are in Set B. Test shapes 53 and 55 have no identical shapes and so belong to neither set.

Display 12

56. Neither set; **57.** Set B; **58.** Set A; **59.** Set B; **60.** Neither set

Explanation

In Set A, if you see a white circle, you also see a black circle. If no white circle is present, no black circle is present either. However, multiple black circles can exist – the absence of a white circle only prevents the existence of a *single* black circle.

In Set B, if you see a white square, you also see a black square. If no white square is present, no black square is present either. However, multiple black squares can exist – the absence of a white square only prevents the existence of a *single* black square.

Test shape 58 is in Set A. Test shapes 57 and 59 are in Set B. Test shapes 56 and 60 obey neither set's rules.

Display 13

61. Set A; **62.** Set B; **63.** Neither set; **64.** Neither set; **65.** Set A

Explanation

This question's set rules are complex. In both sets, the default nature of the arrow is to be vertical and double-headed. In Set A, if you see a white square, the arrow points up. If you also see a white circle, the arrow points right.

In Set B, a white square causes the arrow to point down. If you also see a white circle, the arrow points left.

Test shape 61 is in Set A because of the upward-pointing arrow in the presence of a white square (with no white circle). Test shape 65 is also in Set A because the arrow points right in the combined presence of both a white square and a white circle. Test shape 62 is in Set B because of the downward-pointing arrow in the presence of a white square but the absence of a white circle. Test shapes 63 and 64 have the default arrows despite the absence of white squares and (in the case of shape 64) white circles and so belong to neither set.

Decision Analysis

Answer 1
B – Pass the ball to the striker.

= Ball, Pass, Striker

= Ball pass to striker

= Pass the ball to the striker

Answer 2
C – Pass to midfield, then to the striker, then shoot.

$$\hookleftarrow\underline{\downarrow}\ \triangle\ \underline{\downarrow}\ \hookleftarrow,\ \blacktriangleright,\ \lightning$$

= Pass, Midfielder, Pass, Striker, Shoot

= Pass to midfield, pass to the striker, shoot

= Pass to midfield, then to the striker, then shoot

Answer 3
E – Keep possession

$$\rightrightarrows(\blacktriangle,\ \hookleftarrow,\ \blacktriangledown,\ \blacktriangle)$$

= Increase(Cannons, Pass, Ball, Cannons)

= Do more of (Cannons passing the ball to each other)

= Keep possession

Answer 4
D – The referee is an idiot

$$\rightrightarrows \frown,\ \circlearrowleft$$

= Increase Disapprove, Referee

= Greatly disapprove of referee

= The referee is an idiot

This translation takes some liberties with the literal decoded translation, forcing you to equate a general sense of great disapproval with considering the referee to be stupid, but the answer is the best fit of the options available and conveys the gist of the message.

None of the other options fit the code. There is nothing to suggest 'soon', as mentioned in Option A. Options B and C are too specific for the code, mentioning the opposition or the manager's players. Option E discusses bribery, a concept not included in the code.

Answer 5
A – Send off that opposition player, referee!

$$\circlearrowleft,\ \smile,\ \rightrightarrows(\frown \leftrightarrows),\ \blacktriangledown$$

= Referee, Whistle, Increase(Disapprove Talk), Opponent

= Referee, blow whistle and severely tell off opposing player

= Referee should blow whistle and send off opposition player

= Send off that opposition player, referee!

You need to translate the code into a casual vernacular phrase. Sending off a player is not the same as severely telling off the player, but the two phrases share something of the same meaning. None of the other options remotely fits the code. You don't need to know the rules of football, or even know what sending off means, to decode this message because you can eliminate the other options as unsatisfactory translations.

Answer 6
E – I want two defenders to stay near the goalposts to defend this corner.

$$\blacktriangleleft \blacktriangleleft (\,\diagdown\,), \leftarrow \nwarrow$$

= Defender Defender (Goalposts), Defend Corner

= Two defenders at goalposts, defend corner

= I want two defenders to stay near the goalposts to defend this corner

Answer 7
C – Midfield needs to attack faster.

$$(\triangle \triangle), \rightarrow \circlearrowleft$$

= (Midfielder Midfield), Attack Fast

= Midfielders plural, attack fast

= Midfield needs to attack faster

Answer 8
A – We need to score one more than them.

$$(\blacktriangle \,\Updownarrow\,) \rightrightarrows, \blacktriangledown \,\Updownarrow$$

= (Cannons Score) Increase, Opponent Score

= Our score needs to be more than the opposition's score

= We need to score one more than them

Answer 9

B – Referee, the opposing defender handballed!

$$\circlearrowleft, \blacktriangledown \blacktriangleleft, \ \shortmid\!\leftarrow\!\blacktriangledown$$

= Referee, Opponent Defender, Hand Ball

= Referee, the opposing defender handballed!

Option A lacks the specificity of mentioning the defender. Option C adds in more elaboration than necessary compared to Option B. Options D and E contain elements of distracting the referee, which are not included in the code.

Answer 10

C – Tell that idiot striker to just hit the ball into the net!

$$\lightning\!\blacktriangledown, \wedge, (\,\widehat{} \rightrightarrows\,)\blacktriangleright$$

= Shoot ball, Net, (Disapprove Increase)Striker

= Shoot the ball into the net, (I disapprove greatly) striker

= Tell that idiot striker to just hit the ball into the net!

Answer 11

E – The keeper saves from the striker, but the midfielder scores on the rebound.

$$\blacktriangleright\!\lightning, \triangledown\!\leftarrow, \triangle\!\Updownarrow$$

= Striker Shoot, Goalkeeper Defend, Midfielder Score

= The striker shoots, the goalkeeper defends, the midfielder scores

= The keeper saves from the striker, but the midfielders scores on the rebound

Options C and D convey something of the same message. Option D omits elements of the code and option C gets the order of events wrong.

Answer 12

A. ⇆, (⇆ ↔)▶, ◀

= Talk, (Talk Walk) Striker, Defender

= Tell me, (tell walk) striker, defender

= Tell me if I need to tell the striker to walk, for a defender

= Tell me if you want me to substitute a striker for a defender

Option C is superficially similar, but lacks the crucial element of asking the person receiving the message to talk to the manager about whether it would be a good idea for the manager to request the substitution.

Answer 13
D – Run into their half.

↺ ↔, ▼ ‡

= Fast Walk, Opponent Halfway Line

= Run, their side of the halfway line

= Run into their half

Answer 14
C – Score two goals in this half.

(⇪ ⇪)(‿ ‡)

= (Score Score)(Whistle Halfway Line)

= Score twice (whistle halfway line)

= Score twice when the whistle is halfway

= Score twice in this half

The need to transpose a pitch object (the halfway line) into a time (this half) underlines how ambiguity can creep into decoding from a symbolic cipher, but this answer is the best (or least-worst) option out of the list.

Option A has the essential element of scoring twice, but specifies that this should happen in each half. The code, even stretched to its limit, only talks about one half. Option B has two goals in total, but spreads them across the two halves, whereas their grouping together in the code is best interpreted as scoring closer together. Option D discusses winning, which is not in the code. Option E mentions a rematch, which is not hinted at by the code.

Answer 15

$$ \text{A. } \blacktriangledown\nwarrow, \circlearrowleft_{\smile}, \Updownarrow $$

= Ball Corner, Referee Whistle, Score

= Ball on corner spot, referee blows his whistle, then score

= Place the ball on the corner spot and score when the referee blows his whistle

Answer 16
B – Midfield needs to pass up to the striker so he can head a goal.

$$ (\triangle\,\triangle)\vdash, \; \blacktriangleright, \; \rightarrow\!\Updownarrow $$

= (Midfielder Midfielder) Pass, Striker, Head Score

= Midfielders pass to striker, head a goal

= Midfield needs to pass up to the striker so he can head a goal

Answer 17
D – I need everyone to run faster, pass more and get the ball to the strikers.

$$ \blacktriangle\,(\rightrightarrows((\leftrightarrow\circlearrowleft),\hookrightarrow)), \; \blacktriangleright\blacktriangleright $$

= Cannons (Increase ((Walk Fast), Pass)), Striker Striker

= Cannons (increase (run, pass)), strikers

= Cannons (run faster, pass more), strikers

= I need everyone to run faster, pass more, and get the ball to strikers

In this case, the manager omits the code for ball, as he implies the meaning in his request for passing. The manager may have used the code for 'Fast' to encourage his players to run faster; by using the code for 'Increase' instead, he can apply the term to both 'Run' and 'Pass', saving a little bit of code-writing time.

Answer 18
E – Well done, lads; now attack, attack, attack!

$$\searrow \blacktriangle , \, \rightrightarrows \rightarrow$$

= Approve Cannons, Increase Attack

= Well done, lads; now attack, attack, attack!

Answer 19
B – The referee will blow his whistle any minute now; hang on!

$$\circlearrowleft \rightrightarrows (\circlearrowright \smile), \, \rightrightarrows \leftarrow$$

= Fast Increase(Referee Whistle), Increase Defend

= Imminent (referee will blow whistle), more defending

= The referee will blow his whistle any minute now, defend more until then

= The referee will blow his whistle any minute now; hang on!

Answer 20

A – We need our defence to slow the game down.

$$\blacktriangle (\blacktriangleleft \blacktriangleleft), \circlearrowleft \rightleftarrows$$

= Cannons (Defender Defender), Slow Increase

= Our defence, more slow

= We need our defence to slow the game down

Answer 21

C – Get our midfield to send more penetrating crosses to the strikers.

$$\rightleftarrows, \quad \blacktriangle (\triangle \triangle), \rightarrow (\llcorner \hookrightarrow), \blacktriangle (\blacktriangleright \blacktriangleright)$$

= Talk, Cannons (Midfielder Midfielder), Attack (Pass Pass), Cannons (Striker Striker)

= Talk, our midfield, attacking passes, our strikers

= Get our midfield to send more penetrating crosses to the strikers

Answer 22

E – The opponents managed to get the referee to send our defender off the pitch.

$$\blacktriangledown \blacktriangledown, \rightleftarrows, \circlearrowright, (\smile \stackrel{\nearrow}{}) \leftrightarrow, \blacktriangleleft$$

= Opponent Opponent, Talk, Referee, (Whistle Disapprove)Walk, Defender

= The opponents, talk, referee to blow his whistle in disapproval to walk defender

= The opponents talked to the referee to get him to send off our defender

= The opponents managed to get the referee to send our defender off the pitch

Option D conveys a similar meaning, but the code includes the symbol for referee, so the optimal translation should explicitly include that if possible. Option E is therefore a closer translation, making it the correct answer.

Answer 23

C – Owner

And

D – Sell

You can't possibly convey these two terms using the current code. You can convey the term 'Play' by combining all the elements of a game (attack, defend, score, pass). You can convey 'better' by using 'Approve' and 'Increase'. You can convey 'lot of you' simply by using the code for 'Cannons'. Conveying property rights isn't really possible with the limited code.

Answer 24

A – Match

And

D – Calm

This cliché-ridden bit of manager-speak requires you to translate the essential meaning of the idioms rather than trying to translate them literally. 'Over the moon' requires you to convey a sense of extreme happiness, which you can do through judicious use of the terms for 'Approve' and possibly 'Talk'. You can convey 'giving 110%', or trying one's hardest, using the terms for 'Attack', 'Defend' and 'Increase' – and possibly 'Approve' too.

Conveying a sense of taking each match as it comes is much harder. You need to translate a calm and methodical approach to each game. 'Calm' is therefore a useful term to have. The term 'Match' is also helpful. Although you can just about use a similar technique to the one we describe in Answer 23 to group all the elements of a Match to translate the concept, doing so is more convoluted than the solution for the other potential answers in the list (Calm excepted).

Answer 25

A – Get one of our defenders to cover the goalpost nearest the corner, and another to stand next to the keeper and block the net.

$$▲ ◀ (\nwarrow \ \urcorner \ ), \ (▲ ◀ ▽) ← \wedge$$

= Cannons Defender(Corner Goalpost), (Cannons Defender Keeper)Defend Net

= One of our defenders (Corner Goalpost), (another of our defenders and our keeper) defend the net

= Get one of our defenders to cover the goalpost nearest the corner, and another to stand next to the keeper and block the net

Answer 26

C – It's the last minute of the match, we have a corner . . . and score!

$$↺ ⇉ (⤵ \ ⌣ \ ), \ ▲ \nwarrow , \ ⇪$$

= Fast Increase (Referee Whistle), Cannons Corner, Score

= The referee's about to blow his whistle, we have a corner, score

= It's the last minute of the match, we have a corner . . . and score!

Part IV
The Part of Tens

In this part . . .

Every *For Dummies* book ends with a Part of Tens. It's a chance for us to give you some tips that we couldn't find the space or opportunity to mention in the rest of the text.

In Chapter 12, we explain our top ten steps to get you into medical school. And in Chapter 13, we'll let you know our top ten ways to manage your stress levels during the application process, and then on through your medical career.

Use Chapter 12 to make sure you stay on the right path to get into medical school, and use Chapter 13 to make sure you don't regress into a terrified, quivering ball of fear on the way there!

Chapter 12

Ten Steps to Help You Get into Medical or Dental School

. . . .

In This Chapter

▶ Approaching the application process

▶ Prioritising your time

▶ Staying on track when the going gets tough

. . . .

The UKCAT is only one part of the overall process of getting into medical or dental school. You need to retain a broader perspective on the challenge you face. In this chapter, we offer some suggestions to help you on the other parts of your journey to medical or dental school.

Deciding Whether Medicine or Dentistry is Right for You

Medicine and dentistry are popular competitive courses and socially valued professions, but this doesn't mean that one of them is right for you. Make sure that you head down the path of medicine or dentistry because *you* want to, not because other people want you to. To decide whether these fields are for you, try the following:

✔ Work out whether you can see yourself thriving as a doctor or dentist.

✔ Think about the emotional pressure involved in caring for people in pain.

✔ Think about the personal sacrifices it may involve. For example, it may involve temporarily living and working in a part of the country you don't like, especially in the early years. It can sometimes mean postponing having children until you feel more settled in your career, and maybe not seeing as much of your family as you'd like.

✔ Do some meaningful work experience across a few different settings.

✔ Talk to current students and doctors or dentists.

Achieving the Best Grades

To be successful in your application for medical or dental school, you need to be academically very able. You need excellent GCSEs and a firm expectation of excellent A-levels. Be honest with yourself: If you're not reasonably confident of getting those A-level results, all the work experience – and even the best UKCAT score – in the world won't make a difference.

Doing Your Research

Order – and read – university prospectuses. Go on open days. Think about attending courses like ours at Get into Medical School (www.getintomedical school.org), which explain the medical application process in detail. Know what exams you need to take, when you need to take them, and how to apply for them.

Get Your Personal Statement Right

Start thinking about your UCAS (University and Colleges Admission Service) personal statement from an early stage. Identify gaps in your work experience and skills, and plug those gaps before the submission deadline, so your statement is fully rounded. Don't try to do it all in the last minute; personal statements need to be drafted and redrafted many times.

Revising for Your Exams

Both the UKCAT and BMAT exams reward students who've taken the time to familiarise themselves with the tests. This book helps you with the UKCAT, but if you want to apply to a medical school that also requires the BMAT, don't forget to revise for that exam too.

Practising Your Interview Skills

Interviewing is nerve-wracking, especially if you've little experience. Make sure that you get plenty of practise in before the big day. Practising interviews with friends is good. Practising interviews with teachers and professionals who are used to interviewing people is better. And practising interviews with people who've already been through medical or dental school interviews is best of all.

Staying Up-to-Date with Medicine and Dentistry

Medical and dental schools expect candidates to be enthusiastic about medicine and dentistry. You need to have at least a passing familiarity with the world of healthcare and some of the latest news in the field. We set up the free website www.getintomedicineuk.com, which we regularly update with recent healthcare news, highlighting some areas for you to think about.

Sticking to the Timescale

The medical and dental application processes contain a lot of interacting hurdles, many of which have their own submission deadlines and internal administrative annoyances. Use the timeline that we show in Figure 1-1 in Chapter 1 to help you draw up an individualised schedule for your own application.

Reducing Your Anxiety

The application process is long and frustrating. Anxiety is natural but exhausting. Planning ahead, accepting the anxiety as normal, and practising relaxation techniques help reduce your physical and mental agitation. Detailed information and more examples can be found in Chapter 13.

Having a Life beyond Medicine or Dentistry

You may well get into medical or dental school. But you may not. Regardless of which camp you eventually find yourself in, medicine and dentistry aren't the be all and end all of your life. Try hard to retain a sense of personal identity and self-esteem that isn't just tied up with being a doctor or dentist. You'll be a happier and wiser person – and a more effective clinician – if you can manage this.

Chapter 13

Ten Ways to Stay Cool Under Pressure

In This Chapter
▶ Using breathing and relaxation techniques to keep calm
▶ Visualising a positive future
▶ Accepting that some stress is part of the application process

The combination of applying to medical or dental school and sitting exams such as the UKCAT is stressful. Staying calm during the application process is important, however – not only do you feel better, but also you perform better. In chapter, we suggest ten ways to relax under pressure; you may even find some of these methods are useful in later life if you work as a doctor or dentist.

Keeping Things in Perspective

Becoming a doctor or dentist isn't the totality of your life existence. The idea is important to you right now, but that doesn't mean it will always be an all-consuming part of your life. Remember that billions of people live happy, productive, fulfilling lives without working in medicine or dentistry.

Accepting That It's Your Choice

You're voluntarily putting yourself under stress because the potential outcome is something you want to achieve: being a doctor or dentist. You're in control. Acknowledging fundamental truth places the focus of control back in your hands and away from the application system. Your future is yours to decide.

Sticking to Your Plan

You need to be well organised to succeed as a doctor or dentist. Think about when you want to work on your application and exams and when you want to relax.

Draw up a timetable to help you feel in control. Try not to be neurotic about your plan – it should cover your time in just enough detail to give you a sense of direction without feeling suffocating.

Breathing Deeply

When you feel stressed, your body reacts accordingly, with the so-called *flight or fight reaction*. Your pulse quickens, your muscles tense up, and your breathing becomes faster and shallower. The good news is that relationship is two-way: if you can notice these changes and act to control them, you can make yourself feel calmer. By consciously slowing down your breathing and making each breath deeper and more controlled, you can calm and focus your thoughts.

Try breathing in deeply through your nose, and then breathing out slowly through slightly pursed lips, taking about five seconds to complete an entire cycle. You don't need to actively time your breathing – just breathe a little more slowly than normal, but not so slow that you feel uncomfortable.

The first time you try this, you'll probably lose concentration after a few breaths, but if you keep practising you'll get better at the technique. Eventually, the technique becomes second nature when you're stressed and can really work wonders in relaxing your mind and body.

Relaxing Progressively

Consciously relaxing your muscles reduces the tension that builds up with prolonged stress. Practise alternately tensing and relaxing your muscles under conscious control. To do this, follow these steps:

1. **Start off by scrunching up your feet, holding them tensed for a few seconds, and then letting them gradually relax over another few seconds.**

2. **Repeat Step 1 with your feet a few times and move on to your calf muscles, your thighs, your fists, arms, and so on, all the way up to your forehead muscles.**

   The whole sequence can take some minutes – but think of as a break from working and worrying.

Like deep controlled breathing, your relaxation technique will improve with practise, so keep trying.

Trying Visualisation Exercises

You can use visualisation techniques to help you relax and to build your confidence.

To use visualisation for relaxation, follow these steps:

1. **Sit or lie down for a few moments.**

2. **Close your eyes and think of a time and a place when you were very happy.**

   Try to recall all the physical, sensory, and emotional details of the event. Relive the event as closely as you can.

3. **Rest within the moment.**

   You can supplement the visualisation with the deep breathing techniques to boost its relaxing effect.

4. **When you feel rested, slowly open your eyes, let yourself become aware of your surroundings again and take another deep breath before returning to work.**

To build your confidence with visualisation, focus on the successful outcome. Imagine yourself in the position of passing your exams with flying colours, getting into medical or dental school, and qualifying as a doctor or dentist. If feels like 'tempting fate', challenge fear of failure instead of leaving it to fester in your subconscious mind. Aim for success and give yourself permission to see yourself as a successful person. Many of the world's top sportspeople use visualisation techniques like before major competitions to help them focus.

Becoming Familiar with the Application Process

The unknown is a terrifying empty space. You project your deepest and darkest fears into that empty space. If you haven't practised enough UKCAT questions or revised for your A-levels, your fear of the unknown can overwhelm you. By familiarising yourself with all the elements of the medical or dental school application process, you get comfortable with the steps you need to take. familiarity acts as a reassuring protective shield around you. If you haven't researched the application process much, Part I and Chapter 12 of book are good places to start.

Steering Clear of Denial

Stress and anxiety are a normal part of life – and of university applications. Many of the other tips in chapter can help you control your stress and anxiety. In the meantime, however stressful you find the process of applying to medical or dental school, don't try to run away or use alcohol or drugs to block things out – denial never works in the long term and can even lead to more problems and distress.

Avoiding Upsetting Other People

When you feel stressed, you may take out your pent-up frustration on other people – usually those closest to you. Your friends and family love you, so we hope they forgive you to some extent if you don't act yourself when you're applying for medical or dental school. But instead of upsetting people, try to use some of the stress-busting techniques included in chapter. After all, distressing your family and friends only adds to your stress.

Taking a Break

Remember that the application process is a marathon, not a sprint. If you work at 100 per cent effort throughout the process, you'll burn yourself out. Take time out to do the things you love doing and to be with the people you like. By unwinding and relaxing, you'll be much more effective when you have to work again.

Index

• Q •

FOR DUMMIES®

Making Everything Easier!™

UK editions

BUSINESS

Bookkeeping For Dummies
978-0-470-97626-5

Persuasion & Influence For Dummies
978-0-470-74737-7

Starting & Running a Business All-In-One For Dummies
978-1-119-97527-4

REFERENCE

British Politics For Dummies
978-0-470-68637-9

DIY For Dummies
978-0-470-97450-6

Dad's Guide to Pregnancy For Dummies
978-1-119-97660-8

HOBBIES

Growing Your Own Fruit & Veg For Dummies
978-0-470-69960-7

Keeping Chickens For Dummies
978-1-119-99417-6

Beekeeping For Dummies
978-1-119-97250-1

Asperger's Syndrome For Dummies
978-0-470-66087-4

Basic Maths For Dummies
978-1-119-97452-9

Body Language For Dummies, 2nd Edition
978-1-119-95351-7

Boosting Self-Esteem For Dummies
978-0-470-74193-1

British Sign Language For Dummies
978-0-470-69477-0

Cricket For Dummies
978-0-470-03454-5

Diabetes For Dummies, 3rd Edition
978-0-470-97711-8

Electronics For Dummies
978-0-470-68178-7

English Grammar For Dummies
978-0-470-05752-0

Flirting For Dummies
978-0-470-74259-4

IBS For Dummies
978-0-470-51737-6

Improving Your Relationship For Dummies
978-0-470-68472-6

ITIL For Dummies
978-1-119-95013-4

Management For Dummies, 2nd Edition
978-0-470-97769-9

Neuro-linguistic Programming For Dummies, 2nd Edition
978-0-470-66543-5

Nutrition For Dummies, 2nd Edition
978-0-470-97276-2

Organic Gardening For Dummies
978-1-119-97706-3

Available wherever books are sold. For more information or to order direct go to www.wiley.com or call +44 (0) 1243 843291

11–37870

FOR DUMMIES®

Making Everything Easier!™

UK editions

SELF-HELP

978-0-470-66541-1

978-1-119-99264-6

978-0-470-66086-7

STUDENTS

978-0-470-68820-5

978-0-470-974711-7

978-1-119-99134-2

HISTORY

978-0-470-68792-5

978-0-470-74783-4

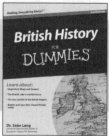

978-0-470-97819-1

Origami Kit For Dummies
978-0-470-75857-1

Overcoming Depression For Dummies
978-0-470-69430-5

Positive Psychology For Dummies
978-0-470-72136-0

PRINCE2 For Dummies, 2009 Edition
978-0-470-71025-8

Project Management For Dummies
978-0-470-71119-4

Psychometric Tests For Dummies
978-0-470-75366-8

Renting Out Your Property For Dummies, 3rd Edition
978-1-119-97640-0

Ruby Union For Dummies, 3rd Edition
978-1-119-99092-5

Sage One For Dummies
978-1-119-95236-7

Self-Hypnosis For Dummies
978-0-470-66073-7

Storing and Preserving Garden Produce For Dummies
978-1-119-95156-8

Study Skills For Dummies
978-0-470-74047-7

Teaching English as a Foreign Language For Dummies
978-0-470-74576-2

Time Management For Dummies
978-0-470-77765-7

Training Your Brain For Dummies
978-0-470-97449-0

Work-Life Balance For Dummies
978-0-470-71380-8

Available wherever books are sold. For more information or to order direct go to www.wiley.com or call +44 (0) 1243 843291

11-37870

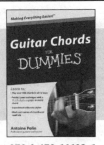

FOR DUMMIES®

Making Everything Easier!™

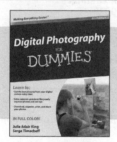

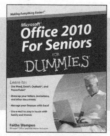